# Cook and Love It

A Collection of Favorite Recipes
and Entertaining Ideas

*Published by*
THE LOVETT PARENT ASSOCIATION
THE LOVETT SCHOOL
Atlanta, Georgia

# Cook and Love It

| | |
|---|---|
| *First Printing—October 1976* | *5,000* |
| *Second Printing—November 1976* | *5,000* |
| *Third Printing—May 1977* | *5,000* |
| *Fourth Printing—November 1978* | *10,000* |
| *Fifth Printing—May 1980* | *10,000* |
| *Sixth Printing—May 1982* | *10,000* |
| *Seventh Printing—May 1985* | *7,500* |
| *20th Anniversary Edition—February 1996* | *15,000* |

ISBN 0-9610846-3-4

Printed in the USA by

**WIMMER**

The Wimmer Companies, Inc.

Memphis

# *Foreword*

Visit the kitchens of Atlanta's finest cooks, and you're sure to find a well-worn copy of *Cook and Love It*. This cookbook, a compilation of southern recipes passed down through generations of Lovett families, is regarded as a must for any cook's collection. Unavailable for many years, *Cook and Love It* is now reprinted complete with all the original recipes due to an overwhelming demand.

First published in 1976 by the Lovett Mothers' Club, *Cook and Love It* was an instant success. Filled with recipes from many members of the school community, the book sold out after each of the seven printings. Today, the Lovett Parent Association is pleased to offer *Cook and Love It* once again, in celebration of the 20th anniversary of its first publication and the 70th anniversary of The Lovett School. This year also offers us a special opportunity to share these wonderful age-old southern treasures with the many cooks from around the world who visit Atlanta in 1996 during the Centennial Olympic Games.

### *1995-96 Cookbook Committee*
Business Chair, Liz Thorneloe

Marketing Chair, Sue Martin

Treasurer, Beth Alexander

Research Chair, Barbara Slick

### *1995-96 Lovett Parent Association Executive Board*
President, Joan Plunkett

Vice President, Debbie Henderson

Treasurer, Mary Justice

Secretary, Cathy Wilson

Finance Advisor, Frances Arnoult

Program Advisor, Lynne Nelson

Immediate Past President, Carter Morris

Administrative Liaison, Paula Lesley

# WHAT READERS SAY ABOUT <u>COOK AND LOVE IT</u> . . .

"Mother's Cookbook is a winner! I would say it is one of the best"

> Beth Tartan
> Journal Home Economist
> Winston-Salem Journal
> Winston-Salem, North Carolina

"Delightful . . . informative . . . *Cook and Love It* is the perfect cookbook for busy and involved people."

> Dot Hartsfield
> Feature Editor
> Buckhead Atlanta

". . . more good recipes than you can shake a stick at!"

> Jean Thwaite, Food Editor
> The Atlanta Constitution

". . . worth buying for sheer reading pleasure. The 'Loving Touches' (numerous household hints scattered throughout the book) . . . are as good as having your own grandmother at your elbow as you cook."

> Norma Bidwell, Food Writer
> The Hamilton Spectator
> Ontario, Canada

". . . praise for its clarity, completeness and menus coordinated for special occasions."

> Kathryn Grayburn
> The Northside Neighbor
> Atlanta, Georgia

"There are enough menus given to last the most energetic hostess an entire year . . . and a chapter on gifts from the kitchen for which Southern women are well known."

> The Los Angeles Times

"Each recipe is better than the one before it!"

> Jean Huffaker
> Novato, California

"It is the nicest cookbook I have ever seen!"

> Arlene Pirozzoli
> North Canton, Ohio

# Contents

# *Blessings*

O Give Thanks Unto The Lord, For He Is Good:
For his Mercy Endureth Forever.   Psalms 107:1

When we gather around the table to eat and drink together, we are expressing our commonness with all people; for while man cannot live by bread alone, we all must have bread to live.

We therefore pause before a meal to reflect upon our membership in the human family and to offer thanks to the Source of our commonness, the Source of food and life.

The following prayers to be used before meals are suggested as blessings that represent various religious traditions.
James D. Curtis

Give us grateful hearts, our Father, for all thy mercies, and make us mindful of the needs of others; through Jesus Christ our Lord.   Amen.
From *The Book of Common Prayer*

Come, Lord Jesus, our guest to be,
And bless these gifts bestowed by thee.
Bless thy dear ones everywhere,
And keep them in thy loving care.
The Moravian Blessing

Bless us, O Lord and these Thy gifts which we are about to receive from Thy bounty, through Christ our Lord.   Amen.
A Roman Catholic Blessing

Blessed art Thou O Lord our God, King of the Universe, who brings forth bread from the earth.   Amen.
A Jewish "Blessing of the Bread"

Thank you for the world so sweet,
Thank you for the food we eat,
Thank you for the birds that sing,
Thank you, God, for everything.    Amen.

Lovett Pre-School Blessing


The Lord's been good to us
And so we thank the Lord,
For giving us the things we need-
The sun, the rain, and the apple seed.    (Or whatever is appropriate
to the season)

O He's been good to us.    Amen.

Lovett Pre-School Blessing


Our Father, for our daily bread,
Accept our praise and hear our prayer.
By Thee all living souls are fed.
Thy bounty and Thy loving care
With all Thy children let us share.    Amen.


Father, we thank you for this meal, for our lives, for other people, for beautiful things, for goodness, and for you.    Amen.


Father, thank you for these and all our many blessings; and forgive us for our sins. May this food nourish our bodies that we may more fully serve thee.    Amen.


Would that you could live on the fragrance of the earth and like an air plant be sustained by the light.

But since you must kill to eat, and rob the newly born of its mother's milk to quench your thirst, let it then be an act of worship.

And let your board stand as an altar on which the pure and the innocent of the forest and plain are sacrificed for that which is purer and still innocent in man.

from The Prophet by Kahlil Gibran

# Appetizers

DAVID SAPP

## AVOCADO SAUCE MALATCHIE

½ cup butter (1 stick)
½ cup sugar
3 avocados (halved lengthwise in hull)

½ cup worcestershire sauce
½ cup catsup

Combine sauce ingredients and heat to boiling point. Pour into avocado halves on lettuce beds and serve with crackers as first course. Allow 1 tablespoon of each ingredient for 1 avocado half.

*Mrs. Edward C. Loughlin, Jr. (Bet)*

## BATON ROUGE DIP FOR VEGETABLES

1 pint sour cream
1 cup Hellmann's mayonnaise
1 cup mozzarella cheese, grated
2 tablespoons parmesan cheese
1 tablespoon fresh chopped parsley
1 teaspoon Accent

1 teaspoon sugar
½ teaspoon garlic salt
1 tablespoon onion, grated
1-2 tablespoons anchovy paste
Lawry's seasoning salt

Mix all ingredients. Refrigerate several hours. Serves 8 for dip.

*Mrs. Edward C. Loughlin, Jr. (Bet)*

## BROCCOLI DIP

*Well-liked by all*

1 box frozen chopped broccoli, cooked and drained
1 medium onion, minced
2 stalks celery, minced
1 (4 ounce) can chopped mushrooms, drained

1 roll Kraft garlic cheese
1 can mushroom soup
1 teaspoon worcestershire sauce
Salt and sherry to taste
Dash each of red pepper and red hot sauce

Saute onion, celery and mushrooms in small amount of butter. Melt cheese in double boiler, add mushroom soup and all other ingredients. Serve hot in chafing dish with Fritos. Serves 12.

*Mrs. John Stephens (Jane)*
*Mrs. William Perry (Anne)*
*Mrs. Dixon Driggs (Lollie)*
*Mrs. James Ney (Carol)*

## CLAM DIP

1 (8 ounce) package cream cheese
1 can minced clams, drained
2-3 tablespoons chopped chives

Worcestershire sauce, to taste
Dash salt and pepper
1 teaspoon lemon juice

Soften cream cheese and add small amount of clam juice to thin. Add other ingredients and mix well. Serve with chips or crackers. May also spread on white bread, which has been cut into rounds, and broil until lightly browned.

*Mrs. Benjamin T. Selman, Jr. (Mary Jean)*
*Mrs. James Wilcox, Jr. (Betty)*

## HOT CLAM DIP

*Different*

3 tablespoons butter
1 small onion, finely chopped
½ green pepper, finely chopped
1 large jar Cheese Whiz
  (or 2 small ones)

2-4 cans minced clams, drained
½ cup catsup
2 tablespoons worcestershire sauce
1 tablespoon sherry (optional)
¼ teaspoon cayenne pepper

Melt butter in double boiler. Add onion and green pepper and saute 3 minutes over direct heat. Add remaining ingredients and cook in double boiler until cheese melts. Stir often. Serve hot in chafing dish with rye toast or Fritos.

*Mrs. Paul Pater (Polly)*
*Mrs. Stephen Selig (Janet)*

## HOT CRAB DIP

1 (8 ounce) package cream cheese
1 tablespoon milk
1 can crabmeat, flaked
2 tablespoons finely chopped onion

½-1 teaspoon horseradish
¼ teaspoon salt
2 tablespoons sherry (optional)
1/3 cup toasted almonds

Cream cheese with milk. Add crabmeat and other ingredients. Put in oven proof dish and bake at 350 degrees for 20-30 minutes, or until hot. Top with almonds. Serve hot on party rye or crackers.

*Mrs. Robert Crow (Marilyn)*
*Mrs. Robert Hennessy (Nancy)*

## MEXICAN DIP

*Good and spicy*

1 large can tomatoes and green chilies
1 package spiced dried beef

1 (10 ounce) package sharp cheddar cheese
1 (8 ounce) package Velveeta cheese

Melt together cheeses on low heat, stirring every 15 minutes. When melted, add tomatoes and chilies; stir. Shred beef and add to mixture. Serve in chafing dish with Taco chips or Doritos.

*Honey Hays Barnes*

## ORIENTAL VEGETABLE DIP

1 cup mayonnaise
4 teaspoons soy sauce
1 teaspoon ginger

1 tablespoon grated onion
1 teaspoon vinegar
Salt to taste

Mix all ingredients. Good with any raw vegetable.

*Mrs. William Horton (Carol Ann)*

## PICKLE DIP FOR VEGETABLES

½ large jar Heinz genuine dill pickles
2 small onions
3 (8 ounce) packages cream cheese

2 tablespoons mayonnaise
Dash worcestershire sauce
Dash tabasco
Few drops green food coloring

Cut pickles into chunks and puree in blender, (small amounts at a time). Puree onions. Put both in large bowl. Put cream cheese in blender and add small amount of pickle-onion mixture to help blend. Put smooth cheese mixture into bowl. Add other ingredients and stir. Serve in hollowed out purple cabbage head with raw vegetables. Makes 1 quart.

*Mrs. Thomas Warner*

## SMOKED BEEF DIP

1 package Kraft garlic cheese
1 package smoked beef

1 can cream of mushroom soup

Boil beef 3 minutes and drain. Melt cheese in double boiler, add soup and stir. Cut up beef and add to mixture. Keep in chafing dish. Serve with Escort crackers.

*Mrs. William Lummus (Anne Hart)*

4

## SMOKED OYSTER DIP

1 can smoked oysters,
finely chopped
¾ cup chopped celery
½ cup chopped onion
4 slices crisp bacon, crumbled
8 single Premium soda crackers,
crumbled

2-3 tablespoons bacon grease
Juice from oysters
2 hard-boiled eggs, finely chopped
6 tablespoons mayonnaise
Juice of 1 lemon
Salt to taste

Combine the first 6 ingredients and mix well. Add juice from oysters and remaining ingredients to the oyster mixture; blend well. Refrigerate at least 24 hours before serving. Serve with crackers.

*Mrs. John Wright (Joanne)*

## SPINACH VEGETABLE DIP

1 package frozen chopped spinach,
thawed and drained
1 cup mayonnaise

½ cup chopped onion
½ teaspoon salt
2 teaspoons parsley

Put all ingredients in blender. Blend on high for about 2 minutes. Serve with raw vegetables. Make the day before to enhance the flavor.

*Mrs. Victor Pryles (Millie Finch)*

## ARTICHOKE APPETIZER

2 cans artichoke hearts,
drained and shredded
2 cups parmesan cheese,
freshly grated, if possible

2 cups mayonnaise
Dash garlic powder
(optional)

Mix together and sprinkle with paprika. Bake uncovered at 350 degrees for 30 minutes. This can be mixed and served in same dish. Serve with rye toast or crackers.

*Mrs. Victor Pryles (Millie Finch)*
*Mrs. John Dearing (Gail)*
*Mrs. Phil M. Maddox (Linda)*
*Mrs. Timothy Trivers (Helen)*

5

## CAVIAR AND EGG MOLD

| | |
|---|---|
| 4 hard-cooked eggs, mashed | Lemon juice |
| 1/3 cup butter, softened | Salt to taste |
| ¼ to 1/3 cup mayonnaise | ½ cup sour cream |
| 1/3 cup chopped scallions | 1 small jar caviar |

Combine all ingredients except sour cream and caviar. Line small bowl with saran wrap. Pack mixture into bowl and chill well. Unmold on serving platter. Frost with sour cream and top with caviar. Serve with crackers.

*Mrs. Paul Pater (Polly)*
*Mrs. Charles Bartenfeld (Deedy)*

## COLD CRAB MOUSSE

| | |
|---|---|
| ½-1 pound crabmeat (chopped shrimp or lobster may be substituted) | 1 jar pimientos, chopped |
| | 1½ envelopes plain gelatin |
| 1 (8 ounce) package cream cheese | ¼ cup dry vermouth |
| 1 cup celery, finely chopped | 1 teaspoon worcestershire sauce |
| 1 onion, minced | 8-10 drops tabasco sauce |
| 1 can cream of mushroom soup | ½ teaspoon monosodium glutamate |
| 1 cup mayonnaise | |

Let cream cheese stand at room temperature to soften, then whip together with mayonnaise. Add celery and onion. Soften gelatin in vermouth. Heat soup, but do not boil, and add gelatin mixture, dissolving thoroughly. Mix in all remaining ingredients and pour into well-greased molds. After mousse has jelled in refrigerator, it may be frozen and kept for several weeks. If frozen, allow to stand at room temperature for 2 hours before unmolding. Serve with melba rounds or a bland cracker.

*Mrs. Richard L. Childs (Lora)*

LOVING TOUCHES . . .
Low-calorie dip for raw vegetables: equal portions of Kraft Low-Cal French and Blue Cheese Dressings.

6

## SALMON MOUSSE

1½ envelopes unflavored gelatin
2 tablespoons lemon juice
   (more, if desired)
1 small slice onion
½ cup mayonnaise

½ teaspoon paprika
1 teaspoon dried dill, optional
1 (1 pound) can salmon, drained
1 cup heavy cream

Sprinkle gelatin over ¼ cup cold water. Let stand 5 minutes. Spoon gelatin into a sauce pan containing another ¼ cup water. Heat until gelatin is completely melted. Put lemon juice, onion slice, mayonnaise and gelatin into blender. Blend on high speed for 40 seconds. Turn blender off. Add paprika, dill (if used) and salmon. Blend at high speed to a puree. Turn blender off. Add 1/3 of the cream. Blend for a few seconds. Continue until all the cream is used, blending at the end for 40 seconds. Pour into a four-cup mold (you may put a light film of salad oil on mold) and chill until firm. Serves 6. This may be served as an appetizer or as a light luncheon.

*Mr. William Stephens (Bill)*

## FRESH SHRIMP MOLD

*Delicious*

1½ tablespoons plain gelatin
¼ cup cold water
1 can tomato soup
1 (8 ounce) package cream cheese

1½ cups cooked shrimp, chopped
1 cup mayonnaise
¾ cup finely chopped celery
½ cup finely chopped onion

Soften gelatin in cold water. Heat soup and add softened gelatin and cheese. Stir until smooth. When cool, add remaining ingredients. Pour into 4-cup mold. Chill overnight. Serve with crackers.

*Mrs. John J. Henson, Jr. (Marge)*
*Mrs. William Horton (Carol Ann)*

## SHRIMP MOLD

1 (16 ounce) package frozen shrimp
1½ cups Miracle Whip
1 tablespoon gelatin
¼ cup hot water

2 hard-boiled eggs, chopped
½ teaspoon horseradish
1 small onion, grated
Juice of 1 lemon

Dissolve gelatin in hot water. Mix with rest of ingredients. Pour in mold and refrigerate. Serve as an appetizer.

*Mrs. Wade H. Shuford (Nancy)*

7

## SHRIMP SUPREME

*Do-ahead recipe*

1 package plain gelatin
2 tablespoons cold water
Juice of 1 lemon
¾ cup Hellmann's mayonnaise
2 cups shrimp, finely chopped
¾ cup chopped celery

1½ teaspoons grated onion
1 small bottle stuffed olives,
   thinly sliced (15-20)
1 teaspoon catsup
Dash salt and red pepper
½ cup half and half

Soak gelatin in the cold water. Set it in a pan of hot water to liquify. Add lemon juice and mayonnaise. Mix with rest of ingredients. Pour into 1-quart mold. Chill 2 to 3 days. Serve with club crackers.

*Mrs. Richard Perry (Lucy)*

## CHAFING DISH CRAB

6 tablespoons butter
1/3 cup chopped green onions
2 cups fresh mushrooms, sliced
3 tablespoons flour
2½ cups half and half

4 ounces cream cheese
1 pound crabmeat
¼ cup dry sherry or white wine
Juice of ½ lemon
Salt and pepper

Saute onions and mushrooms in butter. Stir in flour; cook until blended. Pour in half and half and cook, stirring constantly, until mixture thickens. Add cream cheese; stir until melted. Add crab, wine, lemon juice, salt and pepper. Serve in chafing dish.

*Mrs. John J. Henson, Jr. (Marge)*

## CHEESE PINEAPPLE

*Can be used as a centerpiece*

2 (8 ounce) packages cream cheese
2 (5 ounce) jars process sharp
   cheddar spread
1 (5 ounce) jar process bleu
   cheese spread

3 tablespoons wine vinegar
Dash of garlic salt
Pineapple - large, with a
   pretty top
Stuffed olives

Blend together cheeses, (which have been softened at room temperature), vinegar and garlic salt. (Leave out the vinegar for a stiffer mixture). Chill. Form the cheese mixture around the pineapple. Chill. Press sliced olives into the cheese to resemble a pineapple. Use crackers or small knife to dip into cheese.

*Mrs. Allan Strand (Anne)*

## CREAM CHEESE AND CHUTNEY

1 (8 ounce) package cream cheese
2/3 cup sour cream
½ cup Major Grey's or Bengal
  hot chutney

3-5 teaspoons curry powder
Dash garlic powder
1 cup chopped, salted cashews

Soften cream cheese; mix with all other ingredients. Serve with crackers. May be frozen.

*Mrs. Coley Evans, Jr. (Mary)*

## OLIVE CHEESE SPREAD

*Very popular*

1 box Ritz crackers
1 (8 ounce) package cream cheese
1 (3 ounce) package cream cheese
2 cups sour cream
1 small onion, chopped
½ small bell pepper, chopped

2 tablespoons lemon juice
1 teaspoon worcestershire sauce
Dash of tabasco sauce
1 teaspoon salt
½ teaspoon paprika
½ bottle olives, chopped

Brush spring pan with butter. Crush crackers and sprinkle on bottom of pan, reserving some for top. Mix rest of ingredients, except olives. Pour into pan. Crumble reserved crackers on top. Arrange olives on top of this.

*Mrs. Harry Lange (Dottie)*

## CHIPPED BEEF SPREAD

1 (8 ounce) package cream cheese
½ pint sour cream
2 tablespoons milk
1 small jar (or package) chipped beef

¼ cup chopped green pepper
2 tablespoons onion flakes
½ teaspoon garlic salt
1 small package chopped pecans

Mix together. Bake 20 minutes at 350 degrees, or until it bubbles. May also warm in a chafing dish. Serve with crackers.

*Mrs. B. W. Cardwell, Jr. (D.D.)*

## LOVING TOUCHES . . .

Serve fresh strawberries in orange juice at breakfast.

## LIVER PATE

1 pound chicken livers
½ pound butter
2-3 tablespoons broth (hot),
   saved from cooking livers
1 small onion, chopped

2 teaspoons dry mustard
1 teaspoon salt
¼ teaspoon grated nutmeg
   (fresh, if possible)

Cook livers until done in small amount of water. Drain, reserving broth. Place all ingredients in blender, and blend until smooth. Mixture will be very thin. Chill in round bowl; may be frozen at this point. Unmold and cover with fresh, chopped parsley, and surround with lemon wheel halves.
*Mrs. George Johnson (Janet)*

## MADRILENE MOLD

*A party favorite*

1 can madrilene, add grated
   onion to taste
1 package Knox gelatin

1 (3 ounce) package cream cheese,
   add grated onion to taste
1 small can liver pate

Soften gelatin in ½ of the madrilene. Heat the other half; mix the two together. Add enough hot water to cheese to make a spreading consistency. Mix about 2 tablespoons mayonnaise with pate. Pour 1/3 madrilene mix into bottom of shallow mold; place in refrigerator. When set, spread cheese mixture over, leaving a small edge of madrilene showing. Add enough madrilene to cover. Set. Repeat the procedure for the pate, ending with the madrilene. Chill well. Serve with small crackers.
*Mrs. Richard B. Jones (Kay)*

## MUSHROOM CAVIAR

*Delicious and easy*

½ medium onion, minced
1 tablespoon butter
¼ pound fresh mushrooms,
   finely chopped
1 tablespoon fresh lemon juice

½ teaspoon worcestershire sauce
Mayonnaise
Salt
Fresh ground pepper

Saute onion in butter until golden. Add mushrooms and saute for 5 minutes. Add lemon juice and worcestershire; mix and remove from heat. Add enough mayonnaise to bind together. Mound on serving plate. Chill and serve with melba toast or crackers. Can be made the day before. Recipe may be doubled.
*Mrs. William A. McClain, III (Rose)*

## STEAK TARTARE

Two pounds prime sirloin,
  finely ground
1 egg
4 anchovy fillets
3 tablespoons finely chopped onion
Salt and pepper

1 teaspoon olive oil
1 tablespoon Dijon mustard
2 dashes worcestershire sauce
3 tablespoons capers
2 tablespoons brandy or madeira

In wooden bowl mash anchovies, capers, onions and mustard with olive oil. (use fork or wooden spoon). Add raw egg and beat just slightly. Add meat, worcestershire sauce, brandy or madeira and salt and pepper. Mix well. Put in oiled decorative mold and chill. Serve on platter garnished with parsley or watercress. Use crackers for hors d'oeuvres or, as first course, place small mound of tartare on bibb lettuce and serve with very thin toast or crackers.

*Mrs. James Cushman (Elkin)*

## CHILIES AND CHEESE PIE

2 (4 ounce) cans El Paso chilies (hot)
2 eggs
1/3 cup milk

½ cup grated sharp cheddar
  cheese
Dash salt

Drain and place chilies in shallow 9 inch baking dish. Beat eggs and milk and pour half of this mixture over chilies. Add salt. Sprinkle grated cheese. Add remaining egg-milk mixture. Bake at 350 degrees for 20 minutes, or until custard consistency. Serve piping hot on thin crackers.

*Mrs. I. S. Mitchell, III (Betty)*

## CHEESE PUFFS

*Melt in your mouth*

½ pound sharp cheddar cheese
1 (3 ounce) package cream cheese
1 stick margarine

Unsliced white bread
2 egg whites, stiffly beaten

Melt cheeses and margarine together in double boiler until mixture reaches fondue-like consistency. Fold in egg whites. Cool. Cut bread in ¾ inch cubes. Coat each cube with cheese mixture (hold cube on fork and swirl on all sides except bottom). Place on waxed paper and freeze. Bake at 425 degrees for 8-10 minutes. Makes 5 dozen.

*Mrs. Lynn Humphries*

## CHEESE WAFERS

*For that unexpected company*

2 cups sharp cheese, grated
2 sticks softened butter
2 cups flour

1 teaspoon salt
Dash tabasco sauce
2 cups Rice Krispies

Work together all the ingredients except the cereal. When well-blended, add the Rice Krispies. Pinch off in small balls and put on ungreased cookie sheet. Bake at 350 degrees for about 16 minutes. Makes 6½ dozen. These keep well in an air-tight container.

*Beverly Wright Clark*
*Mrs. Frank Millians (Helen)*
*Mrs. Joseph White, Jr. (Barbara)*

## HOT CRAB CANAPES

1 loaf French bread, thinly sliced
½ pound crabmeat
½ cup grated cheddar cheese

¼ cup mayonnaise
1 teaspoon grated onion
1 teaspoon horseradish

Saute French bread slices in butter in a skillet until crisp and lightly browned on both sides. Blend crabmeat with remaining ingredients. Spread on toasted French bread rounds and brown in broiler. Makes 3-4 dozen.

*Mrs. Robert Chambers (Wendy)*

## MUSHROOM ROLLS

*Universally liked*

½ pound fresh mushrooms,
   finely chopped
¼ cup butter
3 tablespoons flour
¾ tablespoon salt
½ teaspoon Accent

½ cup light cream
2 tablespoons minced chives
   (frozen)
1 tablespoon lemon juice
Loaf unsliced bread

Saute mushrooms in butter 5 minutes or less. Blend in flour, salt and Accent. Stir in cream (more if needed) and cook until thickened. Add chives and lemon juice, and cool. Cut bread into 25 thin slices and remove crusts. Spread with mixture and roll up. May freeze at this point. Before serving, cut each roll in half or thirds and place under broiler. Serve hot. Makes 50 rolls. May simplify by putting mixture on bread round or in cocktail patty shells.

*Mrs. Dixon Driggs (Lollie)*

## PICKLED MUSHROOMS

2/3 cup tarragon vinegar
½ cup salad oil
1 clove garlic, crushed
1 teaspoon sugar
2 tablespoons water

1½ teaspoons salt
Dash tabasco
Dash pepper
12 ounces fresh, whole mushrooms
1 medium onion, thinly sliced

Combine first 8 ingredients; mix well. Saute mushrooms in butter, and add them, and the sliced onion, to the above mixture. Cover, refrigerate 8 hours or overnight. Drain before serving. This recipe good for pickled beets, too.

*Mrs. W. P. Morgan (Martha)*

## SAUTEED HERB MUSHROOMS

1 stick butter
1 pound mushrooms
¼ teaspoon oregano
½ teaspoon onion powder

Scant ½ teaspoon garlic powder
1 teaspoon (heaping) Accent
¼ teaspoon rosemary
1/3 cup sherry

Wash and drain mushrooms. Melt butter in skillet and add rest of the ingredients. Add mushrooms and simmer 20-25 minutes. Serve as hors d'oeuvre in chafing dish or as condiment to steak. Serves 4.

*Kathy Van Natter Young*

## MARINATED BLACK OLIVES

2 large cans black olives, pitted and drained
1 cup olive oil
1 cup wine vinegar

1 tablespoon Italian seasoning
Salt to taste
Pepper
3 shakes of garlic powder

Combine all ingredients in bowl. Chill for 24 hours.

*Mr. Paul Hensler*

## NACHOS

1 large bag Tortilla chips
1 (4 ounce) can green chilies, diced
1 pound Monterey Jack cheese, grated

½ pint sour cream
1 can frozen guacamole dip, thawed

Cover cookie sheet with foil and spread chips evenly over it. Sprinkle chilies over chips and top with cheese, covering all chips. Place under broiler until cheese melts. Drop mounds of sour cream over hot cheese and top with tablespoons of guacamole. Slide foil onto serving tray.

*Mrs. Jon Shepherd (Kay)*

## CHINESE SWEET BONES

2 pounds sausage
4 tablespoons flour
1 egg, beaten
4 tablespoons butter
½ cup onion, thinly sliced
1½ cups celery, thinly sliced

2 cups water
1 cucumber, sliced
Salt and pepper
1 tablespoon lemon juice
Toasted almonds (optional)

Cut sausage into strips 4 inches long and ¼ inch thick, (or use links or cocktail sausage). Roll in flour, dip in egg, then in flour. Saute in butter. Add 1 cup water, onion, celery. Cover, simmer 20 minutes. Add cucumber with remaining water and lemon juice. Simmer 10 minutes. Serve in chafing dish, garnish with almonds. Provide toothpicks.

*Mrs. Alfred Roach, Jr. (Marchant)*

## LIPTON ONION SOUP STICKS

*Great!*

½ package onion soup (Lipton's)        ½ stick butter

Mix soup and butter and spread on strips of white bread, which has been cut into finger size bites. Brown under broiler and serve hot. Serves 8 with other party foods.

*Mrs. Ervin Williams (Glenda)*

## SWEET AND SOUR MEATBALLS

Meat Balls:
1 pound ground beef
1 egg
½ onion, grated
2 pieces white bread, soaked in water

1 teaspoon Accent
Dash garlic powder
Salt and pepper

Sauce for 1 pound meat:
½ box dark brown sugar
1 can tomato soup
1 teaspoon Accent

¼ cup vinegar
1/8 teaspoon cinnamon

Roll meat mixture into 1 inch balls. Boil sauce ingredients together. Drop meatballs into sauce and simmer 45 minutes to 1 hour. This freezes well.

*Bob Baiter*

14

## COCKTAIL REUBENS

36 slices party rye bread
Thousand Island dressing
Swiss cheese slices

1 or 2 packages thinly sliced
  corned beef
1 can sauerkraut

Spread dressing on bread. Top with piece of folded corned beef. Spread sauerkraut and then cut slice of swiss cheese to fit. Bake 5 minutes at 400 degrees, or until cheese melts. Can be made ahead and cooked at serving time.

*Kathy Van Natter Young*

## ESCARGOTS A LA BOURGUIGNONNE

48 black snails
48 snail shells
½ cup softened butter
½ teaspoon salt
4-6 tablespoons finely chopped parsley

2-6 garlic cloves, minced
2-3 shallots, finely chopped
1 teaspoon white pepper

Place snails in shells. Cream butter until smooth and add rest of ingredients. Mix well. Pack butter mixture on top of snails, and place shells in shallow metal pans. Bake at 400 degrees until butter mixture is lightly browned. Serves 8, as a first course.

*Mrs. David Stacy (Beverly)*

## MARINATED SHRIMP

1¼ cups Wesson oil
¾ cup white vinegar
2 teaspoons salt
2 teaspoons celery seed
Bottle of capers
Shrimp, 3-4 pounds, cooked

Dash of tabasco
3-4 medium onions, thinly sliced
7-8 bay leaves
2 jars marinated artichokes
1 jar button mushrooms

Combine all ingredients, except shrimp, and mix well. Add shrimp and marinate for a day or more.

*Mrs. Dave Davis (Joan)*

## LOVING TOUCHES . . .

Wrap chunks of melon (cantaloupe or honey-dew) with very thin slices of prosuitto ham.

15

## SHRIMP PARFAITS

*Beautiful*

2½ pounds cooked, chilled shrimp
Shredded lettuce
Green mayonnaise
Watercress, lemon slice - garnish

Pimiento (strips)
Hard-boiled eggs (sieved)
Capers, drained

Using 10 parfait glasses, alternate layers of lettuce, shrimp, mayonnaise, pimiento, eggs and capers. Top each parfait with 1 or 2 shrimp. Garnish with watercress and lemon slices. Serves 10.

### Green Mayonnaise

2 cups mayonnaise
2 tablespoons parsley, minced
1 tablespoon chives, snipped

1 tablespoon tarragon, minced
1 teaspoon dill, minced
1 teaspoon chervil, minced

Mix all ingredients together.

*Mrs. Hall Ware (Mary)*

## CRABE DEMOS

1 cup mayonnaise
4 teaspoons prepared mustard
3 teaspoons curry powder
½ teaspoon salt

2 teaspoons lemon juice
6 ounces lump crabmeat
½ cup wild rice, cooked
Parmesan cheese

Mix the mustard, curry, salt, lemon juice with the mayonnaise. Divide the wild rice into 2 sea shells. Cover with the crabmeat. Spread the above mixture over the crabmeat well. Sprinkle with grated parmesan cheese and place in a hot oven for about 20 minutes. Serve each shell as a first course or it may be served as a luncheon dish.

*Stanley Demos' Coach House Restaurant*
*Lexington, Kentucky*

## LOVING TOUCHES . . .

Remember: Line silver dishes with glass bowls, doilies, saran wrap, aluminum foil, etc. against salt, vinegar, mayonnaise and other evil silver spoilers and pitters!

For an easy transition to dinner, serve a first "course" in living room: Soup in mugs, an antipasto plate, an elegant plate of shrimp or caviar.

# Soups

## CREAM CHEESE SOUP

*Very good*

4 (3 ounce) packages cream cheese
2 cups beef consomme

¾ teaspoon curry powder
Red caviar or tiny shrimp

Blend the cream cheese, consomme and curry powder in blender until smooth. Correct seasonings. Chill. Place a teaspoon of red caviar or 6 shrimp in each cup as served. Sprinkle with chopped parsley or chives. Serves 6. This is a delicious cold soup. May be jellied as a salad by adding 1 envelope of gelatin to each pint of liquid.

*Mrs. Moncure Crowder (Jo)*

## CHABLIS CHEDDAR SOUP

*Ideal appetizer*

2 tablespoons butter
3 green onions (with tops), sliced
½ cup finely chopped celery
1 can (10¾ ounce) condensed cheddar cheese soup
½ cup water
½ cup light cream

1 teaspoon instant chicken bouillon
1/8 teaspoon ground nutmeg
¼ cup chablis or other dry white wine
Paprika
Croutons

Melt butter in saucepan. Add onions and celery. Cook about 10 minutes or until tender; remove from heat. Stir cheese soup into onion mixture until smooth. Return to heat. Stir water, cream, chicken bouillon, and nutmeg gradually into soup mixture, until smooth. Cook, stirring occasionally, until thick; about 8 minutes. Stir in chablis. Sprinkle each serving with paprika and garnish with croutons. Serves 4. (½ cup each)

*Mrs. Robert F. Dennis (Peggy)*

## APPLE ONION SOUP

*A pleasing first course*

1 onion, white and quartered
1 apple, seeded and quartered
2 cans chicken bouillon

1 teaspoon curry
Sherry (about ¼ cup or to taste)
¼ cup cream

Cook the onion and apple in the bouillon until tender. Mash and strain. Add curry and sherry to the clear liquid. Reheat. When ready to serve, add cream. Garnish with whipped cream and chives. Serves 4.

*Mr. Robert Saffold*

18

## ASPARAGUS SOUP MARSEILLES

1 pound fresh asparagus spears,
   cut up, cooked, drained
2½ cups milk
1 teaspoon instant minced onion
1 teaspoon salt
1 teaspoon dry mustard

½ teaspoon capers
½ teaspoon juice from capers
Dash of pepper
Shredded lemon peel or chopped
   hard-cooked egg and strips
   of pimiento

In blender place asparagus, milk, onion, salt, mustard, capers, and juice and pepper. Blend at high speed until ingredients are thoroughly combined. Place soup in 2 quart sauce pan and heat to serving temperature. Garnish with lemon peel or egg and pimiento. Yield: 4 cups. 117 calories per cup.                    *Mrs. John C. Portman, Jr. (Jan)*

## BLACK OLIVE SOUP

*Prize-winning*

3 cups chicken stock
1 cup pitted black olives, sliced
1 tablespoon onion powder
1 teaspoon garlic powder

1 cup light cream
1/3 cup flour
2 tablespoons worcestershire sauce
Salt and pepper to taste

Combine in a saucepan, chicken stock, olives, onion and garlic powders. Simmer for 15 minutes. Blend together cream and flour. Add to hot mixture, stirring constantly until mixture thickens and reaches the boiling point. Boil 1 minute. Season with salt and pepper. Stir in worcestershire sauce. Serve hot. Garnish each serving with fresh chopped parsley. Serves 6.                    *Mr. Ed Forio, Jr.*

## ICED BROCCOLI SOUP

1 pound fresh broccoli, trimmed
1 quart clear chicken broth
1 small onion, chopped
2 stalks celery with leaves, chopped
4 or 5 sprigs parsley, chopped
1 large carrot, diced

1 teaspoon salt
¼ teaspoon cayenne pepper
2 tablespoons arrowroot or
   cornstarch
1 cup light cream
1 tablespoon chopped chives

Wash broccoli, cut off the buds and dice the stalks. Put stalks into pot with the chicken broth, onion, celery, parsley, carrot, salt and pepper. Simmer 15 minutes and add the buds. Simmer 5 minutes more and remove the buds. Add to the soup the arrowroot or cornstarch mixed with a little cold water. Simmer and stir until thick. Puree in blender. Chill at least 4 hours. Add light cream. Garnish with broccoli buds and chopped chives. Serves 6.                    *Mrs. Richard L. Childs (Lora)*

## CARROT SOUP

*Pretty, yet filling and good*

5 to 6 peeled, sliced potatoes
7 large carrots
1 large onion, chopped
1½ quarts chicken stock
1 ham hock (or 1 cup leftover ham)

1 tablespoon salt
1 quart heavy cream
Pinch pepper
Chopped chives

Cook potatoes, carrots, onion, and ham in stock until done. Remove hock and put in blender until smooth. Season with salt and pepper. Add cream and chill. Garnish with chopped chives. Serves 10-12.

*Mr. Ed Forio, Jr.*

## CREAM OF CORN SOUP

2 cups fresh corn (or 2 packages frozen)
2 strips finely chopped bacon
2 tablespoons finely chopped onion
2 tablespoons butter

2 tablespoons flour
2 cups milk
1 teaspoon salt
½ teaspoon pepper
2 cups coffee cream

Run corn in blender for 2 minutes. Set aside. Fry chopped bacon until crisp. Add onion and saute until soft. Add corn to onion and bacon and cook until it begins to brown. Add butter, then flour. Cook slowly for 3 minutes. Add milk, salt and pepper and cook until thickened. Add cream and heat until smooth. Serve hot. Serves 6.

*Mrs. Frank Owens, Jr. (Marguerite)*

## COLD AVOCADO SOUP

*Delicate in taste and in color*

1 large, ripe avocado (equivalent to 2 cups pulp)
2½ cups chicken broth
1 tablespoon chopped onion
1 cup sour cream

1 cup heavy cream
Few drops of tabasco
Salt and pepper to taste
1 teaspoon lemon juice

Mash avocado well (or puree in the blender with some of the broth). Add other ingredients and mix well. Chill. Makes 6½-7 cups.

*Mrs. Vernon Sanders (Ann)*

## COLD CUCUMBER – AVOCADO SOUP

*Delightful*

1 cucumber, peeled and seeded
½ avocado, peeled and seeded
2 green onions and tops, chopped
1 cup chicken stock

1 cup sour cream
2 tablespoons lemon juice
Salt and pepper to taste
Paprika

Combine all ingredients in blender for 10 to 15 seconds until smooth. Chill. Sprinkle each serving with paprika. Serves 4-6.

*Mrs. James Cushman (Elkin)*

## CUCUMBER AND WATERCRESS SOUP

3 large cucumbers; peeled, seeded, diced
1 bunch watercress; washed, drained, chopped (remove stems)
3 tablespoons butter

1½ cups cooked, diced potatoes
1 quart rich chicken stock
Salt and white pepper
1 cup heavy cream

Melt butter in 2 quart saucepan. Add cucumbers and watercress. Simmer covered 10 to 15 minutes; stirring occasionally. Add potatoes, chicken stock, salt and pepper to taste. Simmer it covered 10 to 15 minutes more. Stir. Cool soup. Puree in blender until smooth. Add cream (not whipped). Chill. Serves 6-8. (For an extra special touch, place each bowl of soup in a bed of crushed ice.) Garnish with thin slices of cucumbers.

*Mrs. Hall Ware (Mary)*

## WATERCRESS SOUP

3 bunches watercress
3 tablespoons butter
¼ cup minced onion
1½ cups water
1 teaspoon salt
½ teaspoon white pepper

2 tablespoons flour
2 (13 ounce) cans clear chicken broth
2 cups milk
2 eggs
1 cup heavy cream

Rinse and drain watercress. Remove coarse stems. Melt one tablespoon butter in a large saucepan; add onion and cook until golden. Add watercress, water, salt and pepper; cook over high heat for five minutes. Put mixture into a blender at high speed for a few seconds. Melt the remaining two tablespoons of butter in a saucepan and stir in the flour.

(continued)

21

Add the chicken broth and milk and bring to a boil. Stir in the water-cress mixture. Beat egg yolks and heavy cream together. Stir one cup of the hot soup into the egg-cream mixture. Add this combination to the soup, stirring constantly. Heat thoroughly, but do not boil. Serves 8. Serve hot or cold with buttered pumpernickel bread.

*Mrs. Robert F. Dennis (Peggy)*

## SPINACH SOUP
*Serve hot or cold*

1 box (10 ounce) frozen, chopped spinach
1 can beef broth or 10-ounces chicken broth
½ medium onion, chopped

1 cup light cream
Salt and crushed black pepper
Pinch of sugar
MSG

Boil spinach, broth and onion until tender. Pour into blender. Blend. Pour into bowl and add cream. Season with salt, pepper, sugar and MSG. Chill well (or may be heated). Serve with sour cream seasoned with chopped chives, black cracked pepper and pinch of salt. Serves 4.

*Mrs. Paul Pater (Polly)*

## GAZPACHO

1 or 2 cloves garlic, crushed
2 tablespoons olive oil
3 tablespoons wine vinegar
1 teaspoon salt
1 teaspoon worcestershire sauce
¼ teaspoon pepper
6 drops tabasco
2 cups tomato juice

2 tomatoes, peeled and diced
1½ ribs celery, cut fine
½ cucumber, diced
1/3 cup onion, chopped (green)
½ green pepper, diced
1/3 container frozen chives
1/3 container frozen parsley

Mix all ingredients together well. Chill. Serves 6-8.

*Mrs. Thomas Dowden (Wendy)*

LOVING TOUCHES . . .

Save bones and leftovers in a special place in the freezer and combine later for a great soup. Always add one fresh vegetable for a lively taste.

## GAZPACHO VERDE

*A great summer soup*

2 cans cream of celery soup
2 cups milk
1 medium diced cucumber (about 2 cups)
1 cup chopped green pepper

1 cup sliced pimiento stuffed olives
2 tablespoons lemon juice
Dash tabasco
2 cups sour cream

Combine and mix in electric blender soup, milk, cucumber, green pepper, ½ cup olives and dash of tabasco. Blend lemon juice and sour cream into soup mixture. Chill at least 4 hours. Serve in chilled bowls. Garnish with remaining olives and/or chopped parsley, and/or croutons. Serves 8.

*Mrs. L. Newton Turk (Marcy)*

## TOMATO SOUP

*May be served hot or cold*

1½ sticks butter
2 tablespoons olive oil
1 large onion, sliced
½ teaspoon thyme
½ teaspoon basil
Salt and pepper to taste
2½ pounds fresh tomatoes, peeled or substitute with

1 (2 pound 3 ounce) can Italian tomatoes
3 tablespoons tomato paste
¼ cup flour
3¾ cups chicken broth
1 teaspoon sugar
1 cup cream

Combine 1 stick butter and olive oil in pan. Add onion, thyme, basil, salt and pepper. Cook until tender. Add tomatoes and tomato paste. Blend flour into ¾ cup chicken broth and stir into tomato mixture. Add remaining 3 cups chicken broth and simmer 30 minutes. Put soup through blender and strain. When ready to serve, reheat adding sugar and cream. Simmer 5 minutes. Add ½ stick butter. Serves 6-8.

*Mrs. William Benton (Ida)*

LOVING TOUCHES . . .

Soups and stews can be skimmed with pieces of stale bread or a large lettuce leaf.

---

## CURRIED TOMATO SOUP

*Hot or cold*

¼ cup sliced green onions
2 tablespoons melted butter
2 (10¾ ounce) cans tomato soup, undiluted
2½ cups water
¾ teaspoon curry powder

Saute onion in butter until lightly browned. Add tomato soup, water and curry powder. (Add more powder to suit taste). Heat thoroughly, stirring constantly. Garnish with grated egg yolk. Serves 4-6.

*Mrs. James Cushman (Elkin)*


## VICHYSSOISE

*A classic soup*

4 leeks (white part), finely sliced
¼ cup finely chopped onion
¼ cup butter
5 medium potatoes, cut in quarters
1 carrot, sliced
1 quart chicken stock
1 teaspoon salt
2 cups milk
3 cups heavy cream

Saute leeks and onion in butter until yellow. Add potatoes, carrot, chicken stock, and salt. Bring to a rapid boil. Cover. Reduce heat and simmer until potatoes and carrots are soft. Mash and rub through a fine strainer or put in blender. Return to heat and add milk. Season to taste. Cool. Add cream and chill. Serve in very cold cups. Garnish with chives. Serves 8.

*Mrs. James Cushman (Elkin)*
*Mrs. Joseph R. White, Jr. (Barbara)*


## COLD LEMON SOUP

*Delicious on a hot day*

1 tablespoon lemon juice
1 teaspoon lemon rind (grated)
1 egg yolk
4 tablespoons parmesan cheese
4 cups chicken consomme

Combine lemon juice, rind, egg yolk and cheese. Heat consomme. When it reaches a boil, whisk lemon mixture into it. Chill. Top with slice of lemon. Serves 4.

*Mrs. Jay Gilbreath (Skee)*

24

## TIFFANY'S BEAN POT SOUP

*Recipe from old Tiffany's Restaurant and Saloon in Cerrillos*
*near Santa Fe, New Mexico*

2 cups dried pinto beans
1 cup cubed ham
48 ounces tomato juice
2 cups chicken stock
2 medium onions, chopped
1 clove garlic, sliced
¼ cup chopped green pepper

¼ cup brown sugar
1 tablespoon chili powder
1 teaspoon salt
1 medium bay leaf
1 teaspoon celery seed
3 teaspoons fine herbs

Soak beans overnight. Rinse well. Combine with all ingredients and cook slowly for 3 hours. Remove bay leaf. Put in blender. (Thin with tomato juice or water to desired consistency). Reheat. Add 1 teaspoon of sherry to each serving. Top with chopped green onions. Serves 6.

*Mrs. Peter S. Harrower (Irene)*

## FRENCH ONION SOUP

*A husband pleaser!*

6 large yellow onions, thinly sliced
½ cup butter
2 cans condensed beef broth
1 soup can water
1 soup can dry white wine

4 slices French bread, toasted,
cut 1-inch thick
¼ cup fresh parmesan cheese, grated
½ cup Swiss or gruyere cheese,
grated

Saute onions in butter until lightly browned. Add broth, water and wine. Simmer until onions are tender. Add parmesan cheese. Spoon soup into 4 earthenware bowls. Top each with a slice of toasted bread that has been sprinkled with cheese. Broil until cheese melts. Serves 4.

*Mrs. Joseph R. White, Jr. (Barbara)*

## BARLEY, BEEF SOUP

*A hearty vegetable soup that has pleased generations*

2 quarts cold water
3 pounds of short ribs of beef
1 cup medium barley
3 large grated carrots
4 large ribs of celery, chopped
2 large onions, chopped

1 large can whole tomatoes
(1 pound 12 ounces)
1 small can whole tomatoes
(14½ ounce)
1½ tablespoons salt
½ teaspoon pepper

(continued)

Place short ribs of beef, well trimmed of fat, (leave bones in) into water. Bring to boiling point in covered 6 quart pot. Reduce to simmer for 2 hours. Add barley. Return to boiling point, reduce heat and simmer 1 hour. Add carrots, onions, tomatoes, celery, salt and pepper. Bring to boil and then simmer 2 hours covered and 2 hours uncovered. Serve with homemade bread and fresh baked pie. Wonderful winter-day dinner.

*Mrs. Robert Hennessy (Nancy)*

## GROUND BEEF VEGETABLE SOUP

*The more it cooks, the better it gets*

1 pound ground chuck
1 large onion, chopped
3 diced potatoes
1/3 cup raw rice
1 (46 ounce) can V-8 or tomato juice
1 (8 ounce) can tomato sauce
Tabasco (few drops)

1 (10 ounce) package frozen peas and carrots
1 (10 ounce) package frozen succotash (corn and limas) or
2 (10 ounce) packages of mixed vegetables can be substituted
3 cups water
Worcestershire sauce (several shakes)

Brown meat and onions in large pot. Add all other ingredients and salt to taste. Simmer about 30 to 45 minutes, or until potatoes are tender. This makes a lot, but freezes well. It gets thick as it is reheated. If needed, thin with water and bouillon cubes. Serves 8-10.

*Mrs. Bengt Stromquist (Alison)*

## CHICKEN, RICE, PASTINA SOUP

*Thick, nourishing and great for a cold day*

7 cups water
1 large chicken breast split
1¾ teaspoons salt
¼ teaspoon pepper
½ teaspoon celery seed
1 medium onion, chopped

1 2/3 cups celery, chopped plus some tops
½ cup rice
2 tablespoons spinach pastina
1 tablespoon dry parsley

Simmer chicken breast in water seasoned with salt and pepper. When chicken pulls away from bone, remove from liquid. Cut up in bite size pieces and return to stock which has been strained. Bring to a boil and add celery, celery seed, onion, rice, pastina and parsley. Reduce to medium heat and cook until rice is tender. Correct seasonings and add more water if too thick. Serves 6.

*Mrs. Thomas King (Jane)*

## CREAM OF CHICKEN ALMOND SOUP

½ cup blanched almonds
1 tablespoon finely chopped celery
1 tablespoon finely chopped onion
2 tablespoons butter

3 cups hot chicken broth
1 cup diced cooked chicken
1 cup light cream
1/8 teaspoon white pepper

Toast almonds on baking sheet, stirring occasionally until golden, 10 to 15 minutes in 350 degrees oven. Set aside. Cook celery and onion in butter over low heat until tender. Stir 1½ cups chicken broth into vegetables. Heat to boiling; reduce heat. Simmer 5 minutes. Pour remaining 1½ cups broth into blender. Add almonds and chicken. Cover and blend until very smooth. Add chicken mixture to vegetables. Stir in cream and pepper. Cook, stirring occasionally, until very hot for about 5 minutes. Garnish with paprika and sprig of watercress. Makes 7 appetizer servings. (½ cup each)

*Mrs. William Farr, III (Linda)*

## OYSTER SOUP

*A favorite New Orleans Sunday night supper*

6 small green onions with tops, chopped
2 ribs celery, chopped
½ stick butter

Salt and pepper
1 pint oysters
1 quart milk
Worcestershire sauce

Saute onions and celery in butter until tender. Pour in 1 pint of oysters, with liquid; remove from heat. Set aside. Heat milk (don't boil). When ready to serve, reheat both, combine and serve hot. Season to taste with worcestershire sauce, salt and pepper. Serves 4. (Divide oysters evenly into each serving.)

*Josephine Reid*

## LOVING TOUCHES . . .
A dash of nutmeg adds a divine taste to cream soups.

## NEW ENGLAND–STYLE CLAM CHOWDER

*This is a Duke University favorite*

1 quart canned clams, chopped, drained
2 or 3 medium potatoes, diced
2 medium onions, chopped
2 medium green peppers, chopped
8 slices bacon, cooked, diced
1¼ quarts milk
3 tablespoons flour

1 tablespoon bacon drippings
1 quart clam juice
1½ quarts chicken stock (not bouillon)
1 tablespoon worcestershire sauce
1 teaspoon tabasco
Salt and pepper to taste

Fry bacon and boil potatoes. Saute onions and peppers in bacon drippings, reserving one tablespoon for the soup. Heat milk. Make a roux of fat and flour (mix them together), and whip into hot milk. Cook, stirring until slightly thickened. Add clam juice, chicken stock, and all other ingredients (except clams) to this mixture. Heat but do not boil. Turn off heat, add chopped clams and stir. Makes one gallon.

*Valerie Caswell*

## CLAM BROTH WITH WHIPPED CREAM

*Tastes much more complicated than it is*

2 bottles clam juice
1 can minced clams
Salt and pepper

Whipped cream
Curry

Put juice and clams in blender with a little salt and pepper. Strain and chill. Top with a dollop of whipped cream flavored with curry. Serves 4.

*Mrs. Jay Gilbreath (Skee)*

LOVING TOUCHES . . .
Use a wire whisk for smooth blending of canned soups and water.

# Sandwiches

## EGG AND BACON SPREAD

16 hard-boiled eggs, finely minced  
16 slices crisp bacon, crumbled  
4 tablespoons horseradish

4 teaspoons finely minced onion  
1 cup mayonnaise  
4 teaspoons salt

Combine all ingredients and chill until serving time. Serve with Ritz crackers or as a sandwich spread.

*Mrs. Morris L. Shadburn, Jr. (Edyth)*

## BEEF BARBECUE

*Can be cooked in a crock pot*

2-3 pound chuck roast  
¾ bottle Heinz chili sauce  
1½ tablespoons worcestershire sauce  
Salt and pepper to taste

3 tablespoons brown sugar  
1 large onion, chopped  
1 green pepper, chopped

Simmer roast in a kettle, Dutch oven or crock pot in 2-3 inches of water until beef shreds easily. When beef is shredded, remove fat and bones. Combine rest of ingredients and add to the beef. Cook slowly until proper consistency. Serves 4-6.

*Mrs. James Dickson (Mary)*

## BEEF BARBECUE

3 pounds beef roast, cooked and diced  
1 large can tomato sauce  
1 can beef broth  
½ cup vinegar  
3 tablespoons sugar  
1 teaspoon allspice

1 large onion, chopped  
1 teaspoon black pepper  
1 teaspoon chili powder  
½ teaspoon salt  
½ teaspoon nutmeg  
3 or 4 bay leaves

Mix and allow to simmer for several hours, adding more tomato sauce if it seems too thick. Serve on hamburger buns. Serves 6-8.

*Mrs. A. J. Stringer (Martha)*

## WESTERN STYLE BURGERS

1 teaspoon salad oil  
2 tablespoons chopped onion  
½ pound ground beef  
½ cup ripe olives, chopped (optional)  
1 teaspoon prepared mustard

1 cup Swiss cheese, shredded  
1 medium potato, grated  
4 hamburger buns, lighty buttered  
1 teaspoon salt and pepper

Saute onion in oil; brown meat and add all other ingredients. Quickly stir in the meat last. Spoon mixture on bottoms of buttered buns. Cover with bun tops and wrap in aluminum foil. Bake in 350 degrees oven about 40-50 minutes or on outdoor grill. Serves 4.

*Mrs. Kenneth P. Lynch, Jr. (Peggy)*

## CHEESE LOG SANDWICHES

½ cup finely chopped onion
¼ cup mayonnaise
½ cup margarine
2 cups sharp cheese, grated

Dash tabasco
1 small jar pimientos
12 thin slices fresh bread

Spread mixture on bread; reserve 1/3 for tops. Draw opposite corners of bread up to center and spread tops with rest of mixture. Sprinkle McCormick's Italian Seasoning on tops. Pack in pan to hold together and bake at 350 degrees for 10 minutes. Can be made ahead. Serve two or more for luncheon. Serves 6. *Mrs. William Bradshaw (Carolyn)*

## SANDWICH SPREAD

*So easy and so good*

1 small jar (½ pint) Miracle Whip
½ pound Velveeta Cheese

1 can tuna (6½ ounces)

In top of double boiler heat salad dressing and cheese until melted. Add flaked tuna fish. Mix well and store in refrigerator. Serves 6.

*Mrs. Robert Dunlap (Mary Jane)*

## BAKED CHICKEN SANDWICH

6 slices bread
2 cups cooked chicken
¼ cup chopped green pepper
½ cup chopped celery
2 teaspoons chopped onion
Paprika

Parsley
3 eggs
1 pint milk
1 can mushroom soup
8 ounces sharp cheese, grated

Mix together chicken, vegetables, and parsley. Remove crusts from two slices bread and cube. Spread cubes over buttered pan with high sides. Spread chicken mixture over top. Put four slices bread, crusts removed, on top of this. Beat eggs and milk. Add soup to this. Pour over all. Top with cheese and paprika. Bake one hour at 350 degrees. Serves 6.

*Mrs. David F. Apple, Jr. (Jane)*

31

## CHILI OPEN–FACED SANDWICHES

8 ounces extra sharp cheese
8 ounces mild cheddar
8 ounces Monterey Jack
6 English muffins

½ cup chopped green onion
½ cup sliced ripe olives
Miracle Whip to moisten

Grate three cheeses together. Add other ingredients and mix together. Slightly toast English muffin halves and spread mixture on each half. Cook in 400 degree oven, just until cheese mixture is melted and slightly brown on edges. Serves 6. Can be made in advance and will keep indefinitely in refrigerator.

*Mrs. Vernon Sanders (Ann)*

## CRAB SANDWICHES

1 (10 ounce) package refrigerated biscuits
1 (8 ounce) package frozen crab meat

½ cup grated sharp cheddar cheese
3 tablespoons mayonnaise

Separate biscuits. Pat each into a 3½ inch round. Arrange half on greased baking sheet. Mix crab, drained and sliced, with cheese and mayonnaise. Spread on biscuits. Brush tops with melted butter. Let stand 15-20 minutes. Bake at 425 degrees for 15-20 minutes, or until browned. Makes 5 sandwiches.

*Mrs. John M. DeBorde, III (Anne)*

## OPEN–FACED CRABMEAT SANDWICHES

1 stick butter or margarine
3 ounce package cream cheese
4 hamburger buns

1 small can crabmeat
Few drops tabasco

Soften butter and cream cheese and cream together. Add crab and tabasco. Spread on hamburger buns. Cook at 400 degrees until melted and bubbly. Serves 4.

*Mrs. Vernon Sanders (Ann)*
*Mrs. James Stanford (Deenie)*

32

## HOT HAM SANDWICHES

½ pound butter (soft)
3 tablespoons salad mustard
1½ teaspoons poppy or celery seed
1 teaspoon worcestershire sauce

1 medium onion, minced
16 slices ham
8 slices Swiss cheese
8 buns

Mix first five ingredients together. Spread each side of bun with mixture (use plentifully). Place cheese between two slices of ham on each sandwich. Wrap twice in aluminum foil. Bake at 400 degrees for 15 minutes. These are handy to freeze. Bake frozen for 30 minutes. Serves 8.

*Mrs. David Stacy (Beverly)*

## LITTLE PO' BOY SANDWICHES

Bologna
American cheese
Spicy meat
Small French rolls

Swiss cheese
Ham
Pickles (dill slices)

Split small French rolls. On bottom slice put mayonnaise and top with meat, cheese, and pickles. Spread mustard on top half of bread. Secure with a tooth pick. Bake at 450 degrees for 5-8 minutes.

*Mrs. Charles Barnwell (Anne)*

## NUT AND PATE SANDWICHES

¼ cup ground almonds
¼ cup butter

¼ cup pate de foie gras
8 slices sandwich bread

Blend almonds, butter and pate until smooth. Spread between bread slices and trim crusts. For tea sandwiches, cut each large sandwich into quarters. Makes 16 tea, or 4 large sandwiches.

*Mrs. Robert F. Dennis (Peggy)*

**LOVING TOUCHES . . .**

Unusual and delicious sandwich combinations:
Tuna salad with tomato slices and alfalfa sprouts on whole grain bread or pumpernickel roll.

Avocado slices and alfalfa sprouts on French bread, spread with mayonnaise.

33

## ROQUEFORT SANDWICHES

| | |
|---|---|
| ¼ pound roquefort cheese | 1 tablespoon armagnac |
| ¼ pound butter | 8 slices sandwich bread |

Blend cheese, butter and armagnac. Spread between bread slices and trim crusts. For tea sandwiches, cut each large sandwich into quarters. Makes 16 tea, or 4 large sandwiches.

*Mrs. Robert F. Dennis (Peggy)*


## 24—HOUR TOASTIES

| | |
|---|---|
| 2 cans tuna | 2 jars Old English cheese |
| 2/3 cup mayonnaise | ½ cup margarine |
| ½ cup chopped ripe olives | 2 eggs |
| 4 hard-boiled eggs | 24 slices bread |
| Salt and pepper | |

Mix first five ingredients for filling. Mix next three ingredients for frosting. Take crusts off bread. Cut round with tuna can. Use three slices bread for each sandwich. Put filling between bread and cover with frosting - top and sides. Let set overnight. Bake 10 minutes at 450 degrees. Serves 8.

*Mrs. Clifford M. Kirtland, Jr. (Jane)*


## VEGETABLE SANDWICH MIX

*For tailgating at the Steeplechase*

| | |
|---|---|
| 1 cup celery | 2 carrots, finely grated |
| 1 medium green pepper | 1 envelope gelatin |
| 1 medium cucumber | 1 cup mayonnaise |
| 1 medium onion | 1 cup sour cream |
| 2 medium tomatoes, peeled | 2 teaspoons salt |

Chop the vegetables and reserve the juices. Add enough water to the juices to make ¼ cup. Pour liquid over gelatin. Soak gelatin in juices until hard. Dissolve hardened gelatin in ¼ cup boiling water. Cool mixture and add mayonnaise, sour cream and salt. Stir this into chopped vegetables and spread on small bread rounds. To keep bread fresh, wrap sandwiches in damp paper towel and keep in refrigerator until time to serve. Makes about 3 dozen.

*Mrs. Thomas Eddins (Barbara)*

34

# Breads

DAVID SAPP

## BUTTER BATTER BREAD

*A dark health bread*

3 cups whole wheat flour
2 packages dry yeast
2½ cups buttermilk
¼ cup molasses
¼ cup honey
1 tablespoon salt

1/3 cup butter
1½ cups rolled oats
2 eggs
2½ - 3 cups flour
1 cup raisins, optional

Combine whole wheat flour and yeast. Heat buttermilk, molasses, honey, salt and butter until just warm. Add oats, whole wheat-yeast mixture, and eggs. Blend at low speed in electric mixer. Stir in enough flour to make stiff dough. Brush with melted butter. Cover; let rise until double. Punch down, divide into 2 round loaves. Bake in greased 1½ quart round 2½ inch deep casserole at 375 degrees for 25-35 minutes.

*Mrs. George Johnson (Janet)*
*Mrs. Richard Mattison (Sharon)*

## EASTER BRAID

*Greek bread*

1 package dry yeast
¼ cup water
1 cup milk, scalded
½ cup sugar
2 teaspoons salt
½ cup butter, softened

4½ - 5 cups flour
2 eggs
2 teaspoons grated lemon peel
¼ teaspoon mace
1 egg and 1 tablespoon water

Soften yeast in warm water. Combine next four ingredients and cool to lukewarm. Stir in 2 cups flour, eggs and mix well. Stir in yeast, peel and mace, and remaining flour. Let rest 10 minutes. Knead until smooth and elastic. Cover and let rise until double. Punch down and divide into 2 balls. Divide each ball into 3 rolls about 8 inches long. Braid, starting at center and working toward ends. Tuck ends under to seal. Brush with egg-water mixture and bake at 350 degrees for 30 minutes.

*Mrs. Richard Mattison (Sharon)*

## ITALIAN BREAD

2 cups hot water
½ cup Wesson oil
3 tablespoons sugar
1 tablespoon salt
1 egg

8 cups flour
2 packages yeast dissolved in
    ½ cup lukewarm water
Egg whites
Sesame seeds

Let dissolved yeast rise 45 minutes. Combine first 5 ingredients and add to yeast. Add 6 cups flour to combined mixture and beat in mixer for 15 minutes. Knead on board until remaining 2 cups of flour are used. Let rise in bowl for 1½ hours. Shape into 2 long loaves and put on greased cookie sheet. Let rise 1 hour. Brush dough with egg whites and sprinkle with sesame seeds. Bake at 450 degrees for 5 minutes, then at 350 degrees for 30 minutes. Bread may be frozen.

*Mrs. John Dearing (Gail)*

## LIMPA (SWEET RYE BREAD)

| | |
|---|---|
| 1 package dry yeast | 2 teaspoons caraway seeds |
| ¼ cup warm water | ½ teaspoon anise seed |
| ½ cup packed brown sugar | 1½ cups hot water |
| 1/3 cup molasses | 4 cups plain flour, sifted |
| 1 tablespoon grated orange peel | 2 cups rye flour |
| 1 tablespoon salt | |

Soften yeast in ¼ cup water. Add hot water to next 6 ingredients. When lukewarm, add 1 cup plain flour and beat until smooth. Stir in softened yeast mixture, then 3 cups plain flour and 2 cups rye. Allow dough to rest a few minutes, then knead 5 or 10 minutes. Place in covered, greased bowl and let rise until double. Punch down, turn over in bowl, and let rise again until doubled. Divide dough into 2 balls and place on greased baking sheet. Cover and let rise until double. Bake at 375 degrees for 25 - 35 minutes.

*Mrs. Philip Bird (Jane Murray)*

## SPOON BREAD

*Old Virginia recipe*

| | |
|---|---|
| 1 cup yellow meal | 1½ teaspoons salt |
| 2 cups milk | 1 cup milk |
| 2 tablespoons Crisco | 2 tablespoons sugar |
| 3 eggs | 1 tablespoon baking powder |

Bring to a boil the meal, milk, Crisco, and stir until smooth. Beat together eggs, salt, and 1 cup milk. Add to hot meal. Combine sugar and baking powder and add to mixture. Pour into greased 1½ quart casserole. Bake at 400 degrees for 30-35 minutes. Serve with butter. Serves 6-8.

*Mrs. Edward C. Loughlin, Jr. (Bet)*

## YORKSHIRE PUDDING

*Easiest yet .. so good*

3¾ cups flour  
1 teaspoon salt  
1¼ cups milk  

¾ cup water  
4 eggs  
½ cup roast beef drippings  

Into a bowl sift together flour and salt. Add milk, water and eggs. Beat until smooth. Let the batter stand covered for at least 2 hours. In shallow baking dish, heat beef drippings in 450 degree oven for 10 minutes. Pour batter into dish and bake pudding for 15 minutes. Reduce heat to 350 degrees and bake for 20 to 30 minutes more. Serves 10.

*Mrs. Hall Ware (Mary)*

## HEMLOCK INN ROLLS

¾ cup scalded milk  
1/8 cup sugar  
3 tablespoons oil  
1 teaspoon salt  

1 rounded tablespoon yeast  
1 egg, slightly beaten  
3½ cups flour  

Pour milk over sugar, oil, salt, and cool to luke warm. Soften yeast in 2 tablespoons water. Add egg and mix well. Add half of flour and beat well. Add remaining flour and mix well. Let rise until double. Knead lightly, roll out and cut. Let rise again until double and bake at 425 degrees for 20 minutes.

*Mrs. William A. Nix*

## ANGEL BISCUITS

1 package yeast  
2 tablespoons warm water  
5 cups plain flour  
1 teaspoon soda  
3 teaspoons baking powder  

4 tablespoons sugar  
1 teaspoon salt  
1 cup shortening  
2 cups buttermilk  

Dissolve yeast in water. Sift flour with dry ingredients. Cut in shortening. Add buttermilk and yeast mixture. Stir, then knead a few minutes. Roll out to ½ inch thickness. Cut with biscuit cutter and brush with butter. Bake in 400 degree oven about 12-15 minutes. Dough may be kept several days in refrigerator.

*Mrs. Gene S. Cofer (Neta)*  
*Mrs. Ed Andrews (Jan)*

## MUFFIN BISCUITS

2 cups self-rising flour
1 cup milk

4 tablespoons mayonnaise

Mix together in bowl and fill greased muffin tins ½ full. Bake at 450 degrees for 10 minutes. Makes 12.

*Mrs. Edward C. Loughlin, Jr. (Bet)*

## SWEET POTATO BISCUITS

1 (16 ounce) can drained
   sweet potatoes
¼ cup milk

1 tablespoon sugar
1½ cups biscuit mix

Combine potatoes, milk and sugar and beat until smooth. Add biscuit mix, stir with a fork until moistened. Turn out and knead 5 times. Roll out ½ inch thick and cut with 2½ inch cutter. Bake on ungreased baking sheet at 450 degrees for approximately 12 minutes. Makes 10-12 biscuits.

*Mrs. Bengt Stromquist (Alison)*

## BEATEN BISCUIT

*An almost lost art!*

7 cups sifted flour
2 teaspoons baking powder
4 tablespoons sugar
1 teaspoon salt

1 cup lard
2/3 cup milk
2/3 cup ice water

Mix first 4 ingredients. Add lard and work in thoroughly. Combine milk and water and add slowly, kneading until stiff dough is obtained. Divide dough in half for ease of handling. Put dough through beaten biscuit kneader or beat with wooden rolling pin thoroughly. Combine dough batches and repeat beating process at least 75-80 times. A velvety smooth dough about ¼ inch thick is your goal. Cut with 1 inch biscuit cutter, place on cookie sheet, and punch twice, all the way through with a fork. Bake in 300 degree oven for 35 minutes. Reduce heat to 250 degrees degrees for another 10 minutes. They should be slightly pink on top and bottom. Makes 8 dozen.

*Mr. Bud Gould*

## LOVING TOUCHES . . .

Thin slices of baked chicken breasts, watercress and mayonnaise (with chutney and curry powder added) on whole grain bread.

## BEER MUFFINS

3 cups Bisquick
½ cup sugar

12 ounce can beer

Mix and bake in hot greased muffin tins, 2/3 full, at 400 degrees until done. Makes about 2 dozen.

*Mrs. Bengt Stromquist (Alison)*

## CINNAMON NUT MUFFINS

1 cup sugar
2 cups flour
3 teaspoons cinnamon
¼ teaspoon salt
2 teaspoons baking powder

1 cup milk
½ cup Crisco oil
2 eggs, beaten
1 cup chopped nuts

Combine dry ingredients and sift together. Mix all liquids and combine quickly with dry ingredients. Fold in nuts and bake in greased muffin tins at 400 degrees for 20 minutes. Dough keeps well in refrigerator for 7-10 days in Tupperware.

*Mrs. Merritt S. Bond (Suzanne)*

## SIX—WEEK BRAN MUFFINS

15 ounce box raisin bran
3 cups sugar
5 cups flour
5 teaspoons soda
2 teaspoons apple pie spice mix

2 teaspoons salt
4 eggs, beaten
1 quart buttermilk
1 cup Crisco oil
2 teaspoons vanilla

Mix all ingredients together. Store in covered container in refrigerator. Mix will keep six weeks. To bake, fill greased tins 2/3 full and bake in 400 degree oven 10-15 minutes.

*Honey Hays Barnes*
*Mrs. William Farr, III (Linda)*
*Mrs. Charles A. Beard (Mary Crain)*

## HERB BREAD STICKS

8 day-old hot dog rolls, cut
  into 6 sticks
1 stick butter, softened

1 teaspoon basil
1 teaspoon marjoram
½ teaspoon thyme

Mix together butter and herbs, and spread on cut sides of bread sticks. Bake at 250 degrees for 1 hour. Cut off oven and leave in for another hour. May be served hot or cold.     *Mrs. Ed Forio, Jr. (Phoebe)*

## HOT HERB BREAD

1 loaf Italian or French Bread
½ cup soft margarine
1 teaspoon parsley flakes
¼ teaspoon oregano, crumbled

½ teaspoon dill weed
1 clove minced garlic
Grated parmesan cheese

Mix butter and herbs. Spread on bread which has been cut into 1 inch diagonal slices. Sprinkle cheese over loaf. Wrap in aluminum foil and bake at 400 degrees until warmed.

*Mrs. Jerry Tidwell (Dottie)*
*Mrs. Dudley G. Pearson (Neville)*

## HUSH PUPPIES

1 cup water ground white corn meal
1 cup plain flour
1 tablespoon salt
1 tablespoon sugar

1 egg, beaten slightly
¾ cup finely chopped onion
2 teaspoons baking powder
Beer

Mix first six ingredients, add 2 heaping teaspoons baking powder. Moisten with beer to a consistency that will drop off a kitchen spoon in egg-sized balls. Drop into hot oil and turn with slotted spoon so they will brown evenly. Serves 6.

*Mrs. Jay Gilbreath (Skee)*

## ONION BREAD

1 package dry yeast
1 cup cottage cheese
¼ cup lukewarm water
¼ teaspoon soda
1 tablespoon butter
2½ cups plain flour

½ teaspoon salt
2 tablespoons sugar
1 tablespoon minced onion
2 tablespoons dill seed
1 egg

Dissolve yeast in water. Heat cottage cheese to lukewarm. Add salt, soda, and sugar. Then add onion, dill seed, butter and yeast. Add well-beaten egg and flour in small amounts, and mix well. Let stand in buttered bowl 2 hours. Knead well and place in greased loaf pan. Let rise until double and bake at 350 degrees for 40 minutes. Brush with melted butter and spinkle with salt.

*Mrs. Gene Presley (Dianne)*

41

## ZUCCHINI BREAD

3 eggs
2 cups sugar
1 cup vegetable oil
2 cups grated, peeled raw
   zucchini
3 teaspoons vanilla extract

3 cups flour
1 teaspoon salt
1 teaspoon baking soda
¼ teaspoon baking powder
3 teaspoons cinnamon
1 cup chopped walnuts or filberts

Beat eggs until light and foamy. Add sugar, oil, zucchini and vanilla, and mix lightly, but well. Combine flour, salt, soda, baking powder, and cinnamon, and add to egg-zucchini mixture. Stir until well blended. Add nuts and pour into 2 greased (9x5x3) loaf pans. Bake in preheated 350 degree oven for one hour.

*Claudia Lewis*

## BANANA BREAD

1 stick butter
¾ cup sugar
2 eggs
3 bananas, well-mashed

2 cups flour
1 teaspoon soda
1 teaspoon vanilla
1 cup chopped pecans

Cream butter and sugar. Add eggs one at a time. Beat in bananas. Sift flour, reserving 3 tablespoons, with soda. Fold flour in by hand in 3 equal additions. Add vanilla. Dredge pecans in reserved flour and fold into batter. Pour into well-greased and floured standard loaf pan. Bake at 325 degrees for approximately 1 hour 15 minutes. The last 15 minutes of baking you may, if you want a sweeter bread, draw a knife down the center of the loaf twice and pour on a mixture of runny icing made with confectioners sugar and milk. Stud with whole pecans.

*Mrs. Charles B. Rice (Barbara)*
*Mrs. Harry V. Lamon, Jr. (Ada)*
*Linda Murphy Finsthwait*

## LOVING TOUCHES . . .

Homemade biscuits can be undercooked to be "brown 'n serve". To heat: Brush with butter and put in hot oven for five minutes.

Keeping bread in the freezer prevents moldy throw-aways. Bread frozen fresh will thaw to original softness in minutes.

## CARROT BREAD

2 eggs, beaten
1 cup sugar
¾ cup Wesson oil
1 cup grated carrots
1½ cups flour

1 teaspoon baking soda
½ teaspoon salt
1 teaspoon vanilla
½ cup coppped pecans

Blend first 4 ingredients. Add remaining ingredients. Pour into greased 9 inch loaf pan and bake at 350 degrees for one hour or until toothpick stuck in center comes out clean. Freezes well.

*Mrs. Dennis Mollenkamp (Jane)*

## CRANBERRY FRUIT BREAD

2 cups sifted flour
1 cup sugar
1½ teaspoons baking powder
½ teaspoon baking soda
1 teaspoon salt
1 egg, well beaten

¾ cup orange juice
1 tablespoon grated orange rind
3 tablespoons salad oil
½ cup chopped nuts
2 cups chopped cranberries

Sift together flour, sugar, baking powder, baking soda and salt. Combine egg, orange juice, rind, and oil. Make a well in dry ingredients and add egg mixture. Mix only enough to moisten flour. Carefully fold in nuts and cranberries. Spoon into greased (9x5x3) loaf pan and bake at 350 degrees for 1 hour.

*Mrs. Richard Fritto (Mary Kay)*
*Mrs. John B. Gillespie (Vicki)*

## CHRISTMAS FRUIT BREAD

½ cup butter, creamed
3 mashed bananas
1 cup sugar
2 eggs
2 cups flour

1 teaspoon soda
Dash of salt
¼ cup chocolate chips
¼ cup maraschino cherries
¼ cup nut meats

Mix in order given. (Can mix chips, cherries and nuts with flour). Bake buttered loaf pan at 350 degrees approximately one hour.

*Mrs. George Finch (Frances)*

## PEACHY PECAN BREAD

1 (16 ounce) can sliced peaches
6 tablespoons butter, melted
2 eggs
1 tablespoon lemon juice
2 cups all-purpose flour

¾ cup sugar
3 teaspoons baking powder
1 teaspoon salt
¾ cup chopped pecans
2 tablespoons peach preserves

Drain peaches, reserving ¼ cup syrup. Finely chop 1 cup peaches and set aside. In blender combine remaining peaches, butter, eggs, reserved peach syrup and lemon juice. Blend until just smooth. Stir together dry ingredients. Add egg mixture and stir until moistened. Fold in reserved peaches and nuts. Bake in greased (8x4x2) loaf pan at 350 degrees for one hour. Spread with peach preserves. Cool in pan 10 minutes. Remove and cool on rack.

*Libba Finch Sprunt*

## PUMPKIN BREAD

3 cups sugar
1 cup salad oil
4 eggs, well beaten
1 (1 pound) can pumpkin
2/3 cup water
2 teaspoons salt

3½ cups flour
1 teaspoon cinnamon
1 teaspoon pumpkin pie spices
1 teaspoon baking powder
2 teaspoons soda

Cream oil and sugar. Add eggs and pumpkin and mix well. Sift and add dry ingredients alternately with water. Pour into two well-greased and floured (9x5) loaf pans. Bake at 350 degrees for 1 hour.

*Mrs. Thomas M. Johnson, Jr. (Benita)*
*Mrs. John Crenshaw (Patti)*

## BLUEBERRY COFFEE CAKE

1 stick margarine
1 cup sugar
½ pint sour cream
2 eggs
2 cups flour

1 teaspoon baking powder
½ teaspoon baking soda
1 teaspoon vanilla
1 can blueberries

Cream margarine and sugar together. Add eggs one at a time, then sour cream which has been mixed with baking soda first, then vanilla. Sift baking powder and flour together. Add to mixture. Pour ½ batter into an ungreased tube or bundt pan. Pour can of well-drained blueberries over and sprinkle generously with sugar and cinnamon. Then add rest of batter. Bake at 350 degrees for 45 minutes. Allow to cool before removing from pan.

*Mrs. Russell French (Vicki)*

## LOUISIANA BUTTER PECAN COFFEE CAKE

| | |
|---|---|
| 1 cup sugar | Topping: |
| 2 cups sifted flour | ½ cup chopped pecans |
| 3 teaspoons baking powder | 2 tablespoons soft butter |
| 1 teaspoon salt | ¼ cup brown sugar, packed |
| 1/3 cup soft butter | 2 tablespoons flour |
| 1 egg | 1 teaspoon cinnamon |
| 1 cup milk | |

Sift first 4 ingredients together. Add butter, egg and milk. Beat well, about 2 minutes. Pour into greased and floured 9 inch square pan. Blend topping ingredients and sprinkle over cake mixture. Bake at 350 degrees for 35-40 minutes.

*Mrs. David M. Vaughan (Vi)*

## MAKE AHEAD ORANGE COFFEE CAKE

Mix dough as much as 3 or 4 days ahead, refrigerate until needed, then bake.

| | |
|---|---|
| 2 cups flour | ¾ cup orange juice |
| 3 teaspoons baking powder | 1 egg |
| ½ teaspoon salt | 1 teaspoon vanilla |
| ½ cup sugar | ¼ cup vegetable oil |
| 1 teaspoon grated orange rind | |

Mix ingredients in order given and stir until well moistened. Pour into 10 inch cake pan. Sprinkle on topping of: 2 tablespoons grated orange rind, ½ cup sugar, 1 teaspoon cinnamon. Dot with 2 tablespoons butter and bake in 400 degree oven 20-30 minutes.

*Mrs. Gregory Fitz-Gerald (Diane)*

## LOVING TOUCHES . . .

A little broken-up stale bread will enable you to chop the hardest cheese in your blender. (Great for topping casseroles or spreading on toast for broiling.)

## PEANUT BUTTER CRISPS

1/3 cup peanut butter
1/3 cup cooking oil

Pinch of salt
8 slices of bread

Trim bread and save crusts. Cut into strips ½x¼. Place bread strips and crusts in oven and bake at 200 degrees for 1 hour. Dip toasted strips in peanut butter, oil and salt mixture, then in finely crushed bread crumbs made from toasted crusts. Store in air tight container and they will keep crisp forever.

*Mrs. Clifford M. Kirtland, Jr. (Jane)*

## SOUR CREAM COFFEE CAKE

2 sticks margarine
2 cups flour
1 teaspoon baking powder
½ teaspoon vanilla
2 cups sugar
2 eggs

¼ teaspoon salt
1 cup sour cream
Crumb Mix:
¾ cup chopped pecans
3 tablespoons sugar
1 teaspoon cinnamon

Cream butter and sugar. Add eggs and beat well. Sift dry ingredients and add alternately with sour cream - starting and ending with flour. Add vanilla. Pour ½ batter into greased bundt pan. Add ½ crumb mix, then other ½ batter. Sprinkle rest of crumb mix evenly over top and bake in 350 degree oven 50-60 minutes. Serves 12.

*Mrs. Wood Lovell (Carolyn)*
*Mrs. James M. Rupp (Sharon)*
*Mrs. Morris Ewing (Nancy)*

## STREUSEL SWIRL COFFEE CAKE

¾ cup raisins
2 cups biscuit mix
1 teaspoon cinnamon
½ cup sugar
1 egg, beaten

¾ cup milk
Streusel:
3 tablespoons melted butter
2/3 cup brown sugar, packed
¼ cup biscuit mix

Blend together first 6 ingredients. Spread ½ dough in greased 8 inch round pan. Blend streusel ingredients until crumbly. Spread half of mixture over dough, then remaining dough covered with rest of streusel. Bake in 350 degree oven about 35 minutes. May be iced with powdered sugar mixed with milk and drizzled over top while warm.

*Mrs. William Farr, III (Linda)*

# Salads

## and Salad Dressings

## ASPARAGUS SALAD

| | |
|---|---|
| ¾ cup sugar | 1 cup chopped celery |
| ½ cup vinegar | ½ cup chopped toasted nuts |
| 1 cup water | 1 can cut asparagus |
| 2 envelopes plain gelatin | 1 can chopped pimientos |
| ½ cup water | Juice of ½ lemon |
| 1 tablespoon grated onion | Salt to taste |

Combine sugar, vinegar, one cup water, and salt. Bring to a boil and boil 5 minutes. Dissolve gelatin in ½ cup water. Add this to hot mixture. Cool, then add remaining ingredients. Pour into a mold and chill. Serves 6-8

*Mrs. Merritt S. Bond (Suzanne)*
*Mrs. George Hopkins (Betty)*
*Mrs. Allan Strand (Anne)*

## ARTICHOKE — HEARTS OF PALM SALAD

*Good with roast or at a cocktail buffet*

| | |
|---|---|
| 3 cans (14 ounce) hearts of palm, sliced | 1 tablespoon worcestershire sauce |
| 3 cans (15 ounce) artichoke hearts, quartered | 1 teaspoon salt |
| | ½ teaspoon pepper |
| 2 jars (2 ounce) chopped pimientos | ½ cup oilive oil |
| 1 can (4½ ounce) chopped ripe olives | ½ cup tarragon vinegar |
| 1 can (4 ounce) chopped mushrooms | Juice of ½ lemon |
| 2 teaspoons French mustard | Oregano, pinch |
| | Basil, pinch |

Drain first 5 ingredients and place in a bowl. In another bowl stir mustard, worcestershire, salt, and pepper. Add remaining ingredients, stirring well. Pour dressing over salad just before serving. This will keep for a day even after dressing has been added and will not be soggy. Serves 20.

*Mrs. Jerry Tidwell (Dottie)*

## ARTICHOKE — RICE SALAD

*Delicious with roast beef; A favorite with men*

| | |
|---|---|
| 1 package chicken flavored rice mix (Uncle Ben's preferred) | 12 pimiento stuffed olives, sliced |
| 4 green onion, sliced thin | 2 (6 ounce) jars marinated artichoke hearts |
| ½ green pepper, seeded and chopped | ¾ teaspoon curry |
| 1/3 cup mayonnaise | |

Cook rice as directed on package omitting butter. Cool in large bowl. Add green onions, pepper and olives. Drain artichoke hearts, reserving marinade and cut them in half. Combine artichokes with the rice salad and toss with dressing of reserved liquid and mayonnaise. Chill. If you prefer a stronger curry accent, increase. Serves 8 generously.

*Mrs. Sydney Curtis (Ann)*
*Mrs. Jerry Tidwell (Dottie)*

## ASHEVILLE SALAD

2 cans tomato soup
½ pound cheddar cheese, grated
2 packages plain gelatin dissolved
 in 1/3 cup cold water
½ cup chopped celery

½ cup chopped bell pepper
½ cup chopped onion
1 cup mayonnaise
½ cup chopped pecans

Heat soup and cheese, add gelatin while hot. Cool well, add mayonnaise and stir well. Add other ingredients. Pour into oiled mold and refrigerate until firm. Serve on lettuce and top with mayonnaise. Serves 6-8.

*Mrs. Francis B. Sheetz, Jr. (Mandy)*

## ARABIC GREEN BEAN SALAD

*Fine for a buffet supper dish*

½ cup olive oil
1 cup chopped onions
1½ pounds fresh or 2 (10 ounce)
 packages frozen green beans

1 cup canned tomatoes
1½ teaspoons salt
½ teaspoon ground black pepper
½ teaspoon dried oregano

Heat olive oil in sauce pan, add onions and saute for 10 minutes but do not brown. Add the beans, cover and cook over low heat 10 minutes, stirring occasionally. Add the tomatoes, salt, pepper, and oregano. Cook 20 minutes. Chill and serve with lemon wedges. Serves 6-8. Can be doubled.

*Mrs. Jay Gilbreath (Skee)*
*Mrs. Jeffrey S. Muir (Carol)*

## BEETS AND HORSERADISH RING

*An attractive and delicious salad for a luncheon or dinner*

1 package (3 ounce) lemon gelatin
1 medium size can beets, riced
4 tablespoons horseradish

2 cups water mixed with beet juice
Juice of 1 lemon
Salt to taste

Melt gelatin with the water and beet juice - add other ingredients. Pour into round ring and refrigerate. Serves 6. To increase, double everything except horseradish.  *Mrs. Ben C. Finnegan (Dee)*

## BROCCOLI MOLD

*A great side dish for after holiday turkey sandwiches*

2 packages frozen chopped broccoli
1 envelope unflavored gelatin
1 can beef consomme
6 hard-boiled eggs, chopped
¾ cup mayonnaise

½ teaspoon salt
2 tablespoons lemon juice
1 tablespoon worcestershire sauce
8 drops tabasco

Boil broccoli in salted water 3-5 minutes. Dissolve gelatin in ¼ cup consomme. Heat remaining consomme, add to gelatin, cool. Combine other ingredients, pour into a mold or Pyrex (to cut into squares for serving), and refrigerate. Serves 8-10.  *Mrs. J. Randall Akin (Vicki)*
*Mrs. Herbert J. Beadle, Jr. (Jerry)*

## CAESAR SALAD

1 medium garlic clove
6 anchovies
1 teaspoon salt
Peppermill to taste
½ teaspoon Guldens mustard
½ teaspoon worcestershire sauce
1 cup oil

½ cup wine vinegar
1 egg, coddled
½ fresh lemon
½ cup parmesan cheese
2 heads romaine lettuce
Croutons

Paste garlic around wooden bowl. Paste anchovies around bowl. Add all other ingredients to bowl (salt, pepper, mustard, worcestershire, oil, vinegar, and egg) and mix. Set aside in refrigerator. Clean romaine and break into small pieces. Squeeze lemon juice over lettuce. Sprinkle with parmesan cheese. Pour other ingredients over lettuce and toss. Add croutons and serve. Serves 6-8. Dressing may be prepared in advance and kept for at least a week.

*Mrs. Myles J. Gould (Lynn)*

## CHERRY SALAD

*Men especially like this - it's not too sweet*

1 can pitted, sour pie cherries, canned in water
1 package cherry gelatin
1 small can crushed pineapple
1 cup chopped pecans
1 orange rind, grated
1 lemon rind, grated

Drain juice from cherries and add 2 tablespoons sugar to the juice. Heat juice and add gelatin. Add 3 tablespoons sugar to drained cherries. Add pineapple, nuts, and grated rinds. Add to gelatin mixture and mold. Serves 8.

*Mrs. William Horton (Carol Ann)*

## GERMAN COLE SLAW

1 cup white vinegar
1½ teaspoons salt
1 teaspoon mustard
1 teaspoon celery seed
¾ cup oil
1 cabbage, knife shredded
½ cup sugar
2 onions, thinly sliced

Layer cabbage and onion in large bowl and sprinkle sugar over mixture. Do not stir. Combine first 4 ingredients and boil for 1 minute and then add oil. Bring to boil again and pour over cabbage and onion. Do not stir. Cover and refrigerate 4 hours before serving. Serves 8. Keeps about 2 weeks.

*Mrs. Henry Smith (Anne)*

## CREAMY COLE SLAW

2 cups mayonnaise
¼ cup horseradish
1 tablespoon sugar
1 tablespoon lemon juice
1 tablespoon grated onion
2 teaspoons salt
½ teaspoon paprika
3 pounds green cabbage, finely shredded
½ cup shredded radishes
½ pound carrots, shredded

In large bowl, combine first 7 ingredients and mix well. Add the cabbage, radishes, and carrots and toss until well-coated. Refrigerate overnight. Serves 12.

*Mrs. Hall Ware (Mary)*

## MARINATED CARROT SALAD

*Great for picnics and cookouts*

1 (10¾ ounce) can undiluted
   tomato soup
½ cup corn oil
¾ cup herb vinegar or
   cider vinegar
1 cup sugar
1½ teaspoons worcestershire sauce
1 teaspoon dry mustard
1 tablespoon salt

½ tablespoon pepper
1/8 teaspoon red pepper
3 (16 ounce) cans drained
   sliced carrots
1 (8 ounce) can drained
   whole kernel corn
1 cup chopped celery
1 medium onion, chopped
1 medium green pepper, chopped

Combine and mix well and store in refrigerator in covered bowl. Stir occasionally. Drain and serve. Make at least two days before. Serves 10-12. Keeps for 2 weeks in refrigerator.

*Mrs. Harry V. Lamon, Jr. (Ada)*

## CONGEALED FRUIT SALAD

*Different and easy*

1 package lemon gelatin
1 package orange gelatin
1 (No.303) can apricots,
   drained and mashed
1 (No.303) can Kadota figs,
   drained and mashed

1 small can crushed pineapple,
   drained
1 small bottle cherries
1 (3 ounce) package cream cheese
½ cup crushed nuts
1 cup water

Dissolve gelatin in the hot water. Add juices from the drained fruit. Allow to thicken; fold in fruit, cheese, and nuts. Refrigerate. Serves 8.

*Mrs. Rual W. Stephens (Lenora)*

## DIFFERENT CHICKEN SALAD

*Not fattening*

2 whole fryers
3 stalks celery with leaves
2 bay leaves
2 tablespoons parsley flakes
2 onions, chopped
3 chicken bouillon cubes

Sherry
1½ cups chicken broth
½ cup sour cream
1 tablespoon honey
Blanched almonds or pecans

52

Boil fryers in highly seasoned water (celery, bay leaves, parsley, onions, and bouillon) to cover fryers. When chicken is very tender put in collander and drain broth into a pot placed under collander. Pull meat from bone and dice. Sprinkle chicken with some sherry and mix diced chicken with broth, sour cream, and honey. Add almonds or pecans before serving. May need salt. Serves 6 generously. Does not spoil easily.

*Mrs. Thomas M. Johnson, Jr. (Benita)*

## CONGEALED CHICKEN SALAD

*Good for lunch or snacks on crackers*

1 package lemon gelatin (large)
2 teaspoons garlic salt
¾ cup hot water
½ cup sour cream
½ cup mayonnaise
2 cups diced cooked chicken
    (3 chicken breasts)

1½ teaspoons grated onion
Dash white pepper
1 tablespoon vinegar
½ cup chopped pecans
½ cup diced celery

Dissolve gelatin and garlic salt in hot water. Add sour cream, mayonnaise, onion, pepper, and vinegar. Chill until thickened. Add pecans, celery, and chicken. Refrigerate until congealed. Serves 8.

*Mrs. Bert Oastler (Belitje)*

## CRAB AND AVOCADO SALAD

*Fabulous*

3 large avocados, peeled, pitted,
    and cut into 1 inch cubes
2½ pounds lump crabmeat
½ cup finely chopped celery
½ cup thinly sliced radishes
¼ cup lemon juice

¼ cup vinegar
3 tablespoons olive oil
2 tablespoons finely chopped
    green onions
¼ teaspoon cayenne
Salt to taste

Combine all ingredients. Mound on serving dish and surround with bibb or Boston lettuce hearts. Serve with Louis dressing (p. 54). Serves 12.

*Mrs. Hall Ware (Mary)*

## LOVING TOUCHES ...

A good squeeze of fresh lemon or a dash of wine vinegar will help any bottled dressing, mayonnaise, or leftover homemade dressing.

## LOUIS DRESSING

1 cup mayonnaise
¼ cup chili sauce
2 tablespoons chopped parsley
1 tablespoon finely chopped onion

1 tablespoon chopped chives
Dash of cayenne
¼ cup heavy cream, whipped

Add all ingredients to mayonnaise, folding whipped cream in last.

*Mrs. Hall Ware (Mary)*

## CRANBERRY SALAD MOLD

1 package black cherry gelatin
1 cup hot water
1 cup sugar
2 tablespoons lemon juice
1 tablespoon gelatin

1 cup pineapple juice
2 cups chopped raw cranberries
1 orange and rind, grated
1 cup crushed pineapple
1½ cups pecans

Dissolve cherry gelatin in hot water. Add sugar and lemon juice. Dissolve gelatin in pineapple juice and melt over hot water. Add to cherry gelatin mixture. Stir until blended. Add remaining ingredients. Pour into ring mold. Serve on lettuce. Serves 10.

Dressing:
1 cup mayonnaise
1 cup sour cream

Dash lemon juice

Blend together.

*Mrs. I. S. Mitchell, III (Betty)*

## CRANBERRY SAUCE MOLD

*Great for Thanksgiving with turkey*

1 package black cherry gelatin
¾ cup hot water

1 pound whole cranberry sauce
¼ cup ginger ale

Dissolve gelatin in hot water. Stir in cranberry sauce and ginger ale. Pour into greased small mold. Chill several hours. Serves 4-6.

*Mrs. Stanley D. Goldstein (Rita)*

## CRANBERRY SALAD

1 package orange-pineapple gelatin
½ jar cranberry-orange relish

1 small can crushed pineapple
½ cup chopped nuts

Dissolve gelatin in 1 cup boiling water. Add cranberry-orange relish, pineapple, and nuts. Chill. Serves 8.

*Mrs. Lamar Roberts (Shirley)*

## CONGEALED CUCUMBER SALAD

¾ cup shredded cucumber with rind
¾ cup liquid (cucumber juice drained and water)
1 package lime gelatin
1 teaspoon salt
2 tablespoons grated onion
1 package cream style cottage cheese
1 cup mayonnaise
½ cup slivered almonds

Grate cucumber with rind on. Press out juice and strain, adding water to make ¾ cup. Heat juice and dissolve gelatin in it. Cool, add remaining ingredients and chill. Serve on lettuce with mayonnaise. Serves 8.

*Mrs. John C. Portman, Jr. (Jan)*

## FRUIT FREEZE

1 cup mayonnaise
1 (8 ounce) package cream cheese
2 cups (No.303 can) fruit cocktail, drained
½ cup maraschino cherries
Food coloring
2 cups miniature marshmallows
1 cup whipping cream, whipped

Add mayonnaise to cream cheese and blend well. Add fruit and food coloring. Fold in marshmallows and whipped cream. Pour into salad mold and freeze. Serves 12. Can be made days ahead. Use food coloring to match color theme.

*Mrs. Gene Presley (Dianne)*

## GREEK SALAD

6 boiling potatoes
¼ cup finely chopped parsley
½ cup thinly sliced green onions
½ green pepper, thinly sliced
½ cup salad dressing
Salt
1 large head lettuce
12 roka leaves or 12 sprigs watercress
2 tomatoes cut in 6 wedges each
1 peeled cucumber, cut lengthwise into 8 fingers
1 avocado peeled, cut into wedges
4 portions feta cheese
1 green pepper cut into 8 rings
4 slices canned cooked beets
4 shrimp, cooked and peeled
4 anchovy fillets
12 black olives, Greek style
12 medium hot Salonika peppers
4 fancy cut radishes
4 whole green onions
½ cup white vinegar
½ cup each olive and salad oil blended
Oregano

(continued)

Make potato salad with first six ingredients. Line a large platter with the outside lettuce leaves. Place 3 cups of potato salad in a mound in center of platter. Cover with remaining lettuce which has been shredded. Arrange the roka or watercress on top of this. Place tomato wedges around outer edge of salad with a few on the top. Place cucumber fingers in between tomatoes, making a solid base of salad. Place avocado slices around the outside. Arrange feta cheese slices on top of salad with green pepper slices over all. On the very top, place sliced beets with a shrimp on each beet slice and an anchovy fillet on the shrimp. Arrange olives, peppers, green onions as desired. Sprinkle with oil and vinegar and then oregano. Serve at once. Serves 8-10. Good with garlic toasted Greek bread.

*Mrs. Henry C. Standard, Jr. (Marcia)*

## MEXICAN SALAD

*Main dish, good with bread and wine*

| | |
|---|---|
| 1  pound ground beef | 1  head of lettuce, torn in pieces |
| 1  can kidney beans, drained | 4  ounces grated cheddar cheese |
| ¼  teaspoon salt | ½-¾ bottle Catalina salad dressing |
| 1  onion, chopped | ½-1 bag of Doritos, crumbled |
| 4  tomatoes, cut in pieces | 1  avocado, cut in pieces |

Brown beef, add kidney beans and salt. Drain. Mix all ingredients in large bowl and toss.

*Mrs. J. Randall Akin (Vicki)*

## QUICK MANDARIN SALAD

| | |
|---|---|
| 1  medium carton Cool Whip | 1  small carton cottage cheese |
| 1  package (3 ounce) orange jello | 1  can mandarin orange slices, drained |

Mix together all ingredients and mold. Delicious as a salad or dessert Serves 6.

*Mrs. Graydon Leake (Vinita)*

## LOVING TOUCHES ...

To make your own croutons, cut French bread (or leftover bread saved in freezer) into cubes and place in a shallow pan. Pour over melted butter with garlic added and cook at 225 degrees for several hours.

## PICKLED PEAS

*This is modern version of the traditional "black-eyed peas and hog jowl"*
*served on New Year's Day in the South*

2 (No.2) cans cooked dried
  black-eyed peas
1 Italian onion, sliced thin
1 cup salad oil

¼ cup wine vinegar
1 clove garlic
½ teaspoon salt
Fresh ground pepper

Drain peas. Combine with onion in bowl. Mix other ingredients for marinade and pour over peas. Refrigerate for two days to two weeks before serving. Remove garlic after one day. Stir occasionally. Serves 12.

*Mrs. Robert Dunlap (Mary Jane)*

## LESEUR PEA SALAD

*Cold vegetable for picnics*

1 (15 ounce) can large LeSeur peas,
  drained
1 stalk celery, chopped
1 small bell pepper, chopped
½-¾ cup Polish pickles, drained and sliced

1 cup cheddar cheese, diced
1 bunch spring onions, sliced
Mayonnaise to bind mixture
Salt and pepper

Combine all ingredients and chill. Serve on bed of lettuce. Serves 4.

*Mrs. Robert F. Dennis (Peggy)*

## HOT POTATO SALAD

5 cups diced potatoes
1 pound carton cottage
  cheese
1 cup sour cream

1/3 cup green onions chopped,
  stems too
1 small bud garlic
Sharp cheese, grated

Cook potatoes in salted water and drain. Mix all ingredients together and put in large buttered rectangular casserole. Grate sharp cheese on top. Bake at 350 degrees about 40 minutes. Serves 8.

*Mrs. Jerry Tidwell (Dottie)*

## PAUL'S POTATO SALAD

8 large potatoes, diced
¼ cup chopped onions
¼ cup chopped bell peppers
¼ cup chopped celery
1 small jar chopped pimientos
5 tablespoons chopped sweet pickles

6 hard-boiled eggs, chopped
1 cup mayonnaise
4 tablespoons vinegar
1 tablespoon prepared mustard
1 pinch of sugar
Salt and pepper to taste

Boil potatoes until tender. Drain. Combine with remaining ingredients. Chill. Serves 10-12.

*Mr. Paul Hensler*

## PEPPED—UP POTATO SALAD

1½ teaspoons mustard seed
1 teaspoon celery seed
3 tablespoons vinegar
1½ teaspoons salt

½ cup green onion, chopped
with tops
5 cups diced cooked potatoes
¾ cup mayonnaise
2 hard cooked eggs, chopped

Soak mustard seed and celery seed in vinegar (several hours or overnight). Combine seed mixture with salt and green onions, add potatoes and mix lightly. Add mayonnaise and chopped eggs, toss to mix. Chill thoroughly. Serves 6.

*Mrs. William Teem, III (Betty)*

## ORIENTAL SALAD

1 pound fresh spinach
1/3 can (16 ounce) bean sprouts,
drained
1 can water chestnuts, sliced
and drained

2 hard-boiled eggs, chopped
1 cup fresh mushrooms, sliced
4 slices bacon, fried and
crumbled

Wash and dry spinach thoroughly, remove stems, add other ingredients, and use following dressing to toss. Serves 6-8.

### Dressing: puree in blender

1 cup oil
1/3 cup sugar
1/3 cup catsup
½ teaspoon salt

1/3 cup vinegar
2 teaspoons worcestershire
sauce
1 small onion, chopped

*Mrs. B. W. Cardwell, Jr. (D.D.)*
*Mrs. Jon M. Shepherd (Kay)*

## PICKLED PEACH CONGEALED SALAD

1 package lemon gelatin
¾ cup boiling water
1 cup pickled peach juice

4 pickled peaches, cut up
½ cup nuts, chopped

Dissolve gelatin in boiling water. Add other ingredients. Pour into mold and refrigerate. Serves 4.

*Mrs. Robert Jordan (Jay)*


## PINEAPPLE SALAD

2 packages lime gelatin
2 cups boiling water
1 cup crushed pineapple, drained
½ cup black walnuts

1 carton country style
   cottage cheese
1 small package cream cheese, broken
1 small can evaporated milk

Mix gelatin with water and cool. Stir in other ingredients, place in salad mold and refrigerate. Serves 12-15.

*Mrs. A. J. Stringer (Martha)*


## SHRIMP SALAD
*Tangy!*

1 pound shrimp cooked, cut up
1 cup celery, chopped
¼ cup diced green pepper

2 tablespoons horseradish
2 cups tomato juice
1 package lemon gelatin

Heat tomato juice, dissolve gelatin, chill until starts to set, fold in shrimp, celery, green pepper, horseradish, and put in mold. Serve with following sauce.

### Sauce

½ cup heavy cream, whipped
3-4 tablespoons mayonnaise

2 tablespoons horseradish

*Mrs. Robert Barr (Jane)*


## LOVING TOUCHES . . .

Grated provolone cheese adds a special taste to a green salad tossed with Wishbone Italian Dressing.

Toss curly endive, fresh orange slices and fresh onion slices with Italian Dressing for a delicious and different salad.

## SPINACH SALAD

Spinach

Hard boiled eggs, chopped

Garlic croutons

Bacon bits

Clean spinach and tear off stems. Sprinkle with eggs, croutons, and bacon bits.

### Dressing

4 tablespoons olive oil

8 tablespoons wine vinegar

1 teaspoon dry mustard

½ teaspoon seasoned salt

6 dashes soy sauce

Mix all together in a jar and shake well. Chill. Toss with spinach. Makes about ¾ cup of dressing.

*Kathy Van Natter Young*


## STRAWBERRY SOUR CREAM SALAD

2 large packages strawberry gelatin

2 cups boiling water

1 cup cold water

1 cup chopped nuts

1 (No.2) can crushed pineapple, plus juice

1 large carton frozen strawberries

1 pint sour cream

Dissolve gelatin in water; add fruits and juices. Pour half of mixture into (10x15x2) pan. Chill until firm. Smooth sour cream over gelatin. If desired, sprinkle nuts over sour cream. Cover with remaining gelatin mixture. Chill until firm. Cut into squares. Serve on lettuce bed with dash of sour cream and fresh strawberries. Serves 10-12.

*Mrs. John C. Portman, Jr. (Jan)*


## STRAWBERRY SUPREME MOLD

1 large package strawberry gelatin

1 can pink lemonade

1 pint vanilla ice cream

1 quart fresh strawberries

2 cups water

2 (10 ounce) packages frozen strawberries, drained

½ cup pecans, chopped

Follow directions on gelatin package using only 2 cups water. Add melted ice cream and melted lemonade. Add juice from one package of drained strawberries. Add 2 packages drained strawberries, then add pecans. Refrigerate mixture until firm. When serving, fill center of ring mold with fresh strawberries. Serves 8-10.

*Mrs. Robert Crow (Marilyn)*

## SAUERKRAUT SALAD

1 pound can sauerkraut, drained
1 onion, chopped
1 cup diced celery
1 cup sliced green pepper

¼ cup vinegar
½ cup oil
½ cup sugar

Mix all of the above together and refrigerate for at least 8 hours. Serves 6-8.

*Mrs. Oliver P. Ackerman, Jr.*

## TASTY GREEN SALAD

1 head lettuce, shredded
1 medium red onion, sliced in rings
4 hard-boiled eggs, sliced
1 (17 ounce) can green peas, drained

2/3 cup mayonnaise
1/3 cup sour cream
1 cup Swiss cheese, shredded
½ cup bacon, crumbled

Layer ingredients in a large clear salad bowl, (brandy snifter is very attractive,) in the order listed. Marinate, tightly covered, in the refrigerator for 10 hours or overnight. Toss and serve. Serves 10 people. This is an excellant tossed salad for parties as it can be prepared the day before. Put it out still layered and toss it just before serving.

*Mrs. Rayford P. Kytle, Jr. (Jean Horten)*

## QUICK TOMATO ASPIC

2 tablespoons gelatin
  (2 packages)
½ cup cold tomato juice or
  V-8 juice
3½ cups hot tomato juice-
  worcestershire sauce to taste

Juice of ½ lemon
1 teaspoon basil
1 or 2 cups solid ingredients
  as: chopped shrimp, celery,
  peppers, olives

Soak gelatin in cold tomato juice. Dissolve this in heated tomato juice. Add juice from 1 lemon and the basil. When this mixture is about to set, add solid ingredients and pour into mold and return to refrigerator.

*Mrs. M. E. Kilpatrick (Mary Hurt)*

61

## TUNA SALAD

*Ladies light luncheon*

4 hard-boiled eggs, chopped
2 tablespoons India relish
1 cup mayonnaise
1 (7 ounce) can tuna

Lemon juice, to flavor
Grated onion juice, to taste
1 (8 ounce) carton sour cream

Mix all ingredients. Serve on lettuce leaf, garnished with parsley. Serves 4.

*Mrs. John H. Stevens (Fern)*


## VEGETABLE SALAD

1 (16 ounce) can cut green beans
1 (16 ounce) can red kidney beans
1 (7 ounce) can pitted ripe olives
1 (8 ounce) can whole mushrooms
1 (4 ounce) jar diced pimiento

2 (15 ounce) cans artichoke
  hearts, cut in half
1½ cups celery, sliced
  diagonally
1 medium red onion, sliced in rings

Drain all ingredients, place in large salad bowl. In a jar mix the following:

### Dressing

¼ cup tarragon vinegar
1½ teaspoons monosodium glutamate
1¼ teaspoons salt
½ cup salad oil
1 teaspoon sugar

¼ teaspoon tabasco
1 tablespoon Fine Herbs
  (packaged)
¼ cup chopped parsley
2 tablespoons capers

Shake all together until well blended. Pour over mixed vegetables, cover, and refrigerate overnight or up to two days. May need to drain extra dressing. Put into serving bowl and sprinkle with parsley and capers. Makes about 12 cups.

*Mrs. William Perry (Anne)*


## COLD VEGETABLE SALAD

*Easy and quick to make*

1 package frozen mixed vegetables
4 stalks celery, diced
1 onion, diced

½ green pepper, diced
1 can kidney beans, drained
  and rinsed

Cook mixed vegetables 10 minutes, cool, and add other ingredients.

Dressing:

2 tablespoons flour

¾ cup sugar

½ cup vinegar

1 tablespoon salad mustard

In saucepan stir constantly until thick and clear. Cool, mix with vegetables and refrigerate. Serves 6-8. Great for any party table or with barbecue dinner.

*Mrs. Myles J. Gould (Lynn)*

## RED AND GREEN SALAD TOSS

1 large head lettuce, torn
into bite size pieces

1/3 head red cabbage, sliced thinly

1 medium red onion, sliced
in thin rings

### Dressing: can be made well in advance

½ teaspoon salt

¼ teaspoon pepper

4-5 teaspoons sugar

1 teaspoon celery seed

2 tablespoons tarragon vinegar

1 teaspoon prepared mustard

½ cup Hellman's mayonnaise

Just before serving toss dressing with lettuce, cabbage, and onions. Serves 6-8.

*Mrs. Robert Hennessy (Nancy)*

## SEVEN LAYER SALAD

1 medium head lettuce, shredded
(about 6 cups)

1 cup coarsely chopped celery

½ cup coarsely chopped green pepper

1 cup coarsely chopped Spanish onion

1 package frozen green peas, separated

1-1½ cups Hellman's mayonnaise

2 tablespoons sugar

2½ cups shredded mild cheddar
cheese

8 strips bacon, drained, crumbled

Arrange lettuce in bottom of 9x13 pan. In layers add other vegetables. Do not toss! Spread mayonnaise evenly over layer of peas. Sprinkle with sugar and cheddar cheese. Cover and refrigerate at least 4 hours. Sprinkle bacon over salad before serving. Cut into squares. Makes 10-12 servings. This may be made the night before serving.

*Mrs. Richard B. Jones (Kay)*

## LOVING TOUCHES . . .

Before adding dressing, lightly toss a salad with a teaspoon or so of oil. This coats the leaves and helps the salad stay crisp.

## COME BACK SALAD DRESSING

| | |
|---|---|
| 1 cup mayonnaise | 1 tablespoon worcestershire |
| ¼ cup catsup | 1 tablespoon mustard |
| ¼ cup chili sauce | 1 small onion, grated |
| ½ cup Wesson oil | 2 buttons garlic |

Mix together. Store in jar in refrigerator. Keeps forever. Serve over wedges of lettuce.

*Mrs. Jerry Tidwell (Dottie)*

## FRESH FRUIT SALAD DRESSING

| | |
|---|---|
| Juice of one lemon (2 tablespoons) | 1 teaspoon almond extract |
| ½ cup sugar | 2 whole eggs, beaten |
| 2 tablespoons butter | ½ pint whipping cream |

Mix first five ingredients together in a small saucepan and cook over medium heat until thick. Cool. Before serving add whipped cream. Then chill mixture. For a nice luncheon dish serve over a combination of honeydew, cantalope, strawberries, and pineapple, or appropriate fruits in season. Serves 8.

*Mrs. Robert Hennessy (Nancy)*

## FRENCH DRESSING

*This is delicious on spinach salad*

| | |
|---|---|
| 1 cup Mazola salad oil | 1 teaspoon salt |
| 1/3 cup vinegar | 6 cloves garlic |
| ¼ cup catsup | 1 tablespoon worcestershire |

Put all ingredients in a jar and shake well.

*Mrs. David F. Apple, Jr. (Jane)*

## FRUIT SALAD DRESSING

| | |
|---|---|
| ½ cup sugar | 1 small onion, diced |
| ½ cup vinegar | 2 tablespoons celery seed |
| ½ teaspoon salt | ½ teaspoon dry mustard |
| 1 cup vegetable oil | Paprika |

Combine all of above in a jar. Cover and refrigerate several hours. Shake well before using. Will keep in the refrigerator for several days.

*Mrs. Dennis Mollenkamp (Jane)*

## "LOVETT" ITALIAN DRESSING

*This recipe is one the Lower School Faculty got from the cooks at*
*Lovett several years ago.*

1  package Italian dressing mix
1  large onion, chopped
1  tablespoon salt
1  teaspoon ground pepper
1  tablespoon sugar

1  cup lemon juice
1  cup vinegar
1  cup salad oil
½ cup cold water

Mix, add other spices if desired, dill weed, McCormicks Salad Supreme, seasoned salt, etc. If after that it still doesn't have that good old "Lovett" taste, add more onion and pepper. Good on any salad, greens, or tossed salad.

*Mrs. Herbert J. Beadle, Jr. (Jerry).*

## POPPY SEED DRESSING

*Excellent over fruit salad*

1½ cups sugar
2  teaspoons dry mustard
2  teaspoons salt
2/3 cup vinegar

3  tablespoons grated onion
2  cups salad oil
3  tablespoons poppy seed

Mix well.

*Mrs. John Bruner (Barbara)*

## ROQUEFORT DRESSING

*May also be used as a dip with fresh vegetables*

1  (3 ounce) package cream cheese
1  tablespoon lemon juice
¼ teaspoon salt

1/3 cup roquefort cheese
1/3 cup mayonnaise
1/3 cup heavy cream

Cream the cheese, lemon juice, and salt. Add crumbled cheese and mayonnaise alternately. Add cream slowly, beating constantly. Makes 1 cup.

*Mrs. Richard Lea (Robin)*
*Mrs. Ralph Williams, Jr. (Emily)*

## ROQUEFORT DRESSING

2 cups mayonnaise
½ cup chopped parsley
2 cloves garlic, minced
½ cup chopped onion
1 cup sour cream

½ cup roquefort cheese,
   crumbled
1/8 cup vinegar
1/8 cup water
2 tablespoons lemon juice

Mix all ingredients together.

*Mrs. A. J. Stringer (Martha)*

## SALAD DRESSING

*Low - calorie*

1 cup red wine vinegar
1 quart water
1 tablespoon salt
1 tablespoon pepper

1 tablespoon sugar
1 tablespoon paprika
1 tablespoon prepared mustard
1 tablespoon chopped garlic

Makes a large amount and keeps well in refrigerator.

*Mrs. William A. McClain, III (Rose)*

## SPECIAL DRESSING

*Good on chef's salad or submarine sandwiches*

1 cup mayonnaise
¼ cup catsup
2 tablespoons horseradish
1 teaspoon lemon juice

2 tablespoons grated onion
1 teaspoon worcestershire sauce
Salt and pepper to taste

Shake together in a pint jar.

*Mrs. Gregory Fitz-Gerald (Diane)*

## SPINACH SALAD DRESSING

6 ounces salad oil
2 ounces cider vinegar
Juice of 1 lemon
1 whole garlic clove

1 teaspoon salt
¼ teaspoon black pepper
½ teaspoon Accent or available
   seasoned salts

Mix together and serve on any tossed salad, but this is a "must" for spinach salad.

*Mrs. Francis B. Sheetz, Jr.*

66

# Meats

DAVID SAPP

## BEEF WELLINGTON
### Pastry

3 cups flour                          ¾ cup shortening
½ teaspoon salt                       ½ - ¾ cup cold water

Combine flour and salt. Cut in shortening until mixture resembles coarse corn meal. Add water, one tablespoon at a time, stirring with a fork until dough holds together. Shape into a ball, then wrap in wax paper and chill until ready to use.

1  fillet of beef (½ pound per person)
2  (4¾ ounces) cans of liver pate

Trim fat and connective tissue from fillet. Tuck in small end of fillet and tie to make fillet even. Tie pieces of beef suet to the fillet and roast in a hot oven (400 degrees) for 10 minutes per pound. Remove meat from the oven and discard the string and fat.

Roll pastry into a 18x14 inch rectangle. Spread liver pate over pastry leaving a 1 inch edge. Place fillet lengthwise, top side down, in the middle of the pastry. Bring long sides of pastry up to overlap over fillet. Brush the seam with a mixture of one beaten egg with 1 teaspoon of water. Then fold over ends and brush with egg mixture again. Place meat, seam side down, on a lightly greased baking sheet. Brush with egg mixture again. Decorate top with shapes made from pastry trimmings. Brush with egg mixture. Bake at 425 degrees for 30 minutes or until pastry is golden. Serve on a large platter garnished with stuffed mushrooms, tomatoes, and artichoke bottoms.

*Mrs. James Cushman (Elkin)*


## EASY BEEF WELLINGTON

4 (6 ounce) pieces of beef tenderloin    Chopped onion
4 Pepperidge Farm patty shells           Chopped fresh mushrooms
Butter, red wine

Defrost patty shells. Brown meat on both sides. Saute onions and mushrooms in butter and wine. Roll out patty shells. Place piece of tenderloin on pastry, onion and mushrooms on meat and wrap pastry around meat. Bake at 425 degrees for 18 to 20 minutes. Serves 4.

*Mrs. Clifford M. Kirtland, Jr. (Jane)*

68

## FLANK STEAK

Flank steak
½ cup Japanese soy sauce
  (Kikkoman)

½ cup dry white or red wine
Garlic powder
Ginger

Score flank steak on both sides. Combine soy sauce, wine and few shakes each of garlic powder and ginger. Marinate steak in mixture 4-6 hours and charcoal broil.

*Mr. David Kenney*

## LONDON BROIL

½ cup olive oil
¼ cup lemon juice
¼ cup vinegar
1 bay leaf, crushed
1 clove garlic, crushed
1 medium onion, thinly sliced

½ teaspoon dried oregano
1 teaspoon salt
½ teaspoon freshly ground pepper
1½ pounds meat (flank steak, top
  round, or London broil)

Mix all ingredients except meat. Put meat in baking pan and pour marinade over. Let stand at room temperature for four hours or overnight. Broil about 8 minutes per side. Slice very thinly on the diagonal. Serve with brown sauce. Serves 6.

### Brown Sauce

2 tablespoons butter or meat drippings
1 tablespoon minced onion
1 tablespoon minced carrot
½ bay leaf
2 tablespoons flour

1 cup meat stock
Salt
Pepper
1 cup sliced mushrooms, sauteed
1 tablespoon sherry

Melt butter or drippings. Add carrot, onion, and bay leaf and cook over low heat until butter is brown. Stir in flour and cook until bubbly. (About 3 minutes.) Add stock and cook until thick and smooth. Strain. Add the mushrooms and sherry. Makes 1 cup.

*Mrs. Robert F. Dennis (Peggy)*

LOVING TOUCHES . . .
Veal for any recipe must be "pink" when purchased.

## LONDON BROIL

1 flank steak
Marinate in:

1 cup burgundy
½ cup Italian dressing
½ cup oil

Juice of 1 lemon
½ cup soy sauce
¼ cup worcestershire sauce

Cook on grill 6-8 minutes per side. Cut on the bias

*Mrs. John B. Gillespie (Vicki)*

## ROAST FILLET OF BEEF

½ fillet of beef, 3-4 pounds
   (about ½ pound per person)
Salt and pepper
½ cup dry white wine
¾ pound mushrooms, sliced
3 tablespoons butter
1 shallot or small white onion

1 teaspoon meat glaze (BV)
1 teaspoon tomato paste
2 teaspoons potato flour or
   2 tablespoons flour
1 cup stock
½ cup madeira wine

Remove the fat and connective tissue from the meat. Surround it with a thin layer of fat, preferably beef suet, and tie it with string at 1½ inch intervals. Season with salt and pepper. Place in shallow roasting pan and roast in a hot oven at 450 degrees for 10 minutes per pound, or until meat thermometer registers 140 degrees. Remove the meat, pour ½ cup of dry white wine over it and keep it warm while making sauce. Remove string and fat. Saute ¾ pounds sliced mushrooms in 3 tablespoons butter.
Remove all but 2 tablespoons of fat from the pan the meat was cooked in. Saute onion until soft but not brown in this fat. Blend in off the fire 1 teaspoon meat glaze, ½ teaspoon tomato paste and flour. Add 1 cup stock and ½ cup madeira and stir over the fire until mixture comes to a boil. Add the sauteed mushrooms, season and simmer 4-5 minutes. Slice fillet and arrange overlapping each other on a large platter. Serves 6-8.

*Mrs. James Cushman (Elkin)*

**LOVING TOUCHES . . .**
Coca Cola is a great baste for ham.

## BEEF SAUERBRATEN

1 (5-6 pound) rump roast
2 onions, chopped
2 carrots, chopped
3 stalks celery, chopped
1 cup white vinegar
1 bay leaf

Some cloves
Salt and pepper
2 tablespoons sugar
1 cup white wine
2 tablespoons flour
1 cup water

Chop all vegetables and bring to boil with all the herbs, water, vinegar, salt, pepper and sugar. Pour over meat and marinate one day or over night. Brown meat in some fat and add vegetables, marinade and white wine. Cook at 375 degrees for 20 minutes per pound. Thicken gravy with flour when roast is done. This is especially good with red cabbage and potato dumplings.

*Mrs. Edward E. Jackson (Dot)*

## POT ROAST IN WINE SAUCE

4 pound roast (shoulder or chuck)
Salt and pepper
1 clove garlic

1 cup red wine (burgundy)
1 package dry onion soup
1 or 2 cups water

Salt and pepper and insert garlic in center of roast. Put in roaster and brown uncovered at 400 degrees. Pour wine over roast, cover and continue to roast at 325 degrees, basting every half hour. Cook about 45 minutes per pound or until tender. Last 30 minutes sprinkle onion soup over roast and add water, mixing well and basting with other juices. Cover and cook until done. May use gravy as is or add a little cornstarch.

*Mrs. Vincent Sgrosso (Joanne)*

## BARBECUED POT ROAST

*Easy and delicious*

1 chuck roast, 2 inches thick
Blend together next six ingredients:
1 (5 ounce) bottle soy sauce
¼ cup brown sugar
1 tablespoon lemon juice

¼ cup bourbon
1 tablespoon worcestershire sauce
1½ cups water

Refrigerate chuck roast in the marinade for six hours, turning once. Broil on the grill for about 45 minutes. Baste with the marinade.

*Mrs. Joseph R. White, Jr. (Barbara)*

## BARBECUED BEEF

*Fabulous at cocktail parties or served on big hamburger buns.*

Beef brisket (3½ pound) Season meat with salt, pepper and garlic powder. Put meat into a roasting pan filled with:

| | |
|---|---|
| 3  cups water | ¼ cup catsup |
| 2  bay leaves | 3 or 4 whole allspice |
| 3  onions, cut over meat and into water | Salt to taste |

Bake covered at 325 degrees until tender, about 2 hours. Let cool and slice very thin.

### Barbecue Sauce

In one pan:

| | |
|---|---|
| Saute two onions, then add: | 2 tablespoons mustard |
| 1  cup catsup | Salt to taste |
| 2  tablespoons vinegar | 1 green pepper, diced |
| 4  tablespoons brown sugar | ½ cup water |
| ¼ cup lemon juice | 1 tablespoon chili powder or |
| 3  tablespoons worcestershire sauce | 10 drops tabasco sauce |

Simmer 30 minutes.
Pour over sliced brisket and let simmer in oven for two hours. The brisket and sauce may each be prepared ahead of time and frozen. (Simmer the two together before serving.) Three pounds of brisket with the one preparation of sauce serves 6-8.

*Mrs. Myles J. Gould (Lynn)*

## BEEF RAGOUT WITH SOUR CREAM

| | |
|---|---|
| 2  pounds round steak, chuck or sirloin tip cut in 1 inch cubes | Salt and pepper |
| | 2 cups water or consomme (or ½ red wine with either) |
| 2  large onions, sliced | 2 cups sour cream |
| 1  tablespoon curry powder | 1 tablespoon prepared horseradish |

Make in biggest bean pot. Put meat, onions, curry powder, seasonings, consomme in pot. Bring to boil on top of stove. Cover and bake 350 degrees for 1½ - 2 hours or until meat is tender. Remove pot to top of stove. Stir in sour cream and horseradish. Reheat but do not boil. Serves 6. Serve with buttered noodles.

*Mrs. Lawson Calhoun (Aline)*

## PEPPER STEAK

3 cups cooked rice
1 pound lean beef round steak
  or sirloin, cut ½ inch thick
1 tablespoon paprika
2 tablespoons butter or margarine
2 cloves garlic, crushed
1 can beef broth
1 cup sliced green onion
  (including tops)
2 green peppers, cut in strips
2 tablespoons cornstarch
¼ cup each water and soy sauce
2 large fresh tomatoes,
  cut in eighths

While rice is cooking, pound steak to ¼ inch thickness. Cut into ¼ inch wide strips. Sprinkle meat with paprika and allow to stand while preparing other ingredients. Using a large skillet, brown meat in butter. Add garlic and broth. Cover and simmer 30 minutes. Stir in onions and green peppers. Cover and cook 5 minutes longer. Blend cornstarch, water and soy sauce. Stir into meat mixture, cooking until clear and thickened, about 2 minutes. Add tomatoes and stir gently. Serve on rice. Serves 6.

*Patty Taulman Wills*

## SKILLET BEEF SUPREME

*Chinese-Style*

½ pound lean beef
2 tablespoons oil
1 onion, sliced
1 green pepper, sliced
1 cup diced celery
1 cup frozen cut green beans, (slightly defrosted)
4 teaspoons cornstarch
1 tablespoon soy sauce
¾ cup water
4 ounces sliced mushrooms
Pimiento strips

Cut beef into strips and brown in oil. Add onion, pepper, celery and green beans. Cook 3-5 minutes. Combine cornstarch, soy sauce and water. Add to skillet. Stir in mushrooms. Cook about 5 minutes, stirring until liquid is clear and shiny and beans are tender. Salt to taste and garnish with pimiento. Serve with rice. (Recipe can use 1 package frozen snow peas instead of frozen green beans for a more Chinese flavor.) Serves 4.

*Mrs. Stanley Goldstein (Rita)*

## BEEF WITH GREEN PEPPER

| | |
|---|---|
| 1 pound beef steak (sliced thin) | ¼ teaspoon M.S.G. |
| 4 tablespoons soy sauce | 1 slice ginger root |
| 1 tablespoon cornstarch | 4 tablespoons cooking oil |
| 1 tablespoon dry sherry | ½ teaspoon salt |
| 1 teaspoon sugar | 2 green peppers, sliced |

Mix sliced beef with soy sauce, cornstarch, sherry, sugar, and M.S.G. Set aside. Saute peppers in 2 tablespoons oil. Remove to platter and add salt. Add rest of oil and ginger root. Stir in beef mixture turning constantly. Return green peppers to skillet and mix thoroughly. Do not overcook.

*Mrs. Charles E. Bouis (Lois).*

## BEEF STROGANOFF

| | |
|---|---|
| 1½ pounds boneless chuck, cut in 1 inch cubes | 1 (3 ounce) can mushrooms |
| 1 cup sliced onions | 1 cup buttermilk |
| 1 tablespoon shortening | 1 can condensed tomato soup |
| 1 clove garlic, minced | 1 tablespoon cornstarch |
| 1 tablespoon worcestershire sauce | 1 package vermicelli or very thin spaghetti |
| 1½ teaspoons salt | Dash tabasco sauce |
| 1/8 teaspoon pepper | |

Brown meat in shortening. Add onions and saute until onions are soft. Add seasonings, sauces, and mushrooms (with liquids). Simmer for one hour. Before serving, thicken mixture with 1½ teaspoons cornstarch mixed with 3 tablespoons cold water. Serve over lightly buttered spaghetti. Serves 6.

*Mrs. Kenneth Covey (Peggy)*

## BEEF BURGUNDY

| | |
|---|---|
| 3 pounds round steak, cut into small pieces | 1 can beef bouillon soup |
| 1 can cream of mushroom soup | ¾ cup red wine |
| | ½ cup brandy |

Mix together the meat, soups, and red wine. Place in casserole dish uncovered at 350 degrees for about 2½ - 3 hours. The last ½ hour add the brandy. It should be stirred a couple of times while cooking and if it seems too dry, cover with tin foil until done. Serves 6. Serve over medium size noodles.

*Mrs. John B. Commander (Elspeth)*

74

## COMPANY BEEF BURGUNDY

*Easy and almost cooks itself*

4 pounds beef sirloin, cut into 1 inch cubes
4 packages dry onion soup mix

3 (4 ounce) cans of sliced mushrooms
3 cups burgundy wine
2 cans tomato soup (optional)

Place beef cubes, onion soup mix and wine in a dutch oven. Mix well. Cover and bake at 350 degrees for 3 hours. Stir occasionally. Add mushrooms 15 minutes before cooking time is up. Serve over white or wild rice.

*Mrs. Charles A. Beard (Mary Crain)*
*Martha Scott Westervelt*

## ALMOND BEEF HAWAIIAN

1 (1 pound) sirloin steak
1 clove garlic, minced
3 tablespoons salad oil, divided
1 cup diagonally sliced celery
1 medium onion, sliced
¼ cup soy sauce
2 teaspoons cornstarch

1 teaspoon sugar
½ teaspoon ground ginger
½ cup water
½ cup green pepper, chopped
6 cherry tomatoes, halved
½ cup toasted slivered almonds
Hot cooked rice

Cut steak into ¼ inch strips. Cook half the strips with garlic in 2 tablespoons hot oil. Remove steak, discard garlic, and cook remaining steak. Saute celery and onion in 1 tablespoon oil for 1 minute. Combine soy sauce, cornstarch, sugar, ginger and water; stir into onion and celery mixture. Stir in steak, green pepper, tomatoes and almonds. Cover and heat 1 minute. Serves 4.

*Mrs. John B. Jackson, Jr. (Sue)*

## ITALIAN STUFFED STEAKS

*Easy, delicious and different*

2 pounds round steak
1 teaspoon salt
¼ teaspoon pepper
1 teaspoon garlic powder
2 tablespoons chopped parsley

3 tablespoons grated parmesan cheese
¼ cup pignolas (Italian pine nuts)
Marinara sauce (see index)

Have beef sliced into 8 thin, flat pieces. Sprinkle salt, pepper, garlic, parsley, cheese and pignola nuts on each piece of meat. Roll and secure with tooth picks. Brown slowly in Wesson oil. Drain. Place in marinara sauce and simmer until very tender. Serves 6-8.

*Mrs. Vincent Sgrosso (Joanne)*

75

## FAMILY PORK CHOPS

| | |
|---|---|
| 6 pork chops | 2 tablespoons worcestershire sauce |
| Salt and pepper | 2 tablespoons vinegar |
| Onion slices | 2 tablespoons brown sugar |
| ¾ cup catsup | 1 teaspoon paprika |
| 1 cup water | 1 teaspoon chili powder |

Salt and pepper chops and place in a shallow baking dish. Top each with an onion slice. Make a sauce of the remaining ingredients and pour over the chops, cover and bake at 300 to 325 degrees for 1½ hours. Uncover for the last 20 minutes. Serves 6.

This sauce can be made up and kept on hand in refrigerator. It may be used on chicken, meat loaf, spareribs or stew meat. The gravy is good on rice.

*Mrs. Francis B. Sheetz, Jr.*

## SWEET AND SOUR CABBAGE ROLLS

*Easy, quick, and good made in advance*

| | |
|---|---|
| 3 pounds ground beef | 1 large bottle catsup |
| 2 small cabbage heads | ¾ cup brown sugar |
| Salt and pepper | Juice of a large lemon |
| 2 tablespoons white rice, uncooked | 1 cup of raisins |
| 3 medium onions, chopped | 2 eggs |

Core cabbage and put in boiling water until leaves are pliable. Mix meat with eggs, salt, and pepper, and rice. Roll into a small ball and put into a cabbage leaf, folding in the ends.

Sauce: Saute onions in a small amount of butter, then pour in catsup, brown sugar, lemon juice, and raisins. Place cabbage rolls in sauce and bake covered at 300 degrees for 3 hours. Baste at least twice. Serves 8-10. Can be frozen.

*Mrs. Donald Brown (Joan)*

## ITALIAN MEAT LOAF

| | |
|---|---|
| 1 pound ground beef, browned | ½ teaspoon oregano |
| 1 (6 ounce) can tomato paste | 1 (8 ounce) package American |
| 1 (4 ounce) can sliced mushrooms, | sliced cheese |
| drained | 2 medium tomatoes, chopped |
| 1 tablespoon salt | 1 loaf unsliced Italian bread |
| 1 tablespoon minced onion | |

Combine ground beef, tomato paste, mushrooms, onion, salt, oregano. Scoop out center of bread and fill with mixture. Lay cheese on top and cook in 350 degrees oven until cheese is melted. Add tomatoes before serving. Serves 4.

*Mrs. James Magbee (Tia)*

## MEAT LOAF

*May be frozen before or after cooking*

| | |
|---|---|
| 1 pound ground chuck | 1 teaspoon salt |
| 1 slice of bread, crumbled | 1 teaspoon pepper |
| 1 onion, chopped | ¼ can tomato sauce (small) |
| 1 egg, beaten | |

Mix the above ingredients together and put into an ungreased loaf pan.

### Topping

| | |
|---|---|
| 1½ tablespoons vinegar | 1 tablespoon worcestershire |
| ¾ can tomato sauce | sauce |
| 1½ tablespoons brown sugar | 1 teaspoon mustard |

Mix these ingredients together and pour over meat loaf. Bake at 350 degrees for 1 hour and 15 minutes.

*Mrs. William Whitaker (Susan)*

## LAMB CURRY WITH WALNUTS

*Good luncheon dish*

| | |
|---|---|
| 2 cloves garlic, minced | 3 apples, peeled, cored, chopped |
| 4 onions, sliced | 1 cup chopped walnuts |
| ¾ cup butter | 2 lemons, sliced |
| 3 pounds lamb shoulder, cut into 2 inch cubes | 4 tablespoons raisins |
| | Coconut |
| Flour | Brown sugar |
| 3 tablespoons curry powder | ½ teaspoon grated lime peel |

Saute garlic and onions in butter until onions are golden. Roll lamb cubes in flour and saute 10 minutes, stirring frequently. Add curry powder and onions, simmer 5 minutes. Add remaining ingredients and pour 3 cups of water over all, bring to a boil, reduce heat and cover pan. Simmer the mixture 1 hour or until the lamb is cooked through. This dish improves if made ahead and allowed to stand. Serve with rice.

*Mrs. Richard McCamey (Betsy)*

## BEEF KABOBS

| | |
|---|---|
| 1 pound tenderloin or sirloin tip, cubed | 2 tablespoons red wine vinegar |
| 1 cup red wine | 1 clove garlic, sliced |
| 1 cup salad oil | Salt and pepper |
| | 1 bay leaf |

Put 1 inch beef cubes in the above marinade in the refrigerator overnight. When ready to broil, put on skewers, alternating with wedges of nearly ripe tomatoes, onions, bell pepper and fresh mushroom caps. Broil five to ten minutes on each side depending on degree of rareness desired. Serve with rice pilaf.

*Mrs. W. H. Bennett (Louise)*

## MEXICAN DELIGHT

*A one dish luncheon from California*

| | |
|---|---|
| 1 chopped onion | 1 teaspoon chili powder |
| 1 minced garlic clove | 1 teaspoon Accent |
| 1 pound ground beef | 1 teaspoon salt |
| 1 small can tomato sauce | 1 teaspoon sugar |
| 1 small can tomato paste | 1½ teaspoons cumin seed |
| 3 small cans water (tomato sauce can) | Tabasco and pepper to taste |

Brown meat and add the rest of the above ingredients. Simmer for ½ hour. Add a cup of cooked rice before serving. Serve on crushed Fritos and along with bowls of: ½ head of lettuce, chopped; 1-2 tomatoes, sliced; chopped green onions; sliced avocado; ½ pound of grated cheddar cheese; 2 small cans of sliced olives.

*Mrs. William Stone (Gloria)*

## LOVING TOUCHES . . .

To flatten veal for escalops - pound it with the flat side of your heaviest pot.

## ITALIAN MEATBALLS
*Authentic and very tasty*

1¼ pounds ground beef
½ pound ground pork
1 cup Progresso Italian
  bread crumbs
1 tablespoon salt
½ teaspoon pepper
¼ cup chopped parsley
¾ cup water

3 eggs
½ cup grated parmesan
  cheese
1/3 cup pignolas (Italian pine
  nuts) optional
Wesson oil
3 cups tomato sauce
  (marinara) see index

Have meat ground together twice. Mix all the ingredients well. With wet hands, shape lightly into balls about the size of an egg. Fry slowly in Wesson oil until well browned on all sides. Drain on paper towels. Place meatballs in marinara sauce (see index) and simmer for 20 minutes before serving. Serves 6-8 and may be made well ahead.

*Mrs. Vincent Sgrosso (Joanne)*

## CHILI
*Great for freezing*

1 pound ground chuck
1 large onion, chopped
1 small bell pepper, chopped
1 (1 pound) can of tomatoes
1 (1 pound) can kidney beans,
  drained

1 (8 ounce) can tomato sauce
1 teaspoon salt
Dash of pepper
1 to 2 teaspoons chili powder
1 bay leaf
1 beef boullion cube

Brown meat, onion, and bell pepper. Add all other ingredients and simmer at least one hour. Serves 4.

*Mrs. William Whitaker (Susan)*

## FAVORITE PORK CHOPS
*Great last minute dish*

4 - 6 pork chops
1 can mushroom soup
3 tablespoons catsup

3 tablespoons worcestershire sauce
½ cup chopped onions
½ cup water

Brown chops. Mix remaining ingredients and pour in with chops. Simmer 30 minutes. Serve with white rice. Serves 4-6.

*Mrs. Charles A. Beard (Mary Crain)*

## SHERRIED PEARS AND PORK

1 (1 pound) can Bartlett
  pear halves
6 pork chops
1½ teaspoons salt
¼ teaspoon pepper

1 tablespoon cornstarch
½ teaspoon nutmeg
1 cup pear syrup, plus water
½ cup sherry wine
¼ cup raisins

Drain pears, reserving syrup. Add water to pear syrup to measure 1 cup. Set aside. Brown pork chops in heavy skillet. Remove from skillet. Combine seasonings, cornstarch and nutmeg. Dissolve in part of pear syrup. Add remaining pear syrup to skillet with sherry and raisins. Heat to boiling. Stir in cornstarch and simmer until clear. Add pork chops. Simmer 30 minutes. Add pear halves and simmer 15-20 minutes longer or until chops are tender. Serves 6.

*Mrs. Kenneth Covey (Peggy)*

## SKILLET LASAGNA

*The noodles don't have to be cooked separately!*

1 pound ground beef
1 envelope spaghetti sauce mix
1 pound creamed cottage cheese
3 cups egg noodles, uncooked
2 teaspoons basil leaves
1 tablespoon parsley flakes

1 teaspoon salt
1 can (1 pound) tomatoes
1 can (8 ounces) tomato sauce
8 ounces mozzarella cheese,
  in thin pieces

Brown beef, sprinkle with ½ spaghetti sauce mix and spoon cottage cheese over meat. Top with noodles and the rest of the spaghetti sauce mix and seasonings. Pour tomatoes, tomato sauce and 1 cup water over top, making sure all is moistened. Bring to boil, cover and simmer 35 minutes. Sprinkle with cheese and let stand 5 minutes. Serves 6.

*Mrs. Speer Mabry (Judy)*

## SIMPLE GOURMET BEEF BALLS

*Good for family or company*

1 pound ground chuck
1 slice white bread
1/3 cup water
1 egg

1 small slice of onion
4 sprigs parsley
1 teaspoon dry beef boullion
¼ teaspoon pepper

80

Place the ground chuck in a mixing bowl. Prepare crumbs by tearing the slice of bread into a blender and blending until fine. Add the crumbs to the ground chuck. Pour the water into the blender and add egg and seasonings. Blend until onion is chopped and parsley is minced. Pour over the ground beef and mix thoroughly. Shape into 12 meat balls, about ¼ cup each. Roll meat balls in flour. Prepare wine sauce.

## Wine Sauce

| | |
|---|---|
| ¼ cup butter or margarine | 1 can Golden Mushroom Soup |
| ½ cup red wine | ¼ teaspoon Kitchen Bouquet |
| ¼ cup water | |

Melt butter in skillet over low heat. Slowly brown meat balls. Remove meat balls from skillet. Add red wine to the drippings. Allow to simmer until the wine is reduced to about ¼ cup. Add remaining ingredients and blend. Return meatballs to the skillet and simmer for about 5 minutes. Serve with noodles.

*Mrs. Jack R. Walker (Charlotte)*

## BAKED ITALIAN SPAGHETTI

*Loved by all ages*

| | |
|---|---|
| 1 onion, chopped | Dash garlic salt |
| 1 pound ground beef | 1 tablespoon sugar |
| 3 tablespoons oil | ½ teaspoon salt |
| 3 (8 ounce) cans tomato sauce | ¼ teaspoon pepper |
| 1 cup burgundy wine | ½ pound spaghetti |
| ¼ teaspoon each oregano, basil, | (2 inch lengths) |
| rosemary, and marjoram | ¼ pound grated cheddar cheese |

A day or two before serving, simmer onion in oil and brown ground beef; add tomato sauce and next 9 ingredients. Simmer 1 hour covered. Add ½ of cheese and stir into a casserole along with cooked and drained spaghetti. Store covered in refrigerator until serving time. One and ½ hours before serving, bake in 350 degrees oven covered for 45 minutes. Uncover and sprinkle remaining grated cheese over top and continue baking 30 minutes. Serve with a tossed salad and French bread.

*Mrs. John Westmoreland, Jr. (Nevin)*

## VEAL DI NAPOLI

*A good diet dish*

1½ pounds veal cutlets
2 tablespoons salad oil
1 teaspoon salt
1 can (1 pound) tomatoes
1 package (1½ ounces) spaghetti
  sauce mix

1 (6 ounce) can mushrooms
1/3 cup sherry
1 (1 pound) can whole onions,
  drained
1 (1 pound) can peas and carrots,
  drained

Pound cutlets ¼ inch thick with a wooden mallet. Cut into serving-size pieces. Mix spaghetti sauce mix with ¼ cup of liquid from mushrooms. In a large skillet, brown veal quickly in hot oil and season with salt. In the same skillet combine tomatoes, spaghetti sauce mix and sherry. Heat to boiling, cover and simmer for ten minutes stirring occasionally. Add onions, mushrooms, and peas and carrots. Simmer for ten minutes. Garnish with parsley. Serves 6.

*Mrs. David Vaughan (Vi)*

## BUTTERFLY LEG OF LAMB

1 jar Dijon mustard
1 teaspoon rosemary
1 teaspoon ginger
1 boned leg of lamb (extra fat removed)

1 crushed clove garlic
2 tablespoons soy sauce
2 tablespoons olive oil

Mix all ingredients except the leg of lamb. Marinate the meat for one hour. Broil in oven or grill 10-15 minutes on each side. Serve pink. A 5-6 pound lamb serves 6-8.

*Mrs. Lawson Calhoun (Aline)*

## LEG OF LAMB BARBECUED

2 small legs of lamb
  (boned and butterflied)
1 cup dry red wine
1 cup beef stock
2 tablespoons orange marmalade
2 tablespoons wine vinegar

1 tablespoon rosemary
2 tablespoons minced onion
1 tablespoon marjoram
1 large bay leaf, crumbled
1 teaspoon salt
½ teaspoon ginger

Combine all ingredients to make a marinade for the lamb. Simmer marinade for 20 minutes, stirring occasionally. Marinate lamb for 2 hours before cooking, turning frequently. Cook lamb over charcoal for about 40 minutes, basting and turning often. Serves 8.

*Mrs. Richard McCamey (Betsy)*

## ROLLED LAMB WITH ARTICHOKES

Leg of lamb, boned (5 pounds)
Garlic clove
Salt and pepper
2/3 cup onion, chopped
6 tablespoons butter
1 cup coarsely chopped
  artichoke hearts
2 cups fresh bread crumbs

3 cups consomme
4 teaspoons chopped parsley
½ teaspoon salt
¼ teaspoon thyme
¼ teaspoon marjoram
¼ teaspoon chopped fresh dill
¼ teaspoon pepper
4 tablespoons flour

Rub lamb with garlic, salt and pepper. To prepare stuffing: Saute onion in butter until golden. Add artichoke hearts, cook one minute. Add bread crumbs, parsley and remaining seasonings. Mix thoroughly and place inside lamb. Secure with skewers and string. Place on rack in open roasting pan. Roast at 325 degrees about 35 minutes per pound. Baste with consomme 20 minutes before meat is done. Remove lamb to hot platter and make gravy. Skim all but 4 tablespoons of fat from pan drippings. Blend in flour, mix until smooth. Add 2 cups consomme, stirring constantly until gravy is smooth and thick. Season with salt and pepper.

*Mrs. Richard McCamey (Betsy)*

## LOVING TOUCHES . . .

To cook a roast or steak ahead: cook to the rare side of perfection, then using very hot plates and hot "jus" or sauce, serve it *'a point* to guests.

Use a wood or clear plastic cutting board under meats to be carved on a silver tray. Disguise edges with salad greenery, tomato "flowers".

A sharp knife is a "joy forever" and a shrewd investment. A "steel" is easy to learn to use and keeps that edge.

## CHOPPED MEAT SAUCE FOR SPAGHETTI

½ pound each of beef and
  pork, chopped together
1 tablespoon olive oil
1 clove garlic
½ medium onion, chopped
1 teaspoon chopped parsley
1 medium can tomatoes

1 can tomato paste
1/8 teaspoon salt
1/8 teaspoon pepper
½ teaspoon chopped basil
2 bay leaves
1 tablespoon butter

Place chopped meat, oil, garlic, onion and parsley in saucepan and brown slowly, stirring frequently to prevent meat from cooking in lumps. Remove garlic as soon as browned. (If you like stronger garlic flavor, you can crush garlic clove into sauce instead of using whole clove). Add tomatoes, tomato paste, salt and pepper, cover pan and simmer one hour. Add basil, bay leaves and cook one minute longer. Remove from fire and add butter. Makes enough sauce for one pound spaghetti or other forms of macaroni.

*Mrs. Stanley Goldstein (Rita)*

## PORK CHOPS AND APPLES

*Easy and delicious*

6 pork chops
4 unpeeled apples,
  cored and sliced

¼ cup brown sugar
1 teaspoon cinnamon
2 tablespoons butter

Brown chops on both sides in hot fat. Place apple slices in a greased baking dish. Sprinkle with sugar and cinnamon, dot with butter. Top with pork chops, cover and bake 350 degrees for 1-1½ hours. Serves 4-6.

*Mrs. Richard McCamey (Betsy)*

## SKILLET PORK CHOPS

4 pork chops
4 small whole onions, peeled
4 potatoes, peeled and quartered
6 carrots, cut into sticks

2 beef boullion cubes
2 cups boiling water
Salt and pepper

Brown pork chops in margarine. Season with salt and pepper. Add boullion cubes to boiling water and dissolve. Pour over pork chops and simmer for 15 minutes. Add vegetables and additional salt to taste and simmer for 30 minutes more or until vegetables are done. Serves 4.

*Mrs. Russell French (Vicki)*

## BAKED PORK CHOPS

8 center cut pork chops,    ¼ cup vinegar
  1 inch thick    ½ cup barbecue sauce
½ cup worcestershire sauce    2 large onions
½ cup prune juice    Prepared mustard

Salt and pepper chops then rub each chop on both sides with mustard. Sprinkle lightly with flour. Brown on both sides on top of stove in roaster in which they are to be cooked. Cut onions in ¼ inch thick slices, place one on top of each chop. Mix prune juice, worcestershire, and vinegar and pour around chops. Bake in 300 degree oven covered for 30 minutes, then baste every ½ hour, adding teaspoon of sauce to top of each chop. Add water if pan dries out. Cook two hours.

*Mrs. Robert Glenn (Lyn)*

## TAHITIAN PORK CHOPS

*Different and delicious*

8 pork chops    1 clove garlic
¾ cup sherry    ¾ teaspoon ginger
¼ cup soy sauce    ¼ teaspoon oregano
¼ cup salad oil    1 tablespoon maple syrup

Brown pork chops in a skillet. Place in baking dish. Put all other ingredients in blender and process at "mix" until smooth. Pour over chops, cover and bake at 350 degrees 1 to 1½ hours or until tender. Turn chops once during baking time to give both sides added browning. Serves 8.

*Mrs. Vincent Sgrosso (Joanne)*

## CANTONESE PORK

1 pound boneless pork loin    2 tablespoons tomato catsup
2 tablespoons peanut oil    1 can condensed chicken broth
1 green pepper, seeded and cut      (or 1½ cups chicken bouillon)
  into 1 inch triangles    ½ cup white vinegar
1 cup sliced celery    1/3 cup sugar
1 cup well-drained pineapple    2 tablespoons cornstarch
  chunks    4 servings cooked rice

Trim fat from pork and cut into ¼ inch strips. In a large skillet heat oil just until it starts to smoke. Stir quickly over high heat until pork is

(continued)

85

cooked, about 3 minutes. Add remaining ingredients except cornstarch. Cover and cook until vegetables are tender, but crisp, about 12 minutes. Mix cornstarch and ¼ cup water. Stir in quickly. Cook, stirring, until mixture bubbles and thickens. Season to taste with salt. Serve over hot rice. Serves 4.

*Mrs. Kenneth Covey (Peggy)*

## GINGERED PORK

| | |
|---|---|
| 18 (1 inch) pieces pork loin | 2 cups chicken broth |
| Soy sauce | ½ cup sherry |
| 1 tablespoon ginger | Salt and pepper |
| Oil | Cornstarch |
| Butter | |

Marinate the pork in mixture of soy sauce and ginger. Brown in ½ oil and ½ butter. Bake at 350 degrees in chicken broth and sherry, salt and pepper for 1 hour until tender. Thicken with cornstarch; mix with remaining chicken broth. Put back in oven for a few minutes. Serves 6.

*Mrs. Moncure Crowder (Jo)*

## PORK ROAST
*Great flavor*

| | |
|---|---|
| ½ cup soy sauce | 1 tablespoon dry mustard |
| ½ cup sherry | 1 teaspoon ginger |
| 2 garlic cloves, minced | 1 teaspoon thyme |
| 1 (4-5 pound) rolled pork roast | |

Mix all the ingredients except the roast for the marinade. Put all in a plastic bag and let marinate for 4-5 hours. Cook at 325 degrees for 2½-3 hours in an uncovered roasting pan. Baste the last hour.

*Mrs. Richard McCamey (Betsy)*

## HAM BRAISED IN MADEIRA

| | |
|---|---|
| 16 pound ham, skinned and trimmed | 2½ cups madeira |
| 1½ cups sliced onions | 4 cups beef bouillon |
| 1½ cups sliced carrots | 8 parsley sprigs |
| 3 tablespoons butter | 2 bay leaves |
| 2 tablespoons oil | 1 teaspoon thyme |
| | Confectioners sugar |

Preheat oven to 325 degrees. Cook vegetables in oil and butter in roasting pan until lightly browned. Place ham fat side up over vegetables, add wine, bouillon and herbs. Bring to simmer on top of stove. Cook covered for 3½-4 hours. Baste every 20 minutes. When ham is done, drain it and sift confectioners sugar over top and brown in 450 degree oven for 10-15 minutes.

This will serve 60 people if thinly sliced. Serve with small slices of bread.

*Mrs. Hall Ware (Mary)*

## HAM LOAF

2 tablespoons gelatin
½ cup cold water
1 cup boiling water
2 tablespoons lemon juice
1 tablespoon horseradish
2½ cups cooked ham, finely ground

2 teaspoons worcestershire sauce
½ teaspoon grated onion
1 pimiento, finely chopped
Dash of cayenne
Dash of ground cloves
½ cup mayonnaise

Soften gelatin in cold water, add boiling water and dissolve. Add lemon juice, chill slightly. Add remaining ingredients in order given. Turn into loaf pan and chill until firm. Unmold on crisp lettuce and garnish with parsley. Serves 6.

*Mrs. Milwee Owens, III (Carol Pimlott)*

## HAM DIVAN

*Great way to use left over ham*

1 package (10 ounce) frozen
  broccoli spears
4 slices white or French bread
  (toasted and buttered)

1 cup sour cream
1 teaspoon mustard
½ cup grated cheddar cheese
4 large thin slices baked ham

Cook broccoli following label directions, drain well. Place toast slices in single layer in large shallow baking dish or individual baking dishes. Cover each with slice ham, folding ham to fit toast; top with hot broccoli. Blend sour cream with mustard in small bowl, spoon in ribbons over broccoli, sprinkle with grated cheese. Bake in hot oven 400 degrees. for 15 minutes or until heated through and cheese melts. Serves 4.

*Mrs. Wink A. Davis, Jr. (Helen)*

## CANADIAN BACON

*Great for brunch and smells so good as it cooks*

1 whole Canadian bacon                     3 tablespoons pickling spice

Place Canadian bacon in a pot and cover with water. Add pickling spice and boil for 1 hour. Yield will depend on the size of the bacon.

*Mrs. Richard McCamey (Betsy)*


## BARBECUED FRANKS

1 pound frankfurters, cut diagonally
  into 1 inch pieces
1/3 cup chopped onion
1 tablespoon vinegar
1 tablespoon brown sugar

2 tablespoons lemon juice
½ cup catsup
1 tablespoon worcestershire sauce
1/3 cup water
2 tablespoons chopped green pepper

Combine all ingredients except the frankfurters. Simmer for 15 minutes. Add frankfurters and simmer for 10 more minutes.

*Mrs. A. J. Stringer (Martha)*


## PARTY HOTDOGS

*For picnics, informal or formal parties*

Bourbon
Catsup

Brown sugar
Hot dogs

In a large heavy saucepan or kettle, mix equal parts of bourbon, brown sugar and catsup and simmer for 20 minutes over low heat. Depending on your amount, chop and add two or three large onions. Allowing 3-4 hotdogs per person, chop each hotdog into 5 pieces and add to mixture (mixture should cover) and simmer uncovered for 40 more minutes. Serve in a chafing dish or fondue pot with toothpicks.

*Mrs. Charles B. Rice (Barbara)*


## LOVING TOUCHES . . .

Sprinkle a package of dry onion soup over a chuck roast or a standing rib pork roast. Seal in foil and bake until done. (This process makes its own gravy while cooking.)

## SCALOPPINE A LA MARSALA

2 pounds veal escallops, pounded
   to ¼ inch thick
Salt
Freshly ground pepper
Flour
½ cup butter

¾ cup beef stock
¾ cup Marsala wine
2 tablespoons chopped parsley
Pinch oregano
2 tablespoons soft butter
2 cups fresh mushrooms, sliced

Season veal with salt and pepper. Dip in flour and shake off excess. In heavy skillet, melt butter over moderate heat. When foam subsides, add veal and brown for about 3 minutes per side. Remove veal from skillet to plate. Pour off most of the butter into a second skillet, leaving only a thin film on the bottom. In second skillet, saute mushrooms until tender. Set aside. Put first skillet over medium high heat. Add Marsala and ½ cup stock. Boil the liquid briskly for 1-2 minutes. Scrape any browned fragments clinging to bottom and sides of skillet. Return veal to skillet. Add mushrooms, oregano and parsley. Cover, reduce heat and simmer 10-15 minutes, basting veal with pan juices. Transfer veal and mushrooms to heated platter. Add ¼ cup stock to sauce remaining in skillet and boil briskly, scraping the browned bits sticking to the pan. When sauce is reduced and has consistency of syrupy glaze, season to taste. Remove skillet from heat, stir in 2 tablespoons soft butter and pour over veal.

*Mrs. Dale Harman (Kathy)*


## VEAL CUTLETS PARMESAN

*A northern Italian recipe*

1 pound veal cutlets
½ cup butter or oil
½ cup grated parmesan cheese
½ pound mozzarella cheese
1 cup dry bread crumbs

2 eggs beaten
1 (8 ounce) can tomato sauce
¼ teaspoon salt
Dash of pepper

Dip cutlets into eggs combined with salt and pepper, then dip into bread crumbs, mixed with the parmesan cheese. Fry in butter (oil) until brown. (About 8 minutes.) Then place cutlets in a baking dish, pour tomato sauce over them and add slices of mozzarella cheese. Bake at 350-375 degrees for 10-15 minutes. Serves 4. Cutlets may be breaded and fried earlier in the day.

*Mrs. Stanley Goldstein (Rita)*

## VEAL PICCATA

*Easy and elegant*

8 thin slices of veal
¼ stick butter
1 lemon, thinly sliced

¼ cup dry white wine
Parsley sprigs
Lemon wedges

Saute veal briefly in butter with sliced lemon. Remove veal to a hot platter. Add wine to the pan and stir. Pour wine and drippings over veal. Garnish with parsley sprigs and lemon wedges.

*Mrs. Jack Wall (Marion)*

## VEAL CORDON BLEU

4 veal fillets
Salt and pepper
Swiss cheese, thinly sliced
4 thin slices of ham

Flour
Eggs
Bread crumbs
Butter or margarine

Pound veal very thin. Salt and pepper each fillet on each side. Put one slice of ham and one slice of cheese in each fillet and fold over, pressing sides together. Dip into flour, egg, and bread crumbs, in that order. Refrigerate before frying. Fry in butter or margarine for about four or five minutes on each side. Serve with lemon wedges. Serves 4.

*Mrs. Robert D. Hand, Jr. (Kitty)*

## SALTIMBOCCA

*Veal cutlets with procuitto ham and mozzarella cheese*

*Specialty of "Once Upon a Stove Restaurant", New York City*

4 veal cutlets, thinly sliced
½ cup flour
Salt, to taste
¼ cup butter
¼ cup Marsala wine
½ cup chicken stock

4 slices procuitto ham,
  thinly sliced
4 slices mozzarella cheese
Bells poultry seasoning
Fresh parsley, chopped

Saute salted and floured cutlets in butter until lightly browned. (May add a little oil to butter to prevent burning.) Add wine and simmer several minutes. Add stock and stir until sauce thickens. Cover veal with ham, then cheese. Sprinkle with poultry seasoning and place under broiler until cheese melts and mixes with sauce. Keep basting veal with sauce for about one minute. Top with parsley and serve at once. Serves 4.

*Mr. Henry Sgrosso (Hank), Owner*

# Poultry

## and Game Birds

## SAUCY CHICKEN WITH AVOCADO

*Out of this world!*

2 tablespoons butter
1 (2½-3 pound) cut-up fryer
2/3 cup dry sherry
2 tablespoons flour
Watercress or parsley

¾ teaspoon salt
Dash paprika
1¼ cups half-and-half
1 large avocado, sliced

In skillet, brown chicken on all sides in hot butter. Stir in sherry, heat to boiling. Reduce heat to low; cover and simmer 25 minutes or until chicken is fork tender. Remove chicken to platter. Into liquid in skillet, blend flour, salt and paprika. Slowly stir in half-and-half; cook, stirring constantly until thickened. Gently add avocado, heat through, spoon over chicken. Garnish with watercress or parsley. Serves 4.

*Mrs. James Wilcox, Jr. (Betty)*

## EASY BAKED CHICKEN

*You won't believe this one, but it works!*

1 broiler, whole                  Salt and pepper

Salt and pepper chicken inside and out. Place in brown paper bag. Place on cookie sheet in 350 degree oven for one hour, or until done.

*Mrs. F. Stuart Gould, Jr.*

## BARBECUED CHICKEN

1 fryer, cut up
¾ cup flour
2 teaspoons salt
½ cup oil or shortening
½ cup chopped onion
2 tablespoons margarine

¼ cup chopped green bell pepper
1 cup water
2 tablespoons brown sugar
½ cup chopped celery
1 cup catsup
2 tablespoons worcestershire sauce

Coat chicken with flour mixed with salt and brown in oil or shortening. As pieces are brown, arrange in casserole dish. Saute onion in melted margarine until clear. Add all ingredients and bring to a boil. Pour over chicken in casserole. Cover and bake in 350 degree oven about one hour until tender. Serves 4.

*Mrs. E. T. Griffith (Barbara)*

## LEMON BARBECUED CHICKEN

| | |
|---|---|
| 6 split broilers | 1 stick margarine |
| 4 tablespoons oil | Dash paprika |
| 4 tablespoons lemon juice | Garlic salt to taste |
| Salt and pepper to taste | |

Start chicken, skin side away, from low charcoal fire. (Be sure to keep fire low with no flame). After searing on both sides, baste each side. Cook rather slowly so as not to burn. Barbecue chicken for 1 hour basting about every 10 minutes. Pour any remaining sauce over chicken before serving. Serves 6.

*Mr. Russell French*

## BURGUNDY CHICKEN BREASTS

*Very delicious! Good for company!*

| | |
|---|---|
| 4 large chicken breast halves | ½ teaspoon garlic powder |
| Salt and pepper | 1 teaspoon parsley flakes |
| 1 can mushroom soup | ¼ cup burgundy wine |

Season chicken breasts with salt and pepper and place on large square heavy duty aluminum foil for baking. Make sauce of remaining ingredients and pour over chicken. Wrap well and place in 425 degrees preheated oven for 15 minutes. Reduce heat to 325 degrees and bake one hour longer. Unwrap, place chicken on plate and cover with sauce. Serves 4.

*Mrs. Edward A. Pierce (Margery)*

## CATALINA CHICKEN

| | |
|---|---|
| Catalina Kraft Salad Dressing, whole jar | 1 cut-up fryer |
| | *1 jar (small) pineapple jelly |
| 1 package Lipton onion soup | *1 jar (small) apricot jelly |

Mix all ingredients together and pour over chicken in casserole. Cook uncovered in a 300 degree oven for about 1½ hours or until tender.
*Note: Any 10 ounce jar of jelly you have will do. I usually use half of a 10 ounce jar of each of these, as I like the taste. Serves 4.

*Mrs. Charles E. Bouis (Lois)*

## CHARLIE'S CHICKEN

4 to 6 pieces of chicken
1 package "Good Seasons"
  Italian Dressing Mix
1 (8 ounce) package cream cheese
1 cup sauterne wine

Handful of chives
1 (10 ounce) can cream of
  mushroom soup
4 tablespoons butter

Saute 4 to 6 pieces of chicken in butter and sprinkle Italian seasoning mix while turning chicken. (Do this very slowly as herbs cause chicken to burn at high temperatures). Heat mushroom soup and cream cheese. When cream cheese is melted, add chives and sauterne wine. Heat until mixture is smooth. Pour over chicken and bake uncovered at 350 degrees for one hour. Serves 4.

*Mrs. Sallie A. Willis*

## CHICKEN BAKE WITH CHEESE

6 to 8 chicken breast halves
  or cut-up whole chicken
1 can cream of mushroom soup

1 can cream of celery soup
1 cup grated sharp cheese

Place chicken in baking pan. Mix the soups (undiluted) and cheese well and pour over chicken making sure that chicken is covered. (Mixture is thick). Bake at 350 degrees until chicken is tender. This makes a delicious gravy to serve over rice with chicken. Serves 6.

*Mrs. George Hopkins (Betty)*

## CHICKEN CONTINENTAL

3-4 pounds frying chicken or
  4 breasts, halved
1/3 cup flour
¼ cup butter
1 can cream of chicken soup
2½ tablespoons grated onion
1 teaspoon salt

Dash pepper
1 tablespoon chopped parsley
½ teaspoon celery flakes
1/8 teaspoon thyme
1 1/3 cups water
1 1/3 cups Minute Rice
Paprika

Flour chicken and brown in butter. Remove chicken. Stir soup, seasoning, and water into drippings. Cook and stir to a boil. Spread rice (uncooked) into 1¾ quart shallow casserole. Pour all but 1/3 of soup mixture over rice; stir to moisten. Top with chicken and rest of soup. Bake, covered, at 350 degrees for 1 hour. Garnish with paprika. Serves 4.

*Mrs. Merrit S. Bond (Suzanne)*

## CREAMED CHICKEN IN BASKETS

*In a hurry? It's like a pot pie!!*

1½-2 cups cut up chicken
  or turkey, cooked
1 can mushroom soup
Sherry

Egg baskets (found in the
  dairy case)
Salt and pepper

Mix cut-up chicken or turkey with mushroom soup. Add salt, pepper and sherry to taste. Put egg baskets in a muffin tin or individual ramekins and fill with mixture. (There are 4 egg baskets per package.)
Bake at 350 degrees for 15 to 20 minutes.

*Mrs. Thomas Johnson (Benita)*

## CHICKEN CREPES

Crepes:
4 tablespoons flour
1 egg
1 egg yolk
Cayenne pepper (pinch)

1 tablespoon oil
About ½ cup milk
Salt

Place 4 tablspoons flour, 1 egg, 1 egg yolk, 1 tablespoon oil, 4 tablespoons milk, salt and cayenne pepper in a small bowl and beat until smooth. Add enough milk to reduce to the consistency of heavy cream (about ½ cup in all). Place in refrigerator for ½ hour. Meanwhile prepare the chicken filling.

Chicken Filling:
½ pound mushrooms
1 tablespoon butter
¾ cup shredded cooked chicken
2 hard-boiled eggs, chopped

1 teaspoon chopped parsley
3 tablespoons sour cream
Salt and pepper

Slice and saute mushrooms in butter about 5 minutes until lightly browned. In top of double boiler add all ingredients together and place over boiling water to heat through and keep warm while crepes are being cooked.

To cook crepes: Remove batter from refrigerator. If thickened, add more milk. Using a crepe pan or heated cast iron skillet, rub the pan with a little butter. Cover the bottom with a very thin coating of batter. Brown carefully on one side, turn and brown the other using a wide spatula. Place on a cake rack or stack with wax paper in between. Place a spoonful of the filling in the middle of each crepe - fold over edges. Top with melted butter and parmesan cheese.

*Mrs. James Cushman (Elkin)*

## EASY CHICKEN CURRY

¼ cup plus 2 tablespoons butter
½ cup minced onion
¼ teaspoon ginger
2 cups chicken broth
2 cups milk
4 cups cut up chicken

1½ teaspoons salt
1½ teaspoons sugar
1 apple, diced
1 tablespoon curry powder
¼ cup plus 2 tablespoons flour
1 teaspoon lemon juice

Melt butter over low heat in sauce pan. Saute onion, apple and curry powder in melted butter. Blend in flour and seasonings. Cook over low heat until mixture is smooth and thick. Remove from heat. Stir in chicken broth and milk. Bring to boil stirring constantly. Boil one minute. Add chicken and lemon juice. Heat and serve over rice. Serve with choice of condiments. This recipe can be made a day ahead of time. Serves 6.

*Marian Beavers*

## HUNGARIAN CHICKEN

Chicken breast for 4 servings
1 pint sour cream
¼ cup butter

2 medium white onions, grated
½ package Pepperidge Farm
cornbread stuffing mix

Place chicken in baking pan. Cover each piece with mixture of sour cream and grated onions. (This should be very thick - use plenty). Sprinkle thickly with stuffing mix. Cut up butter and top each piece generously. Bake in oven at 375 degrees about 40 minutes or until fork tender. This is divine served over rice. Serves 4.

*Mrs. James Wilcox, Jr. (Betty)*

## CHICKEN LOAF

1 tablespoon plain gelatin
¼ cup cold water
¾ cup chicken broth
1 cup mayonnaise
2 plus cups cooked chopped chicken

½ cup chopped celery
¼ cup pimiento
3 hard-boiled eggs, chopped
Salt and pepper to taste

Combine all ingredients with gelatin, water and broth. Pour in greased mold or loaf pan. Refrigerate for 6 hours or until set. Slice. Serves 6.

*Mrs. Thomas G. Magbee*

## BREAST OF CHICKEN MAGNIFIQUE

4 whole chicken breasts     ½ teaspoon garlic powder
  (preferably boned and split)     Generous dash crushed thyme
¼ cup butter     ½ teaspoon crushed rosemary
2 cups sliced mushrooms     2/3 cup light cream
2 cans cream of chicken soup     Toasted slivered almonds

Brown chicken in butter in a large skillet. Remove. Saute mushrooms. Stir in soup, garlic powder and seasonings. Add chicken. Cover, cook over low heat 45 minutes. Stir now and then. Blend in cream, heat slowly. Garnish with almonds. Serves 6.

Note: This recipe is pretty as well as delicious. Serve over a bed of rice, garnished with parsley. Serves 8.

*Mrs. Gene Presley (Dianne)*


## MARINATED CHICKEN

*Best on outdoor grill*

1 envelope herb salad-dressing     2/3 cup salad oil
  mix (or Italian Good Seasons)     2 broiler chickens (2 pounds
1 envelope garlic salad-dressing       each) split in half length-
  mix (Good Seasons)       wise, or chicken pieces
½ cup dry sherry wine

Combine first four ingredients for marinade, mixing well. Pour over chicken in shallow baking dish and refrigerate covered overnight. Turn once or twice to coat well. Broil over slow coals for 20 to 30 minutes on each side, or until done. (This may be partially baked in oven and then grilled until done and well browned.)

*Mrs. Vincent Sgrosso (Joanne)*


## CHICKEN – MEXICAN STYLE

*Different!*

1 cut-up fryer     1 can tomatoes
1 medium onion, chopped     1½ teaspoons tabasco
1 can cream of mushroom soup     1 cup grated cheese
1 can cream of chicken soup     2 tablespoons butter
1 package Doritos

(continued)

97

Stew chicken, cool, remove from bones. Saute chopped onion in sauce pan in butter. Add soups, tomatoes, tabasco and heat thoroughly. Spread Doritos over bottom of large greased casserole. Place chicken on top of Doritos. Pour sauce over all. Sprinkle grated cheese on top. Bake in 350 degree oven until cheese is melted and casserole good and hot. Serves 6.

*Mrs. Herbert J. Beadle, Jr. (Jerry)*

## ORIENTAL CHICKEN BREASTS

3 whole chicken breasts, split in half
5 tablespoons salad oil
½ cup dark brown sugar
½ cup vinegar
¾ teaspoon salt
1/3 teaspoon ground ginger
2 tablespoons cornstarch

1 (8¼ ounce) can pineapple chunks
1 (11 ounce) can mandarin orange sections, drained
1 green pepper, cut into short strips
½ cup halved maraschino cherries
1 teaspoon soy sauce

Heat oil in skillet over medium heat. Brown chicken breasts on each side. Pour off excess oil. Combine brown sugar, vinegar, salt, ginger and soy sauce. Pour over chicken and simmer 35 minutes covered. Remove chicken. Blend cornstarch and 2 tablespoons pineapple syrup and stir into skillet with remaining pineapple and syrup, orange sections, green pepper and cherries. Bring to a boil. Return chicken to skillet. Cover and simmer 5 to 10 minutes longer or until chicken is tender and pepper is cooked. Serve with rice, if desired. Serves 4.

*Mrs. Kenneth Covey (Peggy)*

## CRUNCHY OVEN–BAKED CHICKEN

*Great and easy!*

1 cut-up fryer or 8 boned chicken breasts
2 cups Ritz cracker crumbs
¾ cup parmesan cheese
1 clove garlic, pressed

2 teaspoons salt
1/8 teaspoon pepper
1 cup margarine, melted
¼ cup chopped parsley

Preheat oven to 350 degrees. Blend cracker crumbs, parmesan cheese, parsley, garlic, salt and pepper. Dip each piece of chicken in melted butter and then in cracker mixture. Arrange in open shallow pan or casserole. Pour remaining butter over chicken and bake one hour at 350 degrees. Do not turn chicken. Serves 4.

*Mrs. Oliver P. Ackerman, Jr.*

*Mrs. William Luesing (Carolyn)*

## HUNGARIAN CHICKEN PAPRIKA

| | |
|---|---|
| 5½ pounds chicken breasts or pieces | 4 tablespoons margarine |
| 4 large onions, thinly sliced | 2 tablespoons paprika |
| 4½ tablespoons butter | Salt |
| 1 pint sour cream | Lemon |
| | 8 ounces noodles |

Rub chicken with salt and lemon. Melt butter in pot and add onions, cooking until soft. Add paprika and the chicken. Cover and cook 30-40 minutes, turning several times. Add sour cream, mix and heat. Cook noodles, drain and add margarine. Serves 6.

*Mrs. Howard Kearns (Mary)*

## CHICKEN PAPRIKA

| | |
|---|---|
| 2 chicken breasts, halved | *1 can cream of onion soup |
| 2 tablespoons paprika | ½ teaspoon worcestershire |
| ½ cup diced green pepper | ¼ teaspoon salt |
| 2 tablespoons butter | ¼ teaspoon pepper |
| ¾ cup water | |

Toss chicken with paprika and saute with green pepper in butter until brown. Blend water, soup and worcestershire together and add to chicken. Simmer 10-15 minutes or until tender. Add salt and pepper and serve with rice using pan drippings as gravy. Serves 2 to 4.

*Note: cream of chicken soup may be substituted.

*Mrs. Richard Huff (Sally)*

## BREASTS OF CHICKEN PARMIGIANA

*Marvelous for buffets*

| | |
|---|---|
| 4 chicken breasts (halved and boned) | 1 tablespoon parmesan cheese |
| 1 egg, beaten | 8 slices mozzarella cheese |
| ¼ cup flour | 1 cup marinara tomato sauce |
| 4 ounces butter | (see index) |
| Salt and pepper | 1 cup bread crumbs |

(continued)

Beat breasts until thin, sprinkle with salt and pepper. Coat in flour and cheese mix, then dip into beaten egg and last in bread crumbs. Fry chicken slowly in butter until brown. Place one tablespoon of tomato sauce in a pyrex casserole under each chicken breast. On top of each breast put 2 tablespoons of sauce and one slice of mozzarella cheese. Place chicken in a 350 degree oven and cook until cheese melts. Serve hot. Serves 8.

*Mrs. Vincent Sgrosso (Joanne)*

## ROQUEFORT CHICKEN

2 (1½ pound) broilers, split
1½ teaspoons salt
¼ teaspoon pepper
3 tablespoons butter

6 ounces roquefort cheese
1 clove garlic, minced
1½ cups sour cream

Rub the broilers with salt and pepper. Melt the butter in a skillet. Brown the chicken. Remove from skillet and place in a baking dish. Mash roquefort cheese with a fork and blend in garlic and sour cream. Spread over chicken. Cover and bake at 375 degrees 45 minutes or until tender. Remove cover for last 5 minutes. Serves 4.

*Mrs. Robert Chambers (Wendy)*

## CHICKEN STUFFED WITH SHRIMP

8 boned chicken breasts
8 slices cheddar cheese
1 pound shrimp
2 cans cream of mushroom soup

½ pint sour cream
6 tablespoons sherry
Salt
Pepper

Lay chicken breasts out flat. Put cheese and then shrimp in center of each one. Roll breasts together and secure with toothpicks. Place in 2 quart shallow casserole. Mix soup, sour cream, sherry and salt and pepper to taste. Pour over chicken. Cook uncovered 2 hours at 225 degrees or 1½ hours at 275 degrees. Serves 8.

*Mrs. Dow Kirkpatrick (Harriet)*

## LOVING TOUCHES . . .

Learn to bone chicken breasts and save half the cost. A boned breast, brushed with lemon juice and butter, cooks in 8 to 12 minutes.

## SMOTHERED CHICKEN

2½ pounds chicken pieces
3-4 tablespoons melted margarine

1 can cream of mushroom soup
1 package Lipton onion soup mix

Dip chicken pieces in melted margarine and place in 1½ quart casserole dish. Pour cream of mushroom soup over chicken. Sprinkle package of Lipton onion soup mix over top. Cover. Cook at 350 degrees for 1 hour. Serve over rice or noodles Serves 4.

*Mrs. Donald Buffington (Buffa)*

## BONED CHICKEN BREAST WITH SOUR CREAM

1 jar Armour chipped beef
6 to 8 chicken breasts, boned
Salt and pepper
Accent

Paprika
Bacon strips uncooked
½ pint sour cream
1 can mushroom soup

Line casserole dish with chipped beef. Sprinkle chicken with salt, pepper, Accent and paprika, then wrap with bacon. Mix sour cream and mushroom soup and pour over casserole. Cover with foil and cook at 300 degrees for 2 hours. Uncover and cook one more hour. Serves 6.

*Mrs. Bert Oastler (Belitje)*

## CHICKEN BREAST SUPREME

4 chicken breasts, boned (have
  butcher run them once through
  cuber)
8 ounces chicken broth
2 tablespoons dry sherry wine
Butter or margarine

4 large mushrooms, sliced
Flour
¼ teaspoon salt
1 package McCormick's
  hollandise sauce (use ¼ cup
  less water than called for)

Prepare this receipe in a skillet that can go in oven. In butter, gently brown slightly flour-coated breasts on both sides. Remove. Add butter if needed and saute mushrooms. Remove. In same skillet in about ¼ cup drippings, add 2 tablespoons flour, salt and broth gradually until smooth and thickened. Add wine (and 1 tablespoon cream if desired.) Place chicken breasts in sauce. Gently simmer (covered) about 20 minutes, or until tender. Add mushrooms. Brown hollandaise-covered chicken in preheated broiler for a few minutes. Serves 4.

*Mrs. John Westmoreland, Jr. (Nevin)*

## SYRIAN STUFFED CHICKEN

½ pound ground lamb (or beef)
1/3 cup oil
1½ cups cooked rice
1/3 cup pine nuts (toasted)
Dash dried thyme

½ teaspoon salt
1/8 teaspoon pepper
¼ teaspoon cinnamon
Dash nutmeg
3 to 3½ pound fryer chicken

In skillet brown lamb in 3 tablespoons oil. Add rice, pine nuts, salt and pepper and spices. Mix well. Stuff chicken with mixture and skewer. Place in a shallow pan and brush with remaining oil. Roast in 375 degree oven for 1¼ to 1½ hours, brushing occasionally with remaining oil. Serves 4.

*Mrs. Michele Aquino (Claudia)*

## TARRAGON CHICKEN WITH MUSHROOMS

1 (3 pound) chicken cut-up or
  6 breast halves
1 tablespoon seasoned salt
½ teaspoon ground pepper
Dash paprika

1 teaspoon tarragon
¼ cup butter
1 medium onion, thinly sliced
½ pound fresh mushrooms,
  sliced

Sprinkle chicken with blended salt, pepper and paprika. Cook slowly to a deep golden brown in butter 20-25 minutes. Turn to brown on all sides. Remove chicken from pan. Add onions and mushrooms. Cook until tender but not brown. Return chicken to pan, sprinkle with tarragon and cover with the vegetables. Cover skillet and cook slowly until chicken is done, 20-30 minutes more. Serves 4.

*Mrs. Robert Chambers (Wendy)*

## LOVING TOUCHES . . .

When whole fryers are "on sale", this is a good way to get tender chicken for casseroles. To cook: Put 2 whole fryers (legs up) in a stew pot. Add water and 1 cup white wine, salt and pepper. Simmer for about 1 hour.

To tenderize chicken and other fowl: Rub inside and outside with lemon juice.

## CHICKEN VERONIQUE

12 chicken breasts, boned
Salt and paprika
¾ cup butter, divided
½ cup chopped onion
½ pound mushrooms, sliced
½ cup flour

2 teaspoons sugar
4 cups chicken broth
¼ cup lemon juice
2 cups seedless green grapes
Grape clusters

Sprinkle chicken breasts with salt and paprika. Melt ½ cup butter in large skillet. Add chicken, brown well on both sides and remove. Melt remaining ¼ cup butter in skillet; add onions and mushrooms. Cook over low heat for five minutes. Blend in flour and sugar. Stir in chicken broth and lemon juice. Bring to boil, stirring constantly. Add chicken, cover and simmer 30-40 minutes, or until tender. Add grapes last five minutes of cooking time. Serves 8. This recipe may be made morning of dinner and simmered after guests arrive.

*Mrs. Solon Patterson (Marianna)*

## CORNISH HEN STUFFED WITH FRUIT

*Delicious served hot or cold*

1 cup chopped celery
1 cup chopped apple
1 cup chopped onion
½ cup raisins
1 cup chopped orange with peel

1 cup whole fresh grapes
Maderia wine
4 cornish hens
1 cup orange juice
1 cup maderia wine

Stuffing: Combine celery, apple, onion, raisins, orange and grapes. Cover with wine and marinate overnight. Hens: Salt and pepper hens. Stuff each with ¼ of above dressing. Bake in 350 degree oven for 2 hours or until the meat pulls away from the bone. Baste occasionally with 1 cup orange juice and 1 cup wine. Halve each hen with poultry shears. Place on platter with some stuffing under each. Garnish with fresh parsley. Serves 8.

*Mrs. Ed Forio, Jr. (Phoebe)*

## LOVING TOUCHES . . .

In the pan juice from cooking a turkey breast, add packaged "Tater Tots" and bake according to directions.

103

## OVEN BAKED QUAIL

12 quail, cleaned
1 stick margarine, melted
1 can cream of mushroom soup

1 stick butter, melted
1 cup flour
Salt and pepper

Dredge birds in flour seasoned with salt and pepper. Brown birds in the melted margarine and butter. Remove to casserole. Make gravy with water, pan juices and add to it one can cream of mushroom soup. Pour over birds. Bake covered one hour in 350 degree oven. Note: May vary by adding mushrooms or dry white wine to taste.

*Mrs. Robert Marchman (Helen)*

# Seafood

DAVID SAPP

## FISH MINUTE

1½ to 2 pounds fish fillets
1 teaspoon salt
¼ teaspoon freshly ground pepper
2 tablespoons finely chopped
    scallions

2 tablespoons minced parsley
¾-1 cup dry white wine
2-3 tablespoons fresh bread
    crumbs
Butter

Place fillets in 1½ quart baking dish. Sprinkle with seasonings, scallions, and parsley. Add enough wine to almost cover fish. Top with bread crumbs and dot with butter. Bake at 450 degrees for 15 minutes or until crumbs are browned and fish flakes easily with a fork. Serve hot in baking dish. Serves 6.

*Mrs. Robert F. Dennis (Peggy)*

## FILLET OF FLOUNDER AMANDINE

2 pounds fresh flounder fillets
Salt and pepper to taste
2 tablespoons lemon juice
¾ pound saltine crackers
¾ cup sliced almonds

3 eggs, beaten
2/3 cup milk
2 cups all-purpose flour
½ cup vegetable oil
½ cup butter

Cut flounder into 6 portions and season with salt, pepper, and lemon juice. Crumble crackers coarsely and mix with almonds. Beat eggs and milk together. Dredge flounder in the flour and dip in egg and milk mixture. Roll in cracker crumbs and almond mixture and pat down firmly so cracker crumbs will adhere. Heat oil and butter. Fry the fish about 5 minutes on each side until it is golden brown. Drain on paper towel or brown paper bag and serve immediately. Serves 6.

*Mr. Albert Redd*

## FLOUNDER GRENOBLAISE

*Great - and easy!*

2 pounds fillet of flounder
1 egg, beaten
1 cup milk
Flour
½ cup butter

1 tablespoon worcestershire sauce
1 tablespoon chopped parsley
¼ cup capers
Salt and pepper to taste
Juice of 2 lemons

Dip flounder fillet in batter of egg and milk. Let drain a moment. Dredge in flour. Melt butter in 9 inch skillet and saute flounder until golden. Add lemon juice, worcestershire sauce, parsley, salt, pepper and capers. Heat through. Serves 4.

*Mrs. William Luesing (Carolyn)*

## HADDOCK FLORENTINE

2 packages frozen chopped spinach
1½ pounds fillet of haddock (I use
   2 packages frozen haddock fillets)
1 bay leaf
1 pinch thyme

1 tablespoon lemon juice
Salt
Pepper
1 cup white sauce
½-1 cup grated Swiss cheese

Cook spinach, drain and spread in shallow oblong buttered baking dish. Add bay leaf, thyme, and lemon juice to enough water to cover fish and cook over medium heat for five minutes or until fish flakes easily when tested with a fork. Remove fish with wide spatula and place on top of spinach. Reserve liquid from fish. Sprinkle fish with salt and pepper. Combine white sauce and 1 cup reserved cooking liquid in small saucepan. Cook over medium heat, stirring constantly until sauce comes to a boil. Cook 1 minute. Remove from heat and add cheese. Stir until smooth. Pour over fish. Bake at 400 degrees for 20-25 minutes or until lightly browned. Serves 4. I use this as a first course sometimes, followed by beef. Serves 6-8 as first course.

*Mrs. Richard Denny (Marg)*

## FILLET OF RED SNAPPER WITH HOLLANDAISE

3 pounds fillet of red snapper
2 egg yolks
½ cup melted butter

¼ teaspoon dry mustard
1 tablespoon tarragon
   vinegar

Place fish in pan with water to cover. Remove fish until water boils, then replace fish and poach until it flakes. Drain snapper and place on warm platter. Keep warm. To make hollandaise sauce, combine yolks, mustard and vinegar. Beat well and gradually add butter. Cook and stir over medium heat until sauce thickens. Spoon over fish and dash with paprika. Serves 4.

*Mrs. William A. McClain, III (Rose)*

## FILLET OF SOLE

1 pound fillet of sole
2 tablespoons butter
½ cup water
2 cubes chicken bouillon

1 tablespoon dried parsley
2 tablespoons dried onion
1 teaspoon dry mustard
½ teaspoon tarragon

Place fillets, in single layer, in greased 9x13 glass pan. Combine other ingredients in pan and heat until butter melts and bouillon dissolves. Pour sauce over fish. Bake at 350 degrees for 20 to 25 minutes. Do not overcook. May be reheated if more sauce is made. Serves 2-3.

*Mrs. Richard McCamey (Betsy)*

## BROILED RAINBOW TROUT

*Men lose their minds over this!*

2 fresh rainbow trout
(10-11 inches long) whole,
cleaned and scaled
Large leaves from outside
head of lettuce
Butter

Salt and fresh ground pepper,
to taste

2 limes, thinly sliced
2 small onions, sliced

If fish have been under refrigeration one day or longer, run under cold water and pat dry with paper towels. Rub fish with butter, salt, and pepper. Place a few onion slices and butter slices in gullet area and all across the top of fish. Put a lime slice on top of each onion slice (except those in gullet). Line cookie sheet with lettuce leaves. Place fish on leaves and broil for approximately 10 minutes. Serves 2. Serve with broiled tomatoes, potato souffle and green garden salad - and, of course, a little vino!

*Bebe McIntyre*

## DEVILED CRAB

1 green pepper, chopped
2 tablespoons margarine
1 pound crabmeat, picked and
flaked
1 small jar pimiento

1 teaspoon dry mustard
¼ teaspoon cayenne pepper
½ teaspoon worcestershire sauce
2 tablespoons mayonnaise

Saute green pepper in margarine and mix lightly with other ingredients. Place in greased shallow casserole dish and bake at 400 degrees until brown. Serves 4.

*Mrs. John R. Strother, Jr. (Elsie)*

## CRAB ESHCOL

1 pound crabmeat
3 tablespoons butter
4 tablespoons flour
½ pint whipping cream
¾ cup grated sharp cheese

5 tablespoons sherry
(or more to taste)
1 (4 ounce) can sliced
mushrooms and juice
Salt and red pepper to taste

Make cream sauce with butter, flour and cream. (Let butter and flour cook 2-3 minutes before adding cream). Stir constantly. Add salt, pepper, mushrooms, juice and sherry. Remove from heat and add crab. Pour into a buttered casserole dish and sprinkle with cheese. Cook in 425 degrees oven until cheese is melted. Serves 6. Very good for dinner with a large tossed salad and French bread or used as a hot dip at a cocktail party.

*Mrs. Dennis Mollenkamp (Jane)*

## CRAB GIOVANNI

1 stick butter or margarine
2 cups chopped onions
½ pound fresh mushrooms, sliced
2 cloves garlic, minced
½ pound spaghetti, cooked
2-3 cups crabmeat
½ teaspoon dried basil

½ cup sliced stuffed green olives
½ pound shredded sharp
cheddar cheese
½ cup sour cream
1 can (1 pound 12 ounces) tomatoes,
broken in pieces
1½ teaspoons salt

Melt butter in a large skillet and slowly saute onions, mushrooms and garlic until tender. Combine with remaining ingredients, stirring into a greased 3 quart casserole. Bake at 350 degrees for 35-45 minutes. Serves 8. Combination of seafood can be used.

*Mrs. John H. Hitchins, Jr. (Margaret)*

## SKILLET CRABMEAT

2 cups tarragon vinegar
1½ cups butter
2 tablespoons chopped chives

2 tablespoons worcestershire
sauce
4 pounds fresh lump crabmeat

Put all ingredients, except crab, in a saucepan and heat. Add crab. Heat through and serve in chafing dish. Serves 12. A good buffet dish for the "something hot."

*Mrs. Jay Gilbreath (Skee)*

## CRAB SOUFFLE

16 slices white bread
3 cans crabmeat (or equal
  amount of fresh crabmeat)
1 medium sized onion, chopped
½ cup chopped green pepper
3 cups milk

1 cup chopped celery
½ cup mayonnaise
1 can cream of mushroom soup
4 eggs, beaten
1 cup grated cheddar cheese

Remove crusts from bread. Butter a baking dish 9x13. Line baking dish with 8 slices of bread. Mix onion, celery, green pepper, mayonnaise and crabmeat. Spread mixture over bread in baking dish. Place on top of this the remaining slices of bread. Beat eggs and milk together. Pour over mixture and bread in baking dish. Cover and refrigerate over night. When ready to cook the souffle, bake in 325 degree oven for 15 minutes. Then spoon the can of cream of mushroom soup over top, a sprinkle of cheese and paprika and bake for 1 hour longer or until golden brown. Serves 8. This is delicious for a luncheon, served with a salad.

*Mrs. J. Marion Crain*

## CRAB – SPINACH QUICHE

3 tablespoons butter
2 tablespoons scallions or shallots
½ package frozen, chopped
  spinach, cooked and drained
¼-½ pound crabmeat
¼ teaspoon salt
¼ teaspoon pepper

2 tablespoons dry vermouth
3 eggs
1 cup heavy cream
¼ teaspoon salt and pepper
1 tablespoon tomato paste
1 (9 inch) pie shell
¼ cup grated Swiss cheese

Precook pie shell at 400 degrees for 5 minutes. Set aside. Saute scallions in butter until transparent. Add spinach and cook until all liquid is absorbed. Add crabmeat and gently stir over medium heat for 2 minutes. Add salt, pepper and vermouth. Raise heat and bring just to boil. In a medium bowl beat together eggs, cream, salt, pepper and tomato paste. Gently fold crab mixture into egg and cream mixture. Bake at 350 degrees in upper 1/3 of oven for 25-30 minutes, until browned and puffed. Serves 6.

*Mrs. Richard McCamey (Betsy)*

## CRABMEAT JUSTINE

½ stick butter
1 cup fresh lump crabmeat
1 hard boiled egg, grated
2 tablespoons sherry

Generous amount of tabasco
½ tablespoon lemon juice
1½ cups hollandaise sauce
4 squares toast

Melt butter, add crabmeat, grated egg, sherry, tabasco, and lemon juice. Heat thoroughly. Place squares of toast in individual casseroles, cover with crabmeat mixture, top with hollandaise sauce. McCormick's Hollandaise Sauce mix is very good and easy. Brown under broiler. Serve immediately. Serves 4.

*Mrs. Francis B. Sheetz, Jr.*

## ROCK LOBSTER CURRY AFRIKAANS

¼ cup butter
1 green apple, peeled, cored, and chopped
1 small onion, chopped
1 clove garlic, minced
1 ripe banana, thinly sliced

¼ cup flour
1 cup light cream
1 cup milk
1 tablespoon curry powder
3 packages (8 ounce) frozen rock lobster tails

Condiments: Coconut, peanuts, chopped egg, chopped green pepper, chutney, pineapple chunks, raisins, avocado slices

Melt butter and saute apple, onion, garlic, and banana until very soft, but not brown. Stir in flour. Gradually stir in cream and milk. Add curry. Cook over low heat stirring constantly until sauce bubbles and thickens. Parboil lobster tails by dropping into boiling salted water. When water reboils, drain immediately and drench with cold water. With scissors cut away underside membrane and carefully pull out meat in one piece. Reserve empty shells to use for serving condiments. Cut meat into ½ inch crosswise slices and add to sauce. Season to taste with salt. Simmer 5 minutes. Serve over rice with condiments. Serves 6. Good for a dinner party. Can be prepared ahead and reheated.

*Mrs. Jane Blume*

## SCALLOPED OYSTERS

1 quart fresh oysters
1 cup butter
¾ cup all-purpose flour
1½ teaspoons paprika
½ teaspoon salt
¼ teaspoon pepper
Dash cayenne

½ clove garlic, minced (optional)
1 medium onion, chopped
2 tablespoons lemon juice
1 tablespoon worcestershire sauce
1 cup Ritz cracker crumbs

Melt butter in a skillet or saucepan over medium heat. Add flour and stir until smooth. Brown the flour until it is a medium brown color. Add paprika, salt, pepper, cayenne, garlic, and onion, and stir constantly. Add oysters, lemon juice, and worcestershire sauce. Stir well. Grease a 2 quart casserole and sprinkle half of bread crumbs on bottom and sides. Pour oysters into casserole and sprinkle with remaining cracker crumbs. Dot top with butter. Bake at 350 degrees until cracker crumbs are brown - about 20 minutes. Serves 6-8.

*Mrs. Albert Redd (Sue)*

## COQUILLES SAINT JACQUES

*A real seafood classic*

1 pound fresh bay scallops
½ cup dry white wine
1 small onion, finely chopped
½ pound fresh mushrooms, sliced
Juice of 1 lemon
½ cup water or less

2 tablespoons butter
2 tablespoons flour
2/3 cup heavy cream
Fine bread crumbs
Grated Swiss or parmesan cheese

Cook scallops in wine with onion for 5 minutes. Drain and save liquid. Cook mushrooms in water and lemon juice. Drain and save liquid. Melt butter, add flour, and cook until almost dry. Blend in cream. Add both reserved liquids, stirring until smooth and thickened. Add scallops and mushrooms. Pile into scallop shells or ramekins. Sprinkle tops with bread crumbs and cheese. Lightly brown in 400 degree oven. Serves 6. This can be served as an appetizer.

*Mrs. William A. McClain, III (Rose)*

## SCALLOPS PROVENCAL

1 pound fresh sea scallops, rinsed and drained
2 tablespoons lemon juice
½ pound fresh mushrooms, sliced lengthwise
5 tablespoons olive oil or salad oil
4 shallots, sliced
4 parsley sprigs, chopped
2 cloves garlic, minced
½ teaspoon salt
Dash of white pepper
½ teaspoon dried thyme leaves
½ teaspoon dried oregano leaves
2 pounds fresh peeled tomatoes or 1 (16 ounce) can whole tomatoes, drained

Toss scallops with lemon juice, then add mushrooms and toss. Set aside. In 2 tablespoons hot oil, saute half of shallots and parsley with garlic. Add salt, pepper, thyme, oregano, and tomatoes. Cook, covered, for 20 minutes, stirring occasionally to break tomatoes. Uncover and cook 5 minutes longer. In another skillet, in remaining 3 tablespoons oil, saute remaining shallots and parsley, stirring until tender. Add scallops and mushrooms. Cook uncovered over high heat for 10 minutes, shaking pan and stirring frequently. Add tomato mixture. Cook 2 minutes longer. Serve at once with rice. Serves 4.

*Mrs. F. Douglas Puckett (Diane)*

## CREAMED SEAFOOD ON RICE

2 tablespoons butter
1 small onion, chopped
1 clove garlic, minced
¼ pound mushrooms, quartered
2½ tablespoons flour
1 cup light cream
¾ cup white wine
¾ teaspoon salt
1/8 teaspoon pepper
1 tablespoon cognac
¾ pound shucked raw oysters
½ pound shrimp, cooked, shelled and deveined
1 (5 ounce) can lobster meat
3-4 cups cooked rice

About 35 minutes before serving: In skillet, melt butter, saute onion, garlic and mushrooms until golden. Stir in flour, slowly add cream and wine. Bring to a boil while stirring, then cook until thickened. Next stir in salt, pepper, cognac, oysters, shrimp, and lobster meat. Heat gently, then serve over rice. Serves 6. Well worth seeking out the ingredients!

*Mrs. William Krenson (Agnes)*

113

## SEAFOOD GUMBO

¼ cup salad oil
2 tablespoons flour
5 onions, chopped
3 cloves garlic, minced
2 (16 ounce) cans tomatoes
4 cups fish or chicken stock
2 pounds raw shrimp,
    peeled and deveined

2 bay leaves
1 tablespoon seafood seasoning
2 (10 ounce) packages frozen
    sliced okra
Salt and pepper to taste
2 pints oysters undrained
½ pound lump crabmeat
1 tablespoon gumbo file

Heat oil in a heavy saucepan over medium heat; add flour very slowly, stirring with a wooden spoon until roux is very brown. Add onions and garlic. Cook until onion is soft, but not brown. Add tomatoes, fish stock, shrimp and bay leaves; simmer 30 minutes, stirring frequently. Add seafood seasoning; simmer 45 minutes. Add okra, salt and pepper, continue to simmer 5 minutes. Add oysters, crab and simmer 10 minutes or until edges of oysters curl. Just before serving, stir in gumbo file. Spoon over rice. Serves 6-8. Consistency is better, if it is made a day ahead. If this is done, oysters should be added when it is reheated for serving. My friends from the bayou tell me this is the best they have ever had!

*Mrs. Carl T. Archbold (Mary Jo)*

## LOBSTER SALAD

*Great do-ahead dish*

1 fresh lobster per person, plus
    1 extra tail per man
Capers
Finely chopped onion
Finely chopped celery

Cooked frozen or fresh green
    peas, cooled
Lemon juice
Salt and pepper, to taste
Mayonnaise

(Choose proportions according to amount needed).

Cook lobsters and tails. Cool and cut up meat to bite size. Take off claws and use meat but clean and keep body shell. Sprinkle meat with lemon juice. Toss all ingredients with mayonnaise. To serve, spoon salad into clean shells. Garnish with paprika and parsley or watercress. (If using all tails, allow 2-3 tails per person. Serve on bibb lettuce, on salad plates, or in a lettuce-lined bowl.)

*Mrs. James Cushman (Elkin)*

## BARBECUED SHRIMP

10 jumbo shrimp per person, tiny onions, cherry tomatoes, green pepper slices

Marinade: (enough for 6 servings)

4 cloves garlic
1 cup oil
2 teaspoons salt
2 teaspoons pepper
6 tablespoons chili sauce

2 tablespoons worcestershire sauce
6 tablespoons vinegar
½ cup parsley
Dash tabasco

Blend garlic and oil in blender; add remaining ingredients and blend. Simmer raw shrimp 7-10 minutes. Peel and devein shrimp. Marinate 24 hours. Place shrimp on skewers with tiny onions, cherry tomatoes and green pepper slices. Cook on outdoor barbecue for a different and delicious summer treat!

*Mrs. A. J. Stringer (Martha)*

## SHRIMP CREOLE

1 medium onion, chopped
½ cup chopped green pepper
½ cup chopped celery
1 clove garlic, minced
3 tablespoons margarine
1 can (16 ounce) tomatoes
1 pound cooked shrimp, peeled and deveined

1 teaspoon salt
1 teaspoon sugar
¼ teaspoon black pepper
1/8 teaspoon paprika
2 teaspoons worcestershire
  sauce

Saute onion, green pepper, celery and garlic in margarine until tender. Add tomatoes and seasonings. Simmer 15 minutes. Add shrimp to hot sauce and heat thoroughly. Serve on hot rice. Makes 6 generous servings.

*Mrs. John C. Portman, Jr. (Jan)*

## CURRIED SHRIMP

1/3 cup butter
½ cup chopped onions
¼ cup chopped green pepper
2 cloves garlic, minced
2 cups sour cream
2 teaspoons lemon juice

1 teaspoon curry powder
¾ teaspoon salt
½ teaspoon ginger powder
Dash chili powder
Dash pepper
3 cups cooked shrimp

(continued)

115

Melt butter and saute onion, pepper and garlic until tender, but not brown (about 7 minutes). Stir in sour cream, lemon juice and seasonings. Add shrimp. Cook over low heat; stirring until well heated. The sauce will be thin. Serve over white rice. Top with condiments such as: grated coconut, peanuts, raisins, chutney, chopped eggs, and chopped green pepper. Serves 4.

*Dovie Wingard Nichols*

## CURRIED SHRIMP AU GRATIN

| | |
|---|---|
| 3 tablespoons butter | ½ teaspoon sugar |
| 1/3 cup chopped onion | 2 cups milk |
| 1/3 cup minced celery | 1 pound cooked shrimp |
| 3 tablespoons flour | 2 tablespoons lemon juice |
| 1 teaspoon salt | 3 cups cooked rice |
| 1 teaspoon curry powder | 1 cup grated cheese |
| 1/8 teaspoon ginger | |

Melt butter. Saute onion and celery until tender, stirring occasionally. Stir in flour and seasonings. Gradually add milk and continue to stir while heating just to boil. Stir in shrimp, lemon juice and ½ of the cheese. Butter a 2 quart rectangular casserole. Cover the bottom with the cooked rice, cover with shrimp mixture; sprinkle remaining cheese over the top. Bake on top shelf of 375 degree oven for 20 minutes or until thoroughly heated. Serves 6.

*Mrs. John S. Stephens (Jane)*

## LOVING TOUCHES . . .

Do not leave cooked shrimp in a wrapper or in a covered container. (It becomes "gassy".) Keep it in an open bowl, with ice cubes under and on top. Rinse with ice water before serving.

Undercooking fish is best. Overcooked fish is "mushy". REMEMBER: The Chinese eat it raw.

Rubbing hands with lemons removes "fishy odor".

# GADO GADO

*Javanese shrimp dish*

Salad:
½ head shredded iceberg lettuce
1 pint fresh bean sprouts
Raw spinach leaves
Unpeeled cucumber, scored with
fork and sliced
1 pound whole string beans,
cooked crisply tender and chilled

6 hard boiled eggs, quartered
18-24 whole cooked jumbo
shrimp
Unpeeled oranges, quartered
Salt and pepper
1 fresh lemon

Sauce:
¼ cup finely chopped onion
2 finely chopped garlic cloves
1½ tablespoons oil
1 cup boiling water
1 cup crunchy style peanut
butter
1 tablespoon brown sugar
½ teaspoon tabasco sauce

Juice and grated rind of
1 lemon
1 teaspoon grated ginger
root
1 bay leaf, crushed
Salt to taste
1 cup milk or unsweetened
coconut milk

Saute onion and garlic in oil until lightly colored. Add water, peanut butter, brown sugar, tabasco, lemon juice and rind, ginger, bay leaf and salt. Blend well. Cook over low heat. Gradually stir in milk and cook until thoroughly blended. Serve sauce warm or cold with the following salad: Cover platter with shredded lettuce and two strips of bean sprouts. Center platter with spinach leaves topped with shrimp. Garnish with cucumber slices, eggs, green beans, and oranges. Season with salt, pepper and lemon juice. Serves 6. Colorful and tasty! A perfect one dish meal for a warm summer evening. Ingredients for salad may vary to some extent.

*Mrs. George Johnson (Janet)*

## LOVING TOUCHES . . .

Easy "she-crab soup:
    1 can condensed split pea soup
    1 can condensed tomato soup
    1 can milk
Heat and pour over fresh lump crabmeat in a soup bowl.

## SHRIMP MARIA STUART

1 onion, minced
2 cups boiled shrimp, shelled
  and deveined
½ cup butter
½ cup brandy
Juice of 1 small lemon
2 tablespoons fresh, chopped
  parsley

1 cup heavy cream
4 tablespoons tomato paste
  or catsup
Salt to taste
Freshly gound pepper
1 tablespoon worcestershire
  sauce

Saute the onion gently in butter until transparent. Add shrimp; stir. Add brandy, heat, and ignite. When flame dies, add lemon juice. Add cream, stirring gently. Then add tomato paste, salt, pepper, chopped parsley, and worcestershire sauce. Simmer a few minutes until blended. Serve with rice. Serves 4.

*Mrs. Sydney Curtis (Ann)*

## SHRIMP NEWBURG

½ stick butter
6 tablespoons flour
½ onion, chopped
1 clove garlic, chopped
3 cups milk
4 tablespoons sherry
Worcestershire sauce

Salt
Pepper
Tabasco sauce
1 pound cooked shrimp
3 hard boiled eggs, chopped
1 (4 ounce) can mushrooms
Chopped parsley

Melt butter. Saute onion and garlic. Add flour and mix to form paste. Gradually add milk, stirring constantly. Cook until sauce thickens. Add sherry, worcestershire sauce, salt and pepper to taste, and a little tabasco. To white sauce add shrimp, eggs, mushrooms, parsley. Stir until heated through over low heat. Serves 4.

*Mrs. David E. Lee, Jr. (Janie Cofer)*

# Main Dish
# Casseroles

DAVID SAPP

## EIGHT LAYER DINNER

*Tasty on a cold, winter evening!*

1½ pounds ground beef
2 onions, sliced
1 can (1 pound) tomatoes, undrained

2 to 3 large potatoes, sliced
1 can (1 pound) green beans
Salt and pepper

In large casserole layer half of meat. Salt and pepper generously. Spread on 1 sliced onion, tomatoes with juice, 1 sliced potato, 1 can green beans with one-half liquid drained. Follow with remainder of meat, salt and pepper, 1 sliced onion and 1 sliced potato. Bake for 2 hours at 375 degrees. Serves 6-8. Serve with green salad and French bread.

*Mrs. Robert Barnett (Martha Ann)*

## THAT CASSEROLE

1½ pounds lean ground beef
Garlic salt to taste
1 (15 ounce) can tomato sauce
6 ounces very thin egg noodles
3 ounces cream cheese

8 ounces sour cream
6 green onions, minced
1 tablespoon minced green pepper
1 cup grated cheddar cheese
   or cottage cheese

Saute ground beef. Add garlic salt and tomato sauce. Simmer about 10 minutes. Cook noodles as directed on package. Drain. Mix together cream cheese, sour cream, and green onions. Layer ingredients in casserole, beginning with noodles, meat sauce, and sour cream mixture, ending with grated cheese on top. Cover and bake 1 hour at 350 degrees. Serves four . . . unless they are teenagers!

*Mrs. T. G. Debrecini (Lois)*
*Mrs. Jon Shepherd (Kay)*

## BEEF AND BEAN CASSEROLE

*Delicious! A meal in itself or great side dish*

1½ pounds ground beef
2 tablespoons butter or margarine
1 onion, finely chopped
1 bell pepper, chopped
½ cup finely chopped celery

2 tablespoons worcestershire
1 tablespoon prepared mustard
2 tablespoons brown sugar
1 (14 ounce) bottle catsup
1 (28 ounce) can pork and beans

Brown onion, pepper and celery in butter. Add beef and brown. Combine all ingredients. Mix well. Pour into baking dish and bake 30 to 45 minutes at 350 degrees. Freezes well. Serves 8 to 10.

*Mrs. John T. Glover (Sandra)*

## BEEF AND EGGPLANT CASSEROLE

3 slices bacon, diced
1 onion, chopped
2 cups ground beef (1 pound)
2 cups canned tomatoes
2 eggs, beaten
1 cup bread crumbs

1 hot pepper (optional)
1 teaspoon salt
½ teaspoon pepper
1 eggplant
1 cup grated cheese

Fry bacon and saute onion in drippings. Brown meat and add salt, pepper, and half the bread crumbs. Peel, cook, and mash eggplant. Combine with meat-onion mixture. Add tomatoes and beaten eggs. Pour into greased casserole. Top with remaining crumbs and grated cheese. Dot with small bits of butter. Bake for 45 minutes in 350 degrees oven. Serves 8.

*Mrs. Herbert J. Beadle, Jr. (Jerry)*

## BEEF AND MACARONI CASSEROLE

½ box elbow macaroni
2 tablespoons bacon fat
1 pound ground beef
1 green pepper, chopped

1 onion, chopped
1 can mushroom soup
1 small can mushrooms, drained
½ cup grated cheese

Cook and drain macaroni. Brown onion and pepper in bacon fat. Add meat and cook until brown. Drain. Mix soup, macaroni, and mushrooms. Stir in meat. Pour into buttered 2½ quart casserole. Sprinkle with cheese. Bake 20 minutes at 325 degrees. Serves 6.

*Mrs. William Lummus (Ann Hart)*

## BEEF AND NOODLE CASSEROLE

1 pound ground chuck
  (more if desired)
2 tablespoons butter or margarine
½ cup chopped celery
½ cup chopped green pepper
1 cup chopped onion

1 tablespoon soy sauce
1 (15 ounce) can tomato sauce
½ cup water
1 envelope beef broth (Herb-Ox)
8 ounces flat noodles
1 cup cubed sharp cheddar cheese

Saute vegetables in butter. Add meat and cook until red disappears. Drain off fat. Add tomato sauce, soy sauce, water, and beef broth. Simmer 20 minutes. Cook noodles as directed. Drain. Combine noodles, sauce and cheese. Pour into casserole. Bake at 350 degrees until heated through and bubbly. Serves 6-8.

*Mrs. James N. Rupp (Sharon)*

## BEEF AND RICE CASSEROLE

1 pound ground chuck
1 cup rice, uncooked
1 small onion, chopped
1 teaspoon salt
½ teaspoon pepper
1 teaspoon paprika

1 small bottle stuffed olives,
  sliced
2 cups tomato juice
1½ cups boiling water
½ cup grated cheddar cheese

Lightly brown together beef, rice and onion. Add seasonings. Add sliced olives, tomato juice, and boiling water. Pour into 9x13 casserole. Cover and bake at 300 degrees for 1 hour. Uncover. Sprinkle with cheese and continue baking about 10 minutes, or until cheese is melted. Serves 10 to 12. Freeze, if desired, before baking.

*Patti Marett Nunnally*

## LASAGNE

1 package lasagne noodles
2 pounds ground chuck
1 onion, chopped
1 green pepper, chopped
1 large can tomato paste
1 large can tomato sauce
1 teaspoon oregano
1 teaspoon thyme

1 small jar sliced black olives
1 small jar green olives
1 package pepperoni
1 package mozzarella cheese
1 small can parmesan cheese
1 carton ricotta cheese
Salt and pepper to taste

Brown meat, onion, green pepper. Add tomato paste, tomato sauce, and seasonings. Simmer until thick. Cook noodles as directed. Grease 2 quart casserole with butter. Layer in casserole as follows: 3 noodles on bottom, then olives, ricotta cheese and 1/3 of sauce; then, 3 noodles, pepperoni, 1/3 of sauce, and mozzarella cheese, then, 3 noodles, remaining 1/3 of sauce, parmesan cheese on top. Bake in 350 degrees oven until bubbling. Serves 6-8. May be frozen.

*Mrs. Ensign Conklin (Tricia)*

## LASAGNE

6 ounces lasagne noodles
½ pound ground beef
1/3 cup chopped onion
1 tablespoon parsley
2 teaspoons oregano
½ teaspoon sweet basil
2 (4 ounce) cans tomato sauce

1 teaspoon salt
1/8 teaspoon pepper
1½ cups creamed cottage cheese
  (large curd)
2/3 cup shredded mozzarella cheese
½ cup grated parmesan cheese

Cook noodles in 3 quarts boiling water with 1 tablespoon salt and 1 tablespoon oil. Boil for 12 minutes, stirring frequently. Drain, rinse in hot water and drain. Brown beef with onion. Add seasonings and tomato sauce. Simmer 10 minutes. Mix together cottage cheese, mozzarella, and parmesan cheeses. Layer in 2 quart shallow casserole starting with sauce, noodles, and cheese. Bake 30 minutes in 375 degree oven. Serves 5-6.

*Mrs. G. Frank Felder (Susan)*

## HOBO LUNCHEON

| | |
|---|---|
| 2 potatoes, sliced | 2 cups grated cheese |
| 1 onion, sliced | ½ cup chopped celery |
| 1 pound ground beef, browned | 1 can stewed tomatoes |
| 1 cup cooked rice | Bread crumbs |
| Salt and pepper to taste | Butter |

In large casserole layer potatoes, onion, beef, rice, salt and pepper, 1 cup cheese and celery. Put tomatoes and remaining 1 cup cheese over that. Top with bread crumbs and dot with butter. Cook covered ½ hour, then uncovered ½ hour at 350 degrees. Serves 6.

*Mrs. James Magbee (Tia)*

## LEFT—OVER ROAST CASSEROLE

| | |
|---|---|
| 2 cups cold cooked meat, cubed | ½ cup uncooked rice |
| 1 cup canned tomatoes | 2 tablespoons butter |
| 2 cups meat stock, bouillon, | 2 medium onions, chopped |
| or consomme | 1 tablespoon worcestershire |
| Salt and pepper to taste | |

Cook tomatoes, stock, 1 onion chopped, worcestershire, and seasonings 10 minutes. Melt butter or margarine. Add onion and uncooked rice. Brown. Combine all ingredients. Bake in buttered casserole at 325 degrees for about forty minutes. Serves 6.

*Mrs. Bengt Stromquist (Alison)*

## LOVING TOUCHES . . .

When adding liquid to a casserole, heat it first. Cold liquids may crack it.

"Butter" a casserole dish with vegetable oil for less sticking.

123

## BREAKFAST CASSEROLE

*Absolutely delicious!*

12 slices white bread
(Pepperidge Farm, extra-thin)
Butter
1 pound fresh sausage

½ pound grated sharp cheddar or
1(6 ounce) package sliced
Swiss cheese
4 eggs
3 cups milk

Trim crusts from bread and lightly butter. Saute sausage until lightly browned. Place 6 slices bread in a 3 quart casserole, buttered side up. Spread ½ sausage and cheese over bread. Place 6 slices of bread on top, followed by rest of sausage and cheese. Lightly beat together eggs and milk. Pour over sausage mixture. Press down till milk comes through. Refrigerate overnight, uncovered. Bake for 1 hour at 350 degrees. Serves 6.

*Mrs. Bert Oastler (Belitje)*
*Mrs. Richard Huff (Sally)*

## CHILI CON CARNE AND FRIJOLES

1 pound red kidney or pinto beans,
or combination
5 tablespoons bacon grease
4 medium onions, sliced
3 garlic cloves, chopped
3 pounds beef chuck
(½ inch cubes)

7 cups stewed tomatoes and juice,
or 2 (28 ounce) cans
2-3 tablespoons chili powder
½ teaspoon oregano
½ teaspoon crushed red pepper
2½ teaspoons cumin seed
2 tablespoons salt

Soak kidney or pinto beans overnight. Brown onion and garlic in hot bacon grease. Add meat and brown. Add other ingredients and simmer approximately 2½ hours uncovered. Meanwhile boil beans until tender about 1 hour. Add to chili and simmer ½ to 1 hour and serve. Serves 12. Good with rice or saltines. Freezes well.

*Mr. John Izard*

## EGG AND HAM COMPANY CASSEROLE

*Grand Sunday night supper*

8 hard boiled eggs
¼ cup melted butter
¼ teaspoon mustard
½ teaspoon worcestershire
1 teaspoon chopped parsley
1 teaspoon chopped chives
1/3 cup (or a bit more) finely
  chopped cooked ham

3 tablespoons butter
3 tablespoons flour
1 cup chicken broth
¾ cup milk
Dash of salt and pepper
1 cup shredded American
  cheese

Cut eggs in half, lengthwise. Remove and mash yolks. Add melted butter, mustard, worcestershire, parsley, chives, and ham. Mix well. Fill whites with mixture. Arrange in 1½ to 2 quart casserole. Melt 3 tablespoons butter, blend in flour, add stock, milk and seasonings. Cook till smooth and thick. Pour over eggs and sprinkle cheese on top. Bake in 350 degree oven for twenty minutes or until cheese melts. Serves 4-6.

*Mrs. Richard C. Estes (Becky)*

## HAM AND CHEESE CASSEROLE

*Great use for left-over baked ham!*

2 cups cubed ham
1 small box elbow macaroni
2 tablespoons butter
2 tablespoons flour
1 cup milk

1 cup heavy cream
1 teaspoon paprika
1 pound grated medium
  cheddar cheese
Salt to taste

Cook macaroni as directed on box. Drain. Pour into 2 quart casserole. Pour on 2 cups of cubed ham. Melt 2 tablespoons butter in saucepan on low heat. Add flour and mix to smooth paste. Add milk, cream, paprika and cook till thick, stirring, about three minutes. Add cheese and cook until cheese melts. Add salt to taste. Pour sauce over noodles and ham. Bake in 350 degree oven 30 minutes. Makes 5 heaping servings.

*Mrs. Carlton Childress*

## LOVING TOUCHES . . .

Casseroles double-wrapped in foil and again in newspaper will stay hot for hours.

The reverse is true for cold foods: Wrap in foil, then in wet newspaper, again in foil, to insulate the chill. (Tie up in a pretty checkered towel to "tote" to picnic).

## HAM, NOODLE, AND BROCCOLI CASSEROLE

3 tablespoons butter or margarine
¼ cup all-purpose flour
½ teaspoon salt
Dash white pepper
½ teaspoon dry mustard
1 tablespoon grated onion
3 cups milk

1 cup sharp cheddar cheese
1 (8 ounce) package noodles
1½ - 2 cups ham, cubed
2 (10 ounce) packages frozen
   broccoli florets, cooked
Grated parmesan cheese for
   topping

Melt butter in saucepan, blend in flour, salt, pepper, dry mustard, and onion. Add milk gradually, stirring constantly. Stir and cook until sauce is thickened. Remove from heat, and blend in cheddar cheese. Stir until cheese is melted. Cook noodles according to package directions. Drain. Add ham, broccoli, and noodles to cheese sauce. Spoon into greased 2 quart casserole. Top with parmesan cheese. Bake at 350 degrees for thirty minutes, or until bubbly. Serves 8.

*Mrs. J. S. Havermale (Harriet)*

## PORK CHOP CASSEROLE

6 T-boned pork chops
1 cup raw rice
2 onions, chopped

2 cans consomme
1 small can mushrooms, drained
½ stick butter

Brown pork chops in butter. Put in casserole. Mix remaining ingredients and pour over pork chops. Cover with foil. Bake 1 hour at 350 degrees. Serves 6.

*Mrs. John O. Knox (Dorothy Anne Smith)*

## SAUSAGE–CHICKEN–ALMOND CASSEROLE

*Men like it!*

2/3 cup uncooked rice
1 chicken bouillon cube
1 package Lipton's chicken
   noodle soup
1¼ pounds HOT pork sausage

1 medium onion, chopped
1 small bell pepper, chopped
½ cup blanched almonds
5 ribs celery, chopped

Cook rice as usual, adding chicken bouillon cube as you cook it. Cook chicken noodle soup according to directions, but using half the amount of water. Cook sausage and break up while frying. Remove when brown and drain well. Saute onion, bell pepper, and celery in sausage grease.

126

Remove and drain. Combine all ingredients. Bake in casserole 1 hour at 350 degrees. Serves 8-10. Can be made day before and baked the next day. Freezes well.

*Rita Traver Fink*
*Mrs. August B. Turner (Teresa)*

## EASY CHICKEN

*Easy, and tastes like you slaved over the stove all day!*

8 to 10 pieces chicken
Butter or margarine
1 (8 ounce) can artichokes
½ cup chopped onions
1/3 cup flour
1½ teaspoons dried rosemary

1½ teaspoons salt
¼' teaspoon pepper
1 cup chicken broth
1 cup dry white wine
1 (6 ounce) can mushrooms, drained

Brown chicken in butter. Place in shallow dish. Arrange artichoke hearts on chicken. Arrange mushrooms evenly over chicken. Add onions to skillet and cook until tender. Blend in flour and seasonings. Add broth and wine and cook until thickened. Pour gravy over all. Bake 55 to 60 minutes at 375 degrees. If chilled, add 25 minutes more cooking time.

*Mrs. Frank Millians (Helen)*

## COUNTRYSIDE CHICKEN BAKE

3 cups cooked rice
1 cup sliced celery
¾ cup chopped onion
2 tablespoons melted margarine
2 teaspoons parsley
¼ teaspoon salt
1/8 teaspoon pepper

3 chicken breasts, split
1 can cream of mushroom soup
2/3 cup Italian salad dressing
¼ cup milk
1 can (1 pound) small whole carrots, drained
Paprika

Combine rice, celery, onion, margarine, parsley, and seasonings. Mix lightly. Spoon into a 3 quart casserole. Top with chicken breasts. Combine soup, salad dressing and milk, and blend well. Pour over chicken. Bake at 350 degrees 45 minutes. Add carrots and sprinkle with paprika. Bake 15 minutes longer or until chicken is tender. Serves 6.

*Mrs. Francis B. Sheetz, Jr.*

## CHICKEN AND BROCCOLI

2 packages frozen broccoli,
  cooked and drained
3 whole chicken breasts
2 cans cream of chicken soup
1 cup mayonnaise
1 tablespoon lemon juice
1 teaspoon salad mustard

½ teaspoon curry powder
½ cup shredded cheddar cheese
1 small can water chestnuts,
  chopped (optional)
½ cup soft bread crumbs
1 tablespoon melted butter

Simmer chicken in water with small onion, a stalk of celery, salt and pepper for 1 hour. Cool and slice or break into pieces. Mix soup, mayonnaise, curry powder, lemon juice, mustard, and water chestnuts, if desired. Layer in casserole dish broccoli, chicken, soup mixture, and cheese. Repeat layers. Top with bread crumbs and pour melted butter on top. For a change, Pepperidge Farm stuffing mix may be sprinkled on top in place of bread crumbs. Bake 45 minutes at 350 degrees. Serves 8-10.

*Mrs. John B. Brown (Anne)*
*Ann Wattles Constantine*
*Mrs. Thomas Davison (Nancy)*
*Mrs. William Whitaker (Susan)*

## CHICKEN AND RICE

2 chickens, cut up
Mayonnaise
1 cup rice
1 medium onion, chopped fine
½ cup chopped celery

1 can chicken and rice soup
1 soup can water
Oregano
Salt

Put rice, onions, celery in broiler pan. Add chicken and rice soup and 1 can water. Season with oregano. Salt chicken and spread generously with mayonnaise. Place in pan over rice, skin side up. Sprinkle with pepper. Bake 2 hours, uncovered, at 300 degrees. Serves 6-8.

*Mrs. Zahner Reynolds (Virginia)*

## CHICKEN AND WILD RICE

4 pounds chicken breasts
1 box wild rice
3 to 4 onions, chopped
2 sticks butter
3 tablespoons flour

2 cans mushroom soup
1 cup milk
1 large can sliced mushrooms
Salt and pepper to taste
1 pound sharp cheese, grated

128

Cook chicken breasts, shred meat. Cook rice as directed. Saute onions in butter, blend in flour, soup and milk for sauce. Add mushrooms and seasonings. In 1 large casserole or 2 small casseroles alternate layers of sauce, rice, chicken and cheese, ending with cheese. Bake at 350 degrees until bubbly. Serves 10.

*Mrs. Robert Glenn (Lyn)*

## CHICKEN SPAGHETTI

1 (5 pound) hen
1 (1 pound) package vermicelli
1 onion, chopped
2 (No.2) cans tomatoes, drained
1 large can mushroom pieces, drained
½ cup chopped ripe olives

1 small garlic clove
1 pound grated sharp cheddar cheese
2 cups chicken broth
2 tablespoons flour
Salt to taste

Boil hen and let cool in broth. Remove and cut into small pieces. Skim fat off broth. Combine broth and flour to make cream sauce. Simmer with onion and garlic 15 to 20 minutes. Discard garlic. Break up vermicelli, and cook as directed on package. Combine all ingredients, except cheese. In buttered (9x13) casserole layer vermicelli mixture, then cheese. Repeat layers, ending with cheese on top. Bake 1 hour at 350 degrees. Freezes well. Thaw before baking. Serves 8.

*Mrs. Dennis Mollenkamp (Jane)*

## CHICKEN TETRAZZINI

1 large hen or 2 whole
  chicken breasts
1 stalk celery
1 small onion
1 can mushroom soup
1 small jar Old English Cheese

1 small package fine spaghetti
1 small can mushrooms
1 tablespoon worcestershire
¾ cup chicken stock
Buttered bread crumbs

Cover chicken with water. Cook with small onion, stalk of celery, and celery leaves. Add salt. Cook until tender (about 2 hours for hen). Combine in sauce pan ¾ cup of stock (may substitute ½ cup stock, ½ cup white wine), mushroom soup, juice from can of mushrooms, cheese, and worcestershire sauce. Cook until smooth. Add mushrooms. Cook spaghetti in chicken stock, adding bouillon cube if not enough stock. Put half of spaghetti in casserole dish, then ½ chicken, then ½ sauce. Repeat layers. Top with buttered bread crumbs. Cook 20 to 30 minutes in 350 degree oven. Serves 8.

*Mrs. Robert M. Holder, Jr. (Betty)*

129

## TURKETTI

1 cup spaghetti, uncooked
2 cups cooked turkey
¼ cup pimiento
¼ cup chopped green pepper
½ cup chopped onion

1 small can mushrooms, drained
½ cup turkey stock
1 can mushroom soup
½ teaspoon salt
½ pound grated cheese

Break spaghetti into 2 inch lengths and boil in salted water until done. Drain. Combine spaghetti, turkey, pimiento, green pepper, onion, and mushrooms. Pour into casserole. Combine soup, broth, salt and pepper, and pour over turkey mixture. Add half of the cheese and toss lightly until mixed. Put rest of cheese on top. Bake for 45 minutes at 350 degrees. Serves 6-8. This can be frozen and baked later.

*Mrs. Edward E. Jackson (Dot)*

## TURKEY TETRAZZINI

1 can cream of chicken soup
¼ cup chicken broth, or water
1 can (4 ounces) sliced
   mushrooms, undrained

2 cups diced cooked turkey
4 ounces spaghetti, uncooked
1 cup shredded American cheese
¼ cup buttered bread crumbs

Blend soup, water, and undrained mushrooms. Cook spaghetti according to package directions. In buttered casserole, alternate layers of turkey, spaghetti, cheese and chicken-mushroom sauce. Top with bread crumbs. Bake 25 to 30 minutes at 375 degrees. Serves 6.

*Mrs. Grady Clark*

## SCALLOP–STUFFING CASSEROLE

1 cup chopped onion
4 tablespoons butter or margarine
½ cup dry white wine
½ cup water
½ teaspoon salt

16 ounces frozen scallops, thawed
4 lightly beaten eggs
2 cups herbed stuffing cubes
4 slices Swiss cheese

Saute onion in butter until tender. Add water, wine and salt. Add scallops, and cook 5 minutes. Combine eggs and stuffing cubes. Stir into scallop mixture. Mix well. Spoon into 4 one-cup casseroles. Bake 25 to 30 minutes at 350 degrees. Remove from oven. Halve cheese slices diagonally to top casseroles. Return to oven to melt cheese. Serves 4.

*Mrs. James Dickson (Mary)*

## SHRIMP AND RICE CASSEROLE

2 cups cooked rice
½ pound fresh shrimp, cooked, or
   2 cans of canned shrimp
2/3 cup buttered bread crumbs

2 cups white sauce
1 pound grated cheddar cheese
Dash of cayenne
3 tablespoons melted butter

Make white sauce in double boiler. Add grated cheese and stir till melted. Add cayenne. Pour half of sauce in greased 1½ quart casserole. Place half of rice on sauce. Arrange prepared shrimp on top. Cover with remaining rice. Pour remaining sauce over all. Top with buttered bread crumbs. Bake 25-30 minutes at 350 degrees until browned. Makes 4 generous portions.

*Mrs. John M. Raine (Ruth)*

## SHRIMP AND WILD RICE CASSEROLE

½ cup thinly sliced onion
½ cup thinly sliced green pepper
1 can mushrooms, drained
½ cup margarine
1 tablespoon worcestershire

4 drops tabasco
2 cups Uncle Ben's brown rice
   and wild rice, cooked
1 pound cooked shrimp
2 cups thin cream sauce

Saute onion, pepper, and mushrooms in margarine. Add seasonings, shrimp, and rice. Make cream sauce, using chicken broth instead of milk. Add sauce to shrimp-rice mixture. Pour into casserole and bake 45 minutes in 300 degree oven. Serves 6.

*Mrs. Arthur W. Gill*

## TUNA—BROCCOLI CASSEROLE

1 (10 ounce) package chopped
   broccoli
1 can clam chowder
1/3 cup parmesan cheese
2 tablespoons lemon juice

½ cup sour cream
¼ teaspoon dried dill
1 (9¼ ounce) can tuna, drained
Almonds (optional)
1 can refrigerator biscuits (5)

Cook broccoli and drain. Mix all ingredients except biscuits. Put into 2 quart casserole. Bake at 375 degrees for 30 minutes. Top casserole with biscuits cut into fourths. Bake 15 minutes longer. Serves 4 to 6.

*Mrs. Thomas Clyatt, Jr. (Rowena)*

131

## SEAFOOD CASSEROLE

| | |
|---|---|
| 1 cup shrimp | 1 cup chopped celery |
| 1 cup crabmeat | ½ cup chopped green pepper |
| 1 cup fresh oysters | ½ cup chopped onions |
| 1½ cups cooked rice | 1 teaspoon salt |
| 1 cup mayonnaise | 1/8 teaspoon pepper |
| 2 tablespoons worcestershire | Potato chips |

Mix together all ingredients except potato chips. Pour into casserole. Top with crushed potato chips. Bake 35 minutes in 350 degree oven. Serves 8.

*Mrs. Lamar Roberts (Shirley)*

## SHRIMP—MUSHROOM—ARTICHOKE CASSEROLE

*Better made the day before!*

| | |
|---|---|
| 2½ tablespoons butter | ¾ cup whipping cream |
| ½ pound fresh mushrooms | ½ cup dry sherry |
| ¾ pound frozen shrimp, cooked | 1 tablespoon worcestershire |
| 1 can artichoke hearts | Salt and pepper to taste |
| 4½ tablespoons butter | ½ cup parmesan cheese |
| 4½ tablespoons flour | Paprika |
| ¾ cup milk | |

Melt butter and saute mushrooms. Place in 2 quart casserole, 1 layer each of artichokes, shrimp and mushrooms. Melt 4½ tablespoons butter, add flour, stirring with wire whisk, then milk and cream. Stir and cook till thickened. Add sherry, worcestershire, salt and pepper. Pour sauce over layered ingredients. Sprinkle with grated cheese, then paprika. Bake 30 minutes in 350 degree oven. Serve over rice. (¼ pound crab can also be added for heartier dish). Serves 6.

*Mrs. John O. Mitchell (Beverly)*

# Vegetables

## ITALIAN STUFFED ARTICHOKES

*Vegetable side dish or hors d'oeuvres*

6 artichokes
2 cups Italian bread crumbs
1 small can black olives,
   chopped
½ cup chopped parsley
1 teaspoon garlic powder

¼ cup parmesan cheese
1 tablespoon salt
Oil to moisten
¼ cup oil, scant
¼ teaspoon pepper
1 clove garlic

Rinse artichokes and cut off tips and stalks. Pound upside down to open leaves, spreading the leaves wide open. Mix bread crumbs, olives, parsley, garlic powder, cheese, salt, pepper and enough oil to moisten the mixture. Fill the artichoke leaves with stuffing and place in a small amount of water in a Dutch oven. Add oil and garlic. Cover the pot and cook slowly until almost all the water has evaporated, approximately 1 hour. Serve hot or cold.

*Mrs. Vincent Sgrosso (Joanne)*

## ASPARAGUS AND NOODLE CASSEROLE

1 can asparagus
¾ soup can of milk
½ small package noodles,
   cooked and drained

1 can mushroom soup
2 hard-boiled eggs, sliced
2-3 slices American cheese,
   cut into strips

Dilute soup with milk. Place a small amount of soup mixture in bottom of greased baking dish. Place in layers: ½ noodles, ½ asparagus, 1 sliced egg and ½ soup mixture. Repeat. Arrange cheese strips on top. Bake at 350 degrees about 20 minutes. Serves 4-6. May be prepared ahead and stored in refrigerator.

*Mrs. David B. Cowles (Joan)*

## ASPARAGUS AND CHEESE CASSEROLE

3 eggs, well beaten
1 can cut asparagus
¼ pound sharp cheddar cheese,
   grated
Small can chopped pimientos

½ cup slivered almonds
1 cup milk
¼ cup melted butter
1 teaspoon salt
1 small chopped onion

Combine ingredients and put into greased casserole. Bake at 325 degrees for 45-60 minutes. Serves 4.

*Mrs. William A. Maner (Sandra)*

## ASPARAGUS AND PEAS CASSEROLE

½ cup margarine, melted
1 box cheese crackers, crushed
   into fine crumbs
10 ounces sharp cheddar cheese,
   grated

1 large can asparagus tips,
   cut in 1 inch pieces
1 can mushroom soup
1 small can English peas

Place ½ of the melted margarine in the bottom of the casserole. Mix cracker crumbs and cheese. Add liquid from asparagus to soup to make two cups. Put layer of cracker mixture, layer of asparagus, and peas. Cover with liquid. Repeat. Top with cracker and cheese layer. Pour remaining margarine on top. Bake at 350 degrees for 30 minutes. Serves 6.

*Mrs. John M. DeBorde, III (Anne)*

## ASPARAGUS PUFF CASSEROLE

2 cans asparagus pieces
1 cup mayonnaise
Butter
1 cup grated medium
   sharp cheese

2 eggs, beaten
1 can cream soup
   (celery, chicken,
   mushroom or asparagus)

Drain asparagus, reserving 2 tablespoons of juice. Place asparagus and juice in blender and blend 1 to 2 minutes. Combine with mayonnaise, soup, cheese and eggs. Dot with butter. Bake at 350 degrees 40-45 minutes, until set. Serves 6.

*Martha Barron Barnes*

## BAKED BUTTER BEANS

*Good at formal dinner or with hamburgers*

2 (10 ounce) packages frozen butter
   beans, cooked & drained
6 slices bacon
1/3 cup minced celery
½ cup minced onion
¼ cup minced bell pepper

2 tablespoons flour
1 cup (little more) tomato sauce
2 tablespoons sugar
Salt & pepper to taste
1 teaspoon garlic powder

Fry bacon. Save grease and saute celery, onion and bell pepper. Add flour, tomato sauce, sugar, salt, pepper and garlic powder. Add butter beans. Cook in casserole with bacon strips across the top. Bake at 350 degrees for 20 minutes, or until hot. Serves 10.

*Mrs. Hayward Pardue (Helen)*

135

## LIMA BEANS

4 cans Seaside dried butter beans
1 teaspoon dry mustard
Dash salt

10 heaping tablespoons brown
  sugar
1 pint sour cream

Drain about half the liquid from each can. Mix all together and bake at 350 degrees for 3 hours. Watch so they don't get too dry. Serves 10-12.

*Mrs. Richard McCamey (Betsy)*

## CREOLE BEANS

*A colorful recipe that goes with almost any meat*

8 slices bacon, crisply cooked
2 cans green beans, drained
1 tablespoon dried onion soup mix

1 (1 pound) can stewed tomatoes
1 teaspoon sugar
1 teaspoon cornstarch

Cook bacon. Pour off all but 3 tablespoons drippings. Add beans and onion soup mix and heat. Snip bacon into small pieces and add half to beans, along with stewed tomatoes and sugar. Stir in cornstarch to thicken juice. Heat and top with remaining bacon. Serves 8.

*Mrs. Gene Presley (Dianne)*

## FRENCH BEAN CASSEROLE

2 cans French style green beans
2 medium ripe tomatoes
1 large onion

1 cup sliced almonds
1 stick butter or margarine
¼ teaspoon salt

In a buttered casserole place a layer of ingredients as listed. Then repeat except for salt. Bake at 350 degrees, for 1 hour. Serves 8.

*Mrs. Joseph Biggers (Eathil)*

## GREEN BEAN CASSEROLE

*This is a dish that never fails to bring requests for the recipe*

1 large onion, chopped
½ cup butter
¼ cup flour
1½ cups milk
¾ pound cheddar cheese, grated
Dash of tabasco
1 can water chestnuts
2 teaspoons soy sauce

½ teaspoon pepper
1 teaspoon salt
3 (10 ounce) packages, frozen,
  French-style green beans,
  cooked and drained
1 small can mushrooms
Chopped almonds

Saute onion in butter. Add flour and then milk. Stir in cheese and tabasco, soy sauce, pepper and salt. Add beans, mushrooms and water chestnuts. Pour into casserole and sprinkle with chopped almonds. Bake at 350 degrees, until thoroughly heated. Serves 12.

*Mrs. Hayward Pardue (Helen)*

## TARRAGON BEANS

| | |
|---|---|
| 1½ pounds young tender beans or | 2 (No.2) cans Blue Lake whole green beans |

Make a marinade of the following:

| | |
|---|---|
| ¾ cup French dressing | ¼ teaspoon red pepper |
| ½ teaspoon salt | ¼ cup tarragon vinegar |
| 1 teaspoon sugar | 2 tablespoons lemon juice |
| ¼ teaspoon paprika | 1/8 teaspoon oregano |
| ¼ teaspoon black pepper | 1/8 teaspoon dried thyme |

Marinate beans in French dressing and spices for several hours or overnight. At serving time cook 4 strips of bacon, crisp. Remove from fat. Pour off all but 2 tablespoons of bacon fat and cook 1 medium chopped onion in it until yellow. Place drained beans in casserole dish containing onions and heat thoroughly. Crumble bacon on top. Serves 4-6.

*Mrs. Cleveland Willcoxon, Jr. (Nancy)*

## BROCCOLI CASSEROLE

*This makes a delicious dish for those who don't like broccoli*

| | |
|---|---|
| 2 packages chopped frozen broccoli, cooked 5 minutes | Scant cup mayonnaise |
| | 2 eggs, well beaten |
| 1 cup grated cheddar cheese | 1 can mushroom soup |
| Ritz crackers, crushed | Butter |

Mix broccoli, cheese, mayonnaise, eggs and soup. Put in greased casserole and sprinkle with Ritz crackers. Dot with butter. Bake at 350 degrees for 30 minutes. Serves 8.

*Mrs. Virgil Wolff (K. Eileen)*
*Patty Taulman Wills*

**LOVING TOUCHES . . .**
Scooped-out vegetables, such as cucumbers and squash make lovely servers for dips, etc.

## BROCCOLI WITH CASHEW NUT SAUCE

2 tablespoons minced onion
2 tablespoons butter
1 cup sour cream
2 teaspoons sugar
1 teaspoon white vinegar

½ teaspoon poppy seeds
½ teaspoon paprika
Dash of salt
2 packages frozen broccoli
1 package cashews

Cook onions in butter until clear. Remove from heat and stir in sour cream, sugar, vinegar and seasonings. Pour over cooked, drained broccoli. Sprinkle with chopped cashews. Served 6-8.

*Mrs. Dudley Pearson (Neville)*

## BROCCOLI AND CORN CASSEROLE

*This can be easily doubled or even made larger*

1 package frozen broccoli, thawed
1 can cream style corn
1 tablespoon onion (instant, minced or fresh chopped)

1 egg
4 tablespoons melted butter
2 slices chopped cooked bacon
1 cup Pepperidge Farm herb stuffing

Mix broccoli and corn with egg and onion. Put in greased casserole. Mix stuffing, bacon and butter. Spread over vegetable mixture. Bake uncovered at 350 degrees for 1 hour. Serves 4-6.

*Mrs. David B. Cowles (Joan)*

## RICE AND BROCCOLI CASSEROLE

*Try this with chicken*

2 tablespoons finely chopped celery
2 tablespoons finely chopped onion
Margarine
1 small jar Cheese Whiz
1 can cream of mushroom soup

1 package chopped broccoli, cooked and drained
1½ cups Minute Rice, cooked
Salt to taste
Water chestnuts, sliced, or slivers of almonds

Saute celery and onion, Stir in Cheese Whiz, soup, broccoli, rice, salt, and nuts. Bake at 400 degrees for 20 minutes.  Serves 6.

*Mrs. Earle Duffey (Jacqueline)*

## BRUSSEL SPROUT CASSEROLE

½ cup chopped pecans
6 tablespoons flour
½ teaspoon nutmeg
3 tablespoons butter (not margarine)
3 packages tiny, frozen brussel sprouts

¾ cup powdered non-dairy
   creamer
1½ cups hot chicken bouillon
   (3 cubes)

### Topping

1 package Pepperidge Farm corn
   bread stuffing

2 tablespoons melted butter

Place ingredients in deep baking casserole. Cover and bake in 350 degree oven for 45 minutes, stirring occasionally to test for tenderness. When done, spoon on topping mixture and brown about 10 minutes. Serves 10-12.

*Mrs. Bud Erickson*


## CARROTS WITH GRAPES

1/8 teaspoon garlic powder
2 teaspoons dried basil
½ cup butter
1 teaspoon crushed chervil
Salt and pepper

2 pounds fresh carrots,
   julienne strips
3 cups seedless white grapes
2 tablespoons fresh lemon juice

Cook carrots with basil in enough water to cover, until just tender. Drain. In the meantime, combine butter, chervil and garlic powder. Add butter mixture to carrots. Just before serving, stir in grapes, lemon juice, salt and pepper. Heat only until grapes are hot. Serves 10-12.

*Mrs. Jon Shepherd (Kay)*


## FESTIVE CARROT PUDDING

*A delicious complement to pork, chicken or turkey*

2 cups cooked mashed carrots
1 teaspoon salt
½ cup sugar
½ stick butter or margarine
1 cup milk

3 eggs, well beaten
2 heaping tablespoons flour
1 teaspoon baking powder
¼ teaspoon cinnamon
½ cup chopped pecans

Mix all ingredients together well. Bake in greased casserole at 350 degrees for about 1 hour. If not nicely brown on top, place under broiler for a minute or two. Serves 6.

*Mrs. Jack R. Walker (Charlotte)*

## CAULIFLOWER CASSEROLE

1 carton sour cream
1 tablespoon mayonnaise
Chives for top
3 packages frozen cauliflower, cooked and drained

2 cans frozen cream of shrimp soup, thawed, or Campbell's cream of shrimp soup

Mix all ingredients except chives and put in casserole dish. Sprinkle chives on top. Bake 30-40 minutes at 350 degrees. Serves 10-12.

*Mrs. William Whitaker (Susan)*

## CELERY CASSEROLE

*A good dinner party dish*

2 cups cut celery
1 can cream of chicken soup
1 can sliced water chestnuts

1 small jar pimientos
A few almonds
Buttered bread crumbs

Parboil celery for 5 minutes. Drain well. Mix with soup, chestnuts and pimientos. Put in 1½ quart casserole and cover with bread crumbs. Sprinkle with almonds. Bake at 350 degrees for 30-40 minutes. Serves 6.

*Mrs. Joseph F. Prescott (Jane)*

## CORN PUDDING

1 package frozen corn
1 cup half and half
3 eggs
2 tablespoons butter

2 tablespoons flour
1 teaspoon salt
1 tablespoon sugar
Dash of white pepper

Blend all ingredients in electric blender. Pour into casserole and bake in a cushion of water at 350 degrees for 1 hour. If doubled it will take about 20 minutes longer to bake. Serves 4.

*Mrs. Erik Schonberg (Ann)*

## STUFFED EGGPLANT

1 eggplant, thinly sliced
2 eggs
½ teaspoon salt
Pepper to taste
1 cup ricotta cheese

½ cup ground beef, cooked
¼ cup chopped mushrooms, sauteed
3 tablespoons fresh parsley, chopped
1 cup tomato sauce
Parmesan and mozzarella cheese

Dip unpeeled eggplant slices into eggs beaten with salt and pepper. Fry in hot salad oil (½ inch deep in large skillet) until golden brown. Drain on a paper towel. Make mixture of ricotta cheese, meat, mushrooms and parsley. Put some of this mixture on each eggplant slice, roll up like crepes and place in long pyrex dish. Cover with tomato sauce, parmesan cheese and small pieces of mozzarella cheese. Put under broiler until cheese melts. (This may be served as an appetizer, vegetable or main course).

*"Once Upon a Stove Restaurant"*
*New York City, New York*
*Mr. Henry Sgrosso, owner*

## EGGPLANT AND CLAM CASSEROLE

½ cup milk
Rind of ½ lemon
3 tablespoons minced onion
¼ cup chopped celery
¼ cup butter or margarine
½ teaspoon salt
1 large eggplant, 6 cups
   pared & cubed
1 (7 ounce) can minced clams
1 egg, beaten
2 tablespoons melted butter
   or margarine
2 tablespoons grated parmesan
   cheese
¼ cup flour
1 cup soft bread crumbs

Parboil eggplant with lemon rind in salted water. Drain and discard lemon rind. Turn eggplant into shallow 1 quart casserole. Saute onion and celery in butter in medium-sized sauce pan. Blend in flour and salt. Stir until smooth. Remove from heat and gradually add milk. Add clams with juice. Cook over medium heat, stirring constantly, until mixture is thickened. In medium bowl add mixture to beaten eggs. Pour over eggplant in baking dish. Toss bread crumbs with butter, and sprinkle with parmesan cheese over eggplant mixture. Bake at 375 degrees for 20 minutes or until crumbs are a delicate brown. Serves 4.

*Mrs. Howard Golden (Joyce)*

## LOVING TOUCHES . . .

Cook rice in only enough water to absorb every drop when finished cooking. (2½ cups water to 1 cup rice.) Salt and butter added to cooking mean no stirring when rice is done. Cook covered, slowly for 20 minutes for perfect rice.

## EGGPLANT PARMIGIANA

*Good vegetable for a buffet*

2 medium eggplants, sliced thin
Cooking oil
Flour for dredging
8 tablespoons parmesan
   cheese, grated

8 tablespoons mozzarella
   cheese, grated
2 cups marinara tomato sauce
   (see index for sauce)

Coat eggplant in flour and fry in oil. Drain. Place a small portion of tomato sauce in long baking dish, next a layer of eggplant. Sprinkle on cheeses and continue with another layer of eggplant, sauce and cheeses. Bake at 350 degrees for 15 minutes. Serves 6-8.

*Mrs. Vincent Sgrosso (Joanne)*

## FETTUCCINI ALFREDO

2 (8 ounce) packages thin egg
   noodles
1 stick butter

1 cup heavy cream
1 cup parmesan cheese

Cook noodles according to directions. Drain and return to pot. Add butter and cream and mix well. Add cheese and toss lightly. Spoon into chafing dish or "keep hot" server. Serve with freshly ground pepper. Serves 8. Lovely with green salad and white wine.

*Mrs. Vincent Sgrosso (Joanne)*

## MUSHROOMS AND SOUR CREAM

1 pound fresh mushrooms
1 small onion, sliced
¼ cup margarine
Pepper to taste

1 cup sour cream
1 tablespoon sherry
1 teaspoon salt

Wash mushrooms and halve if large. Saute onion in melted margarine until limp. Add mushrooms. Cover and cook slowly for 5 minutes. Add sour cream, sherry and seasonings. Simmer until heated. Serves 8 as a side dish. Can be made ahead and reheated.

*Mrs. William Luesing (Carolyn)*

## STUFFED MUSHROOMS

| | |
|---|---|
| 5 slices bacon | 1 pound fresh mushrooms |
| 1 small chopped onion | 1 package Stouffers spinach |
| 2 tablespoons butter or margarine | souffle |

Wash mushrooms. Remove and chop stems. Saute onion and chopped stems in butter. Fry and crumble bacon. Mix bacon, onion and stems, with thawed spinach. Spoon into mushroom caps. Broil until brown. Serves 4-6. These can be made ahead of time. refrigerated, then broiled at last minute.

*Mrs. Bruce Dick (Sylvia)*


## ITALIAN POTATOES IN FOIL

*These may be prepared ahead of time*

| | |
|---|---|
| Baking potatoes, 1 per person | Parsley flakes |
| Garlic powder | Oregano |
| Salt | Parmesan cheese, grated |
| Pepper | Butter |
| Paprika | |

Slice potatoes into strips on foil. Season to taste with garlic powder, salt, pepper, paprika, parsley flakes and oregano. Top each with 3 pats of butter and sprinkle heavily with parmesan cheese. Wrap tightly in individual foil packets. Bake at 350 degrees for 1½ hours.

*Mrs. Myles J. Gould (Lynn)*


## BAKED MASHED POTATO

| | |
|---|---|
| 1/3 cup finely chopped onion | 1 (8 ounce) package cream |
| ¼ cup chopped pimiento | cheese, softened |
| 1 teaspoon salt | 4 cups hot mashed potato |
| 1 egg, beaten | (instant can be used) |
| | Pepper |

Combine cream cheese and hot mashed potato. Add remaining ingredients. Mix well. Bake in 1½ quart casserole dish at 350 degrees for 45 minutes. Serves 6. This can be made ahead. It also holds well at a lower temperature after baking completed.

*Mrs. Ben Read (Polly)*

143

## COLD POTATOES IN GREEN SAUCE

*Specialty of Parma, Italy*

Small, red new potatoes                    Freshly ground pepper
Olive oil                                  Fresh garlic, finely chopped
Lemon juice                                Fresh parsley, finely chopped
Salt

(Choose proportions according to your taste)

Boil potatoes until done, but firm. Cut into quarters or bitesize pieces. Blend other ingredients well in a mortar and pestle. Mix well with potatoes. (This is delicious served with sliced broiled steak covered with parmesan cheese and lemon or with charcoal-broiled lamb chops).

*Mrs. Joseph Conant (Olympia)*

## NUTTY POTATOES

12 medium potatoes                         1  teaspoon salt
2 onions                                   ¼  teaspoon pepper
1 quart half and half                      1/8 pound butter

Grind potatoes and 2 onions into one quart half and half. Add salt, pepper and butter. Put in casserole and bake 325 degrees for 4 hours. Stir occasionally. Serves 12.

*Mrs. Richard McCamey (Betsy)*

## BAKED RICE

1 stick butter                             1  cup uncooked rice
1 medium onion, chopped                    1  can mushrooms (optional)
2 cans beef consomme

Saute onion in butter until tender. Combine other ingredients and pour into large casserole. Cover and bake at 350 degrees for 1 hour. Serves 6.

*Amanda Alston Gregory*

## RISOTTO, "ITALIAN RICE"

2 cans chicken broth                       4 sauteed chicken livers,
1 cup rice (long grain)                       chopped
Pinch saffron                              Grated parmesan cheese
1 small can chopped mushrooms, drained

144

Heat broth in pan. When broth comes to a boil, add rice, saffron, mushrooms and chicken livers. Cover and cook until almost all liquid has evaporated. Stir occasionally. Rice will be firm. Serve with grated cheese. Serves 4-6.

*Mrs. Vincent Sgrosso (Joanne)*

## EASY TOMATO RICE
*Good with ham or barbecue*

¼ pound bacon, diced
1 onion, chopped
1 cup uncooked rice

1 (1 pound) can tomatoes with juice
½ cup water

Saute bacon and onion until bacon is browned. Add rice and stir until rice is lightly browned. Stir in tomatoes and water and bring to a boil. Cover and simmer on low heat 30 minutes. Add water if rice seems too dry or if barbecue chef is slow. Serves 8.

*Mrs. Gregory Fitz-Gerald (Diane)*

## WILD RICE CASSEROLE

8 ounces wild rice
1 pound fresh mushrooms or
  1 large can mushrooms
1 stick butter or margarine
¼ cup flour

2 cups milk
2 (8 ounce) packages cream cheese
½ teaspoon salt

Pre-heat oven to 325 degrees. Wash rice and put in double boiler with pinch of salt. Cover with water, adding more if necessary. Cook slowly over low heat for 2 hours or until tender. Pour rice into colander and drain well. Brown mushrooms in butter and set aside. Melt stick of butter in top of double boiler and add flour stirring until thick paste is formed. Add milk slowly, stirring constantly. Add cream cheese and stir or beat until smooth. Add salt. Butter 2 quart casserole and fill with alternate layers of rice, mushrooms and sauce. Decorate top with whole mushrooms and sauce. Bake in oven for 30 minutes or until mixture is slightly brown and bubbly. Serves 8.

*Mrs. Alex C. King, Jr. (Ross)*

145

## CREAMED SPINACH MIMOSA

5 pounds fresh spinach or
3 packages frozen spinach,
  cooked and drained
6 tablespoons butter

2 cups whipping cream
2 hard boiled eggs, sieved
Nutmeg, salt, pepper to taste
2 pieces of toasted bread

Cook drained spinach in butter until moisture has evaporated. Stir in cream gradually; add seasonings. Simmer over low heat until hot and cream is reduced to desired consistency. Put spinach in a heated deep serving dish and sprinkle with eggs. (Garnish with 2 star-shaped pieces of bread, toasted). Serves 10.

*Mrs. Hall Ware (Mary)*

## SPINACH CASSEROLE

2 packages chopped frozen spinach,
  cooked and drained
1 (3 ounce) package cream cheese

1 can mushroom soup
1 can French fried onion rings

Combine spinach and cream cheese. Stir until melted and blended. Alternate layers of spinach, soup and onion rings in casserole. Bake at 400 degrees for 10-15 minutes, or until bubbly. Serves 6.

*Mrs. David Kenney (Jo)*

## SPINACH AND ARTICHOKE CASSEROLE

2 cans artichoke hearts, drained
2 (8 ounce) packages cream cheese
Crushed fresh garlic
Salt and pepper
7-8 packages frozen chopped spinach, cooked and well drained

1 can water chestnuts, sliced
½ pound butter
Onion flakes
Seasoned bread crumbs

Place artichoke halves in buttered 9x13 casserole. Add water chestnuts. Mix cream cheese and butter together in a double boiler. Then mix together with spinach. Add garlic, onion flakes, salt and pepper to taste. Pour over artichokes and chestnuts. Bake at 350 degrees for 30 minutes. Sprinkle with seasoned bread crumbs and bake 10 minutes more. Serves 12.

*Mrs. Robert J. Bridell (Audrey)*
*Linda Murphy Finsthwait*
*Laura Edmondson Childers*

## BAKED SQUASH PARMESAN

4 acorn squash
8 tablespoons butter
8 teaspoons grated parmesan

Salt and freshly ground
black pepper

Preheat oven to 325 degrees. Scrub squash and cut in half lengthwise. Scrape out seeds and all strings. Put squash, open side up, in baking dish. Sprinkle each with salt and pepper. Put 1 tablespoon butter and 1 teaspoon cheese in each half. Bake for 1 hour or until tender. Serves 8.

*Mrs. Robert F. Dennis (Peggy)*

## SUMMER SQUASH AND ZUCCHINI CASSEROLE

¼ cup white wine
2 tablespoons lemon juice
½ teaspoon salt
½ cup water
¼ cup salad oil

¾ pound zucchini, cut in ½ inch slices
¾ pound yellow squash, cut in ½ inch slices
½ onion, sliced
½ cup walnuts

Saute squash slices with onion in hot oil for 5 minutes. Add wine, lemon juice, salt and water. Simmer for 5 minutes. Add walnuts. Serves 4-6.

*Mrs. James Dickson (Mary)*

## ZUCCHINI CASSEROLE

*Especially good with steak*

4 or 5 zucchini squash
1 medium onion, thinly sliced
2 medium tomatoes, thinly sliced
Parsley and oregano, to taste

4 slices American cheese, cut into strips
4 slices bacon

In a rectangular pyrex dish, layer in this order: zucchini (unpeeled and sliced lengthwise), onion, tomatoes, cheese and bacon (uncooked). Sprinkle with parsley and oregano. Bake at 350 degrees for 30 to 40 minutes. Serves 6-8.

*Mrs. Vincent Sgrosso (Joanne)*

## LOVING TOUCHES . . .

When cooking beans or rice, adding a few drops of vinegar or lemon juice will prevent an aluminum pot from turning dark. This does not change the taste of the food.

## SQUASH CASSEROLE

6 to 8 small yellow squash
1 medium onion
2 stalks celery
1 teaspoon salt
½ stick butter

2 slices bread, cubed and
  browned in butter
1 beaten egg
1 cup milk
1 cup diced cheddar cheese
Buttered cracker crumbs

Chop squash, celery, and onion. Add salt and cook until tender. Drain and mash. Mix with remaining ingredients and pour into buttered casserole dish. Cover with buttered cracker crumbs and bake at 350 degrees for 30 minutes. Serves 6. May be frozen before baking.

*Mrs. Lee H. Webb (Beverly)*
*Lois Miner Yates*

## SQUASH CASSEROLE

1 cup sour cream
1 small grated onion
Salt and pepper to taste
1 package seasoned bread crumbs,
  (Pepperidge Farm)

2 cups cooked mashed squash
1 carrot, grated
1 (10½ ounce) can cream of
  chicken soup
2 eggs

Mix all ingredients except bread crumbs. Sprinkle bread crumbs on bottom of buttered casserole dish, add squash mixture, cover with more bread crumbs and add generous dots of butter. Bake at 350 degrees for 30 minutes. Serves 6.

*Mrs. Walter G. Canipe (Virginia)*
*Mrs. William H. Needle (Valerie)*

## SQUASH SOUFFLE

2 cups cooked squash
2 tablespoons finely chopped
  onion
½ cup milk
8 ounces grated cheese
Dash of tabasco

2 eggs, well beaten
1 small can chopped pimiento
1 tablespoon worcestershire sauce
¼ teaspoon paprika
1 small box well crushed saltines
1 stick melted butter

Mix all ingredients, except for saltines and butter and put into 1½ quart casserole dish. Bake at 350 degrees for 45 minutes or until firm. Cover with mixture of saltines and butter and brown lightly for about 3 minutes. Serves 6. This recipe can be doubled.

*Mrs. Bert Oastler (Belitje)*

148

## STOP!

*(squash, tomatoes, onions, peppers)*

2 tomatoes, sliced
5 squash, sliced
1 red onion, sliced
Pepper

1 stick butter
Salt
1½ large green peppers,
  sliced

Put in layers in a casserole, starting with a thick layer of squash. Then onion, pepper, tomato and repeat. Dot each layer with butter. Sprinkle with salt and pepper. Bake at 350 degrees for 1¼ hours, uncovered. Serves 4-6.

*Mrs. Jerry Tidwell (Dottie)*


## CRUNCHY–TOP SWEET POTATO SOUFFLE

3 cups sweet potatoes, mashed
2 eggs, lightly beaten
½ cup milk
1 teaspoon vanilla

1 cup sugar
½ teaspoon salt
1/3 stick butter, melted

### Topping

1/3 stick butter
1 cup brown sugar

1/3 cup flour
1 cup nuts (pecans or walnuts)

Mix together all ingredients except topping, and beat until fluffy and all potato strings removed. Pour into greased baking dish. Melt butter. Add brown sugar, flour and pecans. Pour over sweet potatoes. Bake at 350 degrees for 35 minutes.

*Mrs. Ed Andrews (Jan)*


## LOVING TOUCHES . . .

A few lettuce or other salad green leaves help give a fresh taste to canned vegetables. Discard before serving.

To remove skins from tomatoes, plunge one at a time in boiling water for about 30 seconds. Skin will slip off easily.

In cooking pasta, the real sin is over-cooking. Cook ¾ time stated in directions - al dente' (firm to the bite, never soft and sticky).

After fresh spinach is washed, the leaves hold all the moisture needed to cook it to perfection.

## FRUITED YAM NESTS

*Great with ham!*

1 cup orange marmalade
2 tablespoons brown sugar
4 teaspoons prepared mustard
1/3 cup dry sherry or orange juice
1 can (20 ounces) pineapple
   chunks, drained
1 cup red maraschino cherries

6 medium yams, cooked, peeled,
   mashed, or 4 (1 pound) cans
   yams, drained and mashed
1 egg
¼ cup sugar
3 tablespoons butter or
   margarine, melted

Melt marmalade over very low heat. Blend in brown sugar, mustard and sherry. Add pineapple chunks and maraschino cherries. Heat. Mix yams, butter, egg and sugar. Using back of spoon, shape yams into nest in individual ramekins, or round casserole dish. Cook at 350 degrees for 20 minutes. Heap fruit and part of sauce into nests. Serve remaining sauce with ham. Serves 6.

*Mrs. Walter G. Canipe (Virginia)*

## SWEET POTATO PUDDING

*So easy to be so good!*

½ stick butter
2½ cups grated sweet potatoes
1½ cups sugar
2 cups milk

3 eggs, not beaten
2 teaspoons cinnamon
½ teaspoon salt
½ teaspoon cloves

Melt butter in baking pan. Add all other ingredients and mix. Bake at 450 degrees for 45 minutes or until done. Serves 6.

*Mrs. Fritz Milner (Missy)*

## SWEET POTATO SURPRISE

*Delicious with ham*

1 (1 pound, 1 ounce) can whole sweet
   potatoes, halved lengthwise
1¼ cups brown sugar
1½ tablespoons cornstarch
¼ teaspoon salt

1/8 teaspoon cinnamon
1 teaspoon shredded orange peel
1 (1 pound) can apricot halves
2 tablespoons butter
½ cup pecan halves

Place sweet potatoes in greased baking dish. In sauce pan, combine brown sugar, cornstarch, salt, cinnamon and orange peel. Drain apricots, reserving 1 cup syrup. Stir syrup into cornstarch mixture. Cook and stir over medium heat until boiling; boil 2 minutes. Add butter and pecans to cornstarch mixture. Arrange apricots in pan with potatoes and pour cornstarch mixture over all. Bake at 375 degrees for 25 minutes, uncovered. Serves 6.

*Mrs. A. J. Stringer (Martha)*

## BROILED TOMATOES

*Men love these - they can replace the tossed salad*

| | |
|---|---|
| 7 tomatoes | 1 can artichoke hearts |
| Salt and pepper | ½ pint sour cream |
| Worcestershire sauce | Parmesan cheese |
| Tabasco | Buttered cracker crumbs |
| Lemon juice | |

Halve the tomatoes. Take out stem end and scoop out seeds. Sprinkle tomato halves with salt, pepper, worcestershire sauce, tabasco and lemon juice. Fill holes with sour cream. Put ½ artichoke heart on top of each tomato and sprinkle again with lemon juice, salt and pepper. Cover with parmesan and buttered cracker crumbs. Put in pan with ½ inch of water. Bake at 325 degrees for 20 minutes. Put under broiler to brown top just before serving. Serves 7.

*Mrs. John Sineath (Nancy)*

## TOMATOES IN SOUR CREAM

| | |
|---|---|
| 1 onion, chopped | 3 tablespoons flour |
| 2 tablespoons butter | 1 cup sour cream |
| 6 firm tomatoes, cut into | Parsley |
| thick slices | Pepper |
| Salt | |

Saute onion in butter until golden. Season tomato slices with salt and pepper and add to pan. Cook tomatoes over low heat for 10 minutes or until juices are reduced by half. Blend 3 tablespoons of the juices with the flour. Add flour mixture to tomatoes and simmer mixture until sauce is thick. Stir in sour cream. Heat thoroughly but do not boil. Garnish with parsley. Serves 10-12.

*Mrs. Victor J. Pryles (Millie Finch)*

## TOMATO GARNISH FOR FILLET OF BEEF

Fresh tomatoes
Salt
Sugar

Butter
Fresh peas, cooked and
buttered

Cut a slice from top of each tomato. Remove pulp and seeds. Sprinkle insides with salt and a pinch of sugar. Invert tomatoes on paper towels to drain for 30 minutes. Pat insides dry with towels and put 1 teaspoon butter in each tomato shell. Fill with fresh buttered peas. Arrange in a buttered baking dish and bake in pre-heated 400 degree oven for 10 minutes.

*Mrs. James Cushman (Elkin)*

## TOMATOES ROCKEFELLER

3 large or 4 medium tomatoes
2 tablespoons minced onion
2 tablespoons finely chopped parsley
2 tablespoons margarine
1 package frozen chopped spinach,
cooked and drained well

Salt
Pepper
Paprika
Garlic powder
Bread crumbs

Slice tops off tomatoes and hollow out centers. Place in shallow baking pan cut side up. Mix the onion, parsley, margarine, spinach, salt, pepper, paprika and garlic powder. Divide and fill each tomato evenly. Top with bread crumbs. Bake at 375 degrees for 15 minutes or until crumbs are browned. Serves 3-4.

*Mrs. Dennis Mollenkamp (Jane)*

## VEGETABLE GARNISH FOR BEEF WELLINGTON

½ pound chopped mushrooms
1 cup chopped onion
Margarine or butter
1½ cups bread crumbs
4 hard boiled eggs, chopped
Salt
Pepper

4 tablespoons sour cream
2 teaspoons chopped parsley
10 mushroom caps
10 small tomatoes, scooped out
10 artichoke bottoms
Melted butter
Parmesan cheese, grated

Saute mushrooms and onions until soft. Add bread crumbs, eggs, salt and pepper and cook about one minute. Remove from heat and blend in sour cream and parsley. Fill mushroom caps, tomatoes and artichoke bottoms. Place on cookie sheet and sprinkle with butter and parmesan. Broil 3 inches from heat until brown and heated. Serves 10.

*Mrs. James Cushman (Elkin)*

## CHINESE VEGETABLE CASSEROLE

*Easy, delicious and goes with any meat!*

| | |
|---|---|
| 1 can mushroom soup | 1 can LeSeuer peas, drained |
| Dash worcestershire sauce | 1 can bean sprouts, drained |
| ½ teaspoon mustard | 1 can water chestnuts, sliced |
| 1 teaspoon lemon juice | 1 can mushrooms, sliced and |
| Dash of salt and pepper | drained |
| Grated cheese for top | 1 can French fried onion rings |

Mix soup with worcestershire sauce, mustard, lemon juice, salt and pepper. Make two layers in casserole of peas, beansprouts, water chestnuts, mushrooms and soup mixture. Bake at 350 degrees for 1 hour. Add onion rings and top with cheese. Heat 5-10 minutes more. Serves 6. Can be made early in day and stored in refrigerator.

*Mrs. Harry V. Lamon, Jr. (Ada)*

## VEGETABLE CASSEROLE

| | |
|---|---|
| 2/3 stick margarine | 1 package frozen green peas |
| 1 cup chopped celery | 1 can cream of mushroom soup |
| 1 cup chopped onion | 1 medium jar pimientos, sliced |
| 1 cup chopped green pepper | 1 can water chestnuts, sliced |
| 1/3 pound sliced, fresh or | Pinch thyme |
| 1 large can mushrooms | Salt and pepper |

In margarine, lightly saute celery, onion, green pepper and mushrooms. Cook green peas less time than suggested on package and drain. Combine all ingredients. Season with thyme, salt and pepper and put in greased casserole. Bake at 300 degrees for 25-30 minutes. Serves 8. This can be made ahead of time and refrigerated or frozen. The recipe can be doubled.

*Mrs. W. H. Bennett (Louise)*

## LOVING TOUCHES . . .

To cook vegetables in the classic French way: Cook uncovered in boiling, salty water for a few minutes, about 8 for most vegetables. (FOR FROZEN: ½ the time suggested.) Drain and rinse quickly in cold water to stop cooking. To serve: heat in butter and lemon juice, salt and pepper.

REMEMBER: Crunchiness is fresh-tasting!

## VEGETABLE CASSEROLE

1 can white shoe peg corn, drained
1 can French style green beans, drained
½ cup chopped green pepper
½ cup grated sharp cheese

½ cup chopped celery
½ cup chopped onion
½ cup sour cream
1 can cream of celery soup
Salt and pepper to taste

### Topping

½ box crumbled Ritz cheese crackers
½ can slivered almonds

½ stick butter

Mix all ingredients, except for topping, in a 2 quart casserole. Add topping and bake at 350 degrees for 45 minutes. Serves 8-10.

*Mrs. Kenneth P. Lynch, Jr. (Peggy)*

## LOVING TOUCHES . . .

To ripen an avocado or tomato quickly, place it in a brown paper bag and store in a dark cabinet.

A few drops of oil added to water while cooking noodles will keep the pot from "boiling over" and will keep noodles from sticking together.

To prevent an unpleasant odor when cooking cabbage or cauliflower, put a piece of bread on top of the pan! (It works!)

Colorful gelatins molded in grapefruit shells - then quartered, make lovely salads.

To wash spinach, fill sink with lukewarm water. Lay spinach on top, swish barely and lift out. Repeat several times; refresh with ice and cold water to which 1 teaspoon "Fruit Fresh" has been added.

A pinch of "Fruit Fresh" in a sinkful of cold water will keep salad greens from going "pink". Shake off excess, wrap in large towel, and keep in refrigerator until needed. "Fruit Fresh" also prevents fresh sliced fruit from turning "brown". ("Fruit Fresh" may be purchased in the canning section of grocery stores).

# Sauces

155

## BORDELAISE SAUCE

2 tablespoons butter
1 green onion, finely chopped
1 garlic clove, finely chopped
1 onion slice
2 carrot slices
6 whole black peppers
1 whole clove
Parsley sprig

1 bay leaf
2 tablespoons flour
1 can bouillon
¼ teaspoon salt
1/8 teaspoon pepper
1 tablespoon chopped parsley
1/3 cup red wine

Combine first nine ingredients and saute for 3 minutes or until onion is golden. Remove from heat and stir in flour until smooth. Cook over very low heat, stirring constantly, until flour is lightly browned, approximately 5 minutes. Remove from heat and stir in bouillon; bring to boil stirring constantly. Reduce heat and simmer uncovered for 10 minutes, stirring occasionally. Strain, add salt and pepper, wine and parsley. Reheat slowly. Makes 1 cup.

*Mrs. Hall Ware (Mary)*

## BEEF TENDERLOIN MARINADE

1½ cups white rum
¼ cup soy sauce
¼ cup worcestershire sauce
2 cans beef bouillon or consomme
1 small can crushed pineapple

3 to 4 bay leaves
½ teaspoon salt
½ teaspoon pepper
6 whole cloves

Marinate overnight in covered container (not metal) making sure entire tenderloin is covered with sauce. Grill and cut into small slices. Save marinade, heat and serve with meat in chafing dish.

*Mr. William A. McClain, III*

## SAUCE FOR CHICKEN DIVAN

*The original, from Divan Parisienne Restaurant, New York*

2 cups white sauce:
  4 tablespoons butter
  3 tablespoons flour
  2 cups milk and/or chicken stock

½ cup mayonnaise
½ cup whipping cream
3 teaspoons sherry
1 teaspoon worcestershire sauce

Make white sauce. Mix with other ingredients and boil, stirring for 15 minutes. Pour over well-drained broccoli and chicken breast slices (or ham slices). Top generously with freshly grated parmesan cheese.

*Mrs. Charles D. Wood (Gene M.)*

## COLD SAUCE FOR FRESH CRABMEAT

½ teaspoon horseradish
1 cup mayonnaise
½ cup chili sauce
¼ tablespoon mustard (to taste)

2 hard-boiled eggs
4 stalks celery
1 dill pickle

Mix first four ingredients. Grind together eggs, celery and pickle. Drain and mix with other ingredients.

*Mrs. Stephen Selig (Janet)*

## CURRY SAUCE

1 can mushroom soup
2/3 cup Hellmann's mayonnaise
½ pint sour cream

¼ teaspoon dry mustard
1 teaspoon curry powder
1 can mushrooms (optional)

Heat soup, then add rest of ingredients. Pour over vegetables or cut-up, cooked chicken. Can serve the chicken curry over rice or in Pepperidge Farm patty shells. Serves 4-6.

*Mrs. Dudley Pearson (Neville)*

## BASIC BARBECUE SAUCE

1 cup catsup
1 cup water
¼ cup cider vinegar
1 tablespoon worcestershire

1 small clove garlic
2 tablespoons brown sugar
2 tablespoons dry mustard
1 tablespoon liquid smoke

Cook 20 minutes over low heat. Stir occasionally. Pour over pork.

*Mrs. James G. Wilson (Jeanie)*

## DURKEE BARBECUE SAUCE

*Different - delicious*

1 large bottle Durkees
½ cup vinegar
¾ cup Real Lemon bottled juice
2 sticks butter
Onion salt to taste

2 tablespoons mustard
2 tablespoons sugar
4 tablespoons mayonnaise
Garlic salt, pepper

Melt butter, add Durkees, add the rest of the ingredients. Stir and simmer for 5 minutes. Baste chicken on the grill.

*Mrs. Dudley Pearson (Neville)*

## HOLLANDAISE SAUCE
*Easy, never fails*

½ stick margarine,             Juice 1 lemon
   cut into quarters          1 egg yolk

Bring water to a boil in double boiler. Turn heat down so water is hot, not bubbling - this is very important so sauce will not curdle. Blend egg yolk and lemon juice in top of double boiler. Add ¼ of the margarine and stir constantly until it is completely melted. Follow above rule for next three quarters. Serves 3.

*Mrs. Joseph R. White, Jr. (Barbara)*

## MARINARA SAUCE
*Basic meatless tomato sauce*

1 large can Italian tomatoes      2 cloves garlic (chopped) or
1 bay leaf                 1 teaspoon garlic powder
1 teaspoon salt          ¼ cup Wesson oil
¼ teaspoon pepper      2 tablespoons chopped parsley
¼ teaspoon oregano (optional)

Heat oil in saucepan. Add garlic and parsley and let simmer, but do not brown. Add tomatoes (crushed), bay leaf, salt, pepper and oregano. Bring to boil, then lower heat and cook 30 minutes. This sauce may be served plain or you may add any one of the following for a superb spaghetti sauce: 1 can minced clams (drained), cooked shrimp or lobster, cooked meatballs. Sauce serves 4-6.

*Mrs. Vincent Sgrosso (Joanne)*

## MAYONNAISE
*100% real flavor*

8 egg yolks              ¼ teaspoon paprika
1 tablespoon salt        1 quart Wesson oil
1 teaspoon dry mustard   ½ cup vinegar
¼ teaspoon white pepper   Juice of 1 lemon

Beat egg yolks until thick. Add salt, mustard, white pepper and paprika. Slowly add Wesson oil, beating continually and alternate with mix of vinegar and lemon juice. Finish with 1 tablespoon boiling water. Recipe may be cut in half. Keeps well in refrigerator.

*Mrs. Sydney Curtis (Ann)*

## SAUCE FOR SPARE RIBS

*Most popular*

1 part soy sauce
2 parts orange marmalade

1 part bourbon
3 parts honey

Mix all ingredients in the specitied proportions. Baste spare ribs and cook over charcoal. Baste several times during cooking. Cook 20 minutes. Season spare ribs with season-salt first.

*Mrs. Myles J. Gould (Lynn)*

## CHICKEN STOCK

4 chicken carcasses
1½ pounds meaty veal bones, if available
1½ teaspoons coarse salt, 6 peppercorns
2 onions, each studded with a clove

2 peeled carrots, in 2 inch chunks
2 celery stalks, in 2 inch chunks
1 leek, split in half
Bouquet garnie (3 parsley sprigs, 1 bay leaf, ¼ teaspoon thyme)

Rinse chicken pieces (anything may be used but the liver). Place in deep, heavy pot with veal bones. Cover with cold water. Slowly bring to a simmer, skimming occasionally. Add remaining ingredients. Simmer at least 3 hours. Skim occasionally. Sieve. Place stock in clean pot over high heat. Boil stock down until it tastes good and flavorful. Cool stock. Pour into 1 cup containers or an ice tray. Chill or freeze.

*Diane Wilkinson*

## LOVING TOUCHES . . .

Half portions of butter and roquefort cheese, melted together makes a tasty sauce for steak, fish, etc.

A good and easy marinade for steaks: dry bouillon mix and soy sauce, both rubbed into meat.

To make a smoother cream sauce, warm the milk before adding into flour and butter roux.

Thicken "pan gravies" with cornstarch instead of flour for a clear, shiny look that is especially appetizing.

159

## BROWN STOCK

6  pounds meaty bones, sawed in
   2 inch pieces
2  large onions, cut in half
2  cloves, studded into onions
2  large peeled carrots,
   in 2 inch chunks

2  celery stalks, in 2 inch chunks
1  large leek, split in half
2  teaspoons coarse salt,
   6 peppercorns
Bouquet garnie (3 parsley sprigs,
   1 bay leaf, ¼ teaspoon thyme)

Ideally, the bones should consist of half beef and half veal. If veal is unavailable, one or two chicken carcasses may be used in its place. Use meaty bones, for if too large a proportion of bones is used, the stock will be cloudy and gummy. (Shanks are ideal.) Place the bones, onions and carrots in one or two roasting pans, so the pieces do not touch each other. Place in a 450 degree oven until very brown, turning to brown all sides. When brown, place in large, deep pot. Cover with cold water. Add 2 cups water to roasting pan and place it over high heat, scraping up all the brown bits. Add this to stock pot. Slowly bring to a simmer, skimming occasionally. Add remaining ingredients. Simmer at least 6 hours, (overnight is fine.) Skim occasionally. Sieve. Place stock in clean pot over high heat. Boil stock down until it tastes good and flavorful. Cool stock. Pour into 1 cup containers or an ice tray. Chill or freeze.

*Diane Wilkinson*

## WHITE SAUCES

Any of these white sauces may be made richer by the addition of heavy cream, egg yolks, or a combination of the two. To enrich a sauce with heavy cream, simply whisk ¼ cup cream into 1 cup sauce before serving. To enrich with yolks, beat 1-2 yolks with ¼ cup of the hot, not boiling, sauce. Beat the yolk mixture back into the hot sauce right before serving. The sauce may not return to a simmer after the yolks are added. For an even richer sauce, beat 1-2 yolks with ¼ cup heavy cream. Beat in gradually ¼ cup of the hot sauce. Beat the yolk mixture back into the remaining ¾ cup hot, but not simmering, sauce.

## Bechamel

2 tablespoons butter
2 tablespoons flour

1 cup milk
Salt, white pepper

Melt butter in a non-aluminum pan. Stir in flour. Cook over low heat 3 minutes without browning. Off the heat, whisk in milk. Bring to a boil, whisking. Simmer to desired thickness. Season to taste (a dash of nutmeg is often added). If desired, enrich as described above. Serve with vegetables or as the base for other sauces.

## Veloute

2 tablespoons butter
2 tablespoons flour

1 cup chicken, veal or
fish stock

Follow directions for Bechamel, substituting stock for milk. (Use chicken or veal stock to sauce vegetables, poultry or veal dishes; use fish stock for seafood dishes). If desired, enrich as described above.

## Sauce Aurore

2 tablespoons butter
2 tablespoons flour
1 cup chicken stock or milk

3½ tablespoons heavy cream
1½ - 2 tablespoons tomato
paste

Follow directions for Bechamel Sauce. Stir in cream and tomato paste. Season to taste. Serve over poached or molded eggs, vegetables (spinach, broccoli).

*Diane Wilkinson*

## QUICK PAN SAUCE

1 cup brown stock (or beef
bouillon)
1 teaspoon meat glaze
2 teaspoons cornstarch or potato
starch, dissolved in a bit of bouillon

½ cup brandy, dry red wine,
or dry madiera
2 tablespoons butter,
softened

Remove steaks or roast from pan in which they were cooked. Blot away any excess fat left in the pan. Place pan over high heat and add stock, meat glaze (Bovril may be used), dissolved starch and spirits. Cook over high heat, scraping up the brown bits from bottom of pan, just until thick enough to nicely coat a spoon. Remove from heat. Strain if desired. Swirl in butter. Serve immediately.

*Diane Wilkinson*

## BEARNAISE

1½ tablespoons finely chopped shallots

1½ teaspoons finely chopped fresh parsley (or ¾ teaspoon dried)

1½ teaspoons finely chopped fresh chervil (or ¾ teaspoon dried)

9 crushed white peppercorns

3 tablespoons tarragon vinegar

Salt

3 tablespoons white wine

3 egg yolks + 1½ tablespoons water, beaten

11-12 tablespoons butter, melted and cooled a bit

¾ teaspoon chopped fresh tarragon, or ¼ teaspoon dried

Drops of lemon juice

In a heavy non-aluminum saucepan or a double boiler, reduce, by boiling over high heat, the first 6 ingredients to about 2 tablespoons. Remove from heat and cool pan a few minutes. Beat in the yolks and water. Return to a very low heat and beat until thick. Slowly whisk in the butter, drop by drop at first. Do not add milky layer on bottom of butter. Strain if desired. Season to taste with salt, tarragon and lemon juice. Serve with eggs, beef, fish. Hold or freeze. (To hold bernaise or hollandaise sauce, cover the bowl with plastic wrap and set it in another pan of lukewarm water. Keep it in a barely warm spot - a pilot lit oven is perfect. This may be held for hours. It may also be frozen in a small container. To use it, thaw in refrigerator. Then carefully rewarm it, covered, in a bowl of lukewarm water on a counter top, occassionally whisking it. It should not get too warm, or it will separate).

*Diane Wilkinson*

## SAUCE APRICOT

1½ cups imported apricot preserves

½ cup water

2 tablespoons sugar

2 tablespoons cognac, apricot liqueur, or Grand Marnier

Bring preserves, water and sugar to a boil in a heavy saucepan. Reduce heat to a simmer. Simmer 5-10 minutes. Strain the sauce and stir in liqueur. Serve on crepes, ice cream, cakes or puddings. (Sauce may be served hot or cold.)

*Diane Wilkinson*

162

# Cookies

DAVID SAPP

## ALMOND COOKIES

2 sticks butter
1½ cups sifted powdered sugar
1 egg
2½ cups flour
Pecans or almonds

1 teaspoon soda
1 teaspoon salt
1 teaspoon cream of tartar
1 tablespoon almond extract

Cream butter and sugar. Add slightly beaten egg. Add dry ingredients and almond extract. Cover and refrigerate one hour. Flour fingers and pinch off small amount of dough. Place on greased cookie sheet and press down with ½ pecan or an almond. Bake 325 degrees - 350 degrees for 12 minutes. Makes 80 to 100 cookies.

*Mrs. George Johnson (Janet)*

## APRICOT DAINTIES

*An old time strudel dessert, great on a cookie tray*

1 cup butter or margarine
2 cups sifted all purpose flour
1¼ cups commercial sour cream
1 cup apricot preserves
1 tablespoon lemon
Confectioners sugar

Filling:
1½ cups chopped nuts
1 cup chopped coconut
½ cup chopped raisins
¼ cup chopped maraschino
cherries

Cut butter into flour until particles are size of small peas. Add sour cream; stir until dough is moist enough to hold together. Wrap dough in foil and chill in refrigerator 5 to 6 hours or overnight.

Combine apricot preserves and lemon juice. Divide dough into four parts. Roll out one part into thin 14x12 rectangle and spread with apricot mixture. Sprinkle with ¼ of nut filling*. Roll tightly as for jelly roll, starting with 14 inch side. Seal edges. Place on ungreased baking sheet. Repeat process with remaining dough. Bake in moderate oven 350 degrees, 30 to 40 minutes until golden brown. Cut in 1 inch slices. Serve warm or cold sprinkled with confectioners sugar.

*Nut filling - mix together nuts, coconut, raisins and cherries (optional).

*Mrs. Bernard Pollock (Elaine)*

## BENNE COOKIES

¾ cup butter or margarine, melted
¾ cup all purpose flour
1½ cups brown sugar, packed
1 teaspoon vanilla
1 egg

1 cup benne (sesame seed
  lightly toasted)
¼ teaspoon baking powder
¼ teaspoon salt

Mix all ingredients thoroughly. Drop by ¼ teaspoon onto a lightly greased baking sheet. Bake until brown, about 6 to 7 minutes at 350 degrees. Cool cookies about ½ minute before removing from baking sheet.

*Ruth Wright*

## BOURBON BALLS

2½ cups rolled vanilla wafers
2 tablespoons cocoa
1 cup powdered sugar
3 tablespoons white Karo syrup

1 cup chopped nuts
¼ cup bourbon (use ½ cup if
  stronger flavor is desired)
Confectioners sugar

Mix all ingredients together well. Roll into small balls and then roll in confectioners sugar. Store in an air tight container for at least one week before serving.

*Mrs. Ervin Williams (Glenda)*

## BROWN SUGAR COOKIES

2 cups brown sugar
1 cup butter or margarine
2 eggs, unbeaten
1 teaspoon vanilla

1 teaspoon baking powder
3 cups flour
Large pinch of salt

Cream butter and sugar. Add eggs, one at a time. Add vanilla. Sift dry ingredients and add to mixture. Blend well. Form into teaspoon size balls, place about 2 inches apart on a greased cookie sheet. Press each ball flat with tines of a fork which has been dipped in flour. Bake 350 degrees for 8 minutes. Makes 6 dozen. Be careful not to overbake. Cookies are done when tops are slightly brown. This is a crisp cookie.

*Mrs. H. L. Shessel (Madelyn)*

## BROWNIES

2 eggs
1 stick butter
3 squares unsweetened Bakers
  chocolate

½ cup chopped pecans
½ cup flour
1 cup sugar
1 teaspoon vanilla

Melt butter and chocolate in top of double boiler. Beat eggs and add sugar. Sift flour and stir into eggs and sugar. Add butter and chocolate. Add vanilla. Stir in pecans. Pour mixture into greased pan. Bake at 375 degrees for 20 to 25 minutes.

*Mrs. Robert M. Holder, Jr. (Betty)*

## CHOCOLATE BROWNIES

1 stick butter
2 squares unsweetened chocolate
¾ cup flour
1 cup sugar
1 cup chopped pecans

1 teaspoon vanilla
2 eggs
¼ teaspoon salt
½ teaspoon baking powder

Melt butter and chocolate. Add sugar, eggs and rest of ingredients. Stir. Add pecans. Pour in well greased and floured pan (8x12). Bake at 325 degrees for 25 minutes. Sprinkle with confectioners sugar.

*Mrs. Carroll Jones (Marjory)*

## RED HOLLY BROWNIES

½ pound butter
2 cups sugar
4 eggs, beaten
¾ cup cocoa

1¼ cups flour
2 cups pecans
1 teaspoon vanilla
Salt

### Icing

2 cups sugar
½ cup milk

½ cup cocoa
¼ pound butter

Cream butter and sugar. Add eggs and beat. Mix flour, cocoa and a dash of salt and add to creamed mixture. Add vanilla and nuts. Place in 9x13 or 8x16 pan. Bake 350 degrees for 30 to 40 minutes. Turn entire pan out onto sheet of aluminum foil and allow to cool before icing. Do not cut before icing.

166

Icing: Mix above ingredients in skillet. Cook over low heat until it comes to a boil. Let boil hard for one minute. Pour into small mixing bowl and let cool 5 minutes. Beat and spread on brownies.

*Martha Barron Barnes*

## BUTTER COOKIES
*Easy - buttery good*

1 pound butter
1 cup sugar
2 eggs

4 cups flour (all purpose pre-sifted)

Cream butter and sugar well by hand. Add eggs and continue creaming until very fluffy. Add flour gradually. (May need a little more flour to reach non-sticky stage.) Use cookie press for desired shapes. Bake on ungreased cookie sheet at 350 degrees until slightly brown. Remove to brown paper to crisp. Makes 80 - 100 cookies.

*Mrs. Louis Sgrosso (Marie)*

## CARAMEL CRUNCHIES

1 box dark brown sugar
1 stick butter
4 eggs
1½ cups flour

1/8 teaspoon salt
1 teaspoon baking powder
1 teaspoon vanilla
1 cup finely chopped nuts

Melt butter and sugar together. Add beaten eggs. Add flour sifted with salt and baking powder. Fold in nuts. Pour into 9x13 pan. Bake in preheated oven 300 degrees for 30 minutes. Makes 24 squares.

*Mrs. M. E. Kilpatrick (Mary Hurt)*

## CHEESECAKE SQUARES
*A fun way to serve cheesecake for parties - delicious too!*

1 1/3 cups graham cracker crumbs
1/3 cup brown sugar
½ cup melted butter
4 (3 ounce) packages cream cheese
2 eggs

½ teaspoon vanilla
½ cup sugar
1 cup sour cream
2 tablespoons confectioners sugar

For crust: mix first three ingredients, spread evenly in 8 inch square pan and bake 350 degrees for 8 minutes.

(continued)

For filling: beat next four ingredients until smooth, pour into crust and bake at 350 degrees for 35 minutes.

For topping: blend and spread last two ingredients on top of filling. Bake 5 minutes, cool, refrigerate, then cut into squares and serve.

*Mrs. Myles J. Gould (Lynn)*
*Mrs. John Dearing (Gail)*

## CHOCOLATE FILLED COOKIES

1 cup butter
½ cup sugar
1 teaspoon vanilla
2 cups sifted all purpose flour

1 package Hershey chocolate kisses
Confectioners sugar

Beat butter, sugar and vanilla until light and fluffy. Add flour, mixing well. Chill dough. Shape dough around kisses, using about 1 tablespoon dough for each one. Bake on ungreased cookie sheet at 375 degrees for 12 minutes or until "set", but not brown. Cool slightly. Roll in confectioners sugar.

*Kathy Van Natter Young*

## CHRISTMAS COOKIES

½ pound chopped candied cherries
½ pound chopped candied pineapple
¼ box golden raisins
1½ pounds chopped pecans
1 cup brown sugar
½ pound butter
4 eggs, slightly beaten

3 teaspoons soda dissolved in 4 ounces whiskey
3 cups flour
3 tablespoons milk
1 teaspoon cloves
1 teaspoon allspice
1 teaspoon cinnamon

Mix fruit, raisins and nuts, set aside. Cream butter and sugar, add beaten eggs. Add spices to flour, then add dry mixture (flour) to egg mixture alternately with whiskey and soda. Add milk last. Batter will seem stringy or rubbery due to whiskey and eggs. Pour over fruit and blend. Drop spoonfuls on greased cookie sheet and bake at 350 degrees for about 10 minutes. Cover unused batter with damp towel between bakings. Makes about 12 dozen and can be frozen.

*Mrs. Penn W. Rooker (Dottie)*

## CHRISTMAS FRUIT BARS

*Better than fruitcake*

2 cups chopped pecans
½ pound chopped, candied cherries

½ pound chopped candied pineapple (green if possible)
1 small box pitted dates, chopped

Mixture:
½ box brown sugar
1 stick butter
2 eggs

Drop of vanilla
1 cup plain flour

Line square pan with brown paper and grease well. Spread pecans over greased paper. Spread mixture over nuts. Sprinkle fruit over top. Bake 300 degrees for one hour. When barely warm, cut into squares.

*Mrs. Thomas J. Warner*

## CHRISTMAS HOLLY COOKIES

*A no-bake favorite*

1 stick margarine
30 large marshmallows
2 teaspoons vanilla
1½ teaspoons green food coloring

4 cups corn flakes
Pinch of salt
Red hot cinnamons

Melt butter and marshmallows. Add vanilla and green coloring. Stir and add corn flakes. Continue stirring until corn flakes are well coated. Drop by teaspoon on waxed paper. Put three red hots (cinnamons) to resemble sprig of holly. Let dry couple of days. Makes about 25.

*Mrs. Oliver P. Ackerman, Jr.*

## CREAM CHEESE COOKIES

6 ounces cream cheese
1 cup butter
1 cup sugar

2 cups flour
1 teaspoon salt
Tart jelly or jam

Use mixer to blend cream cheese and butter. Add sugar and cream thoroughly. Slowly add flour and salt and blend. Drop by teaspoonsful on ungreased cookie sheet. Make a slight hollow and add small amount of jelly. Bake at 350 degrees for 10-15 minutes until slightly brown on edges. Vary with peanut butter, nuts, or fruit.

*Sandra Sherard Bethea*

## CRISP CHOCO–CHIP COOKIES

*A family favorite for years*

| | |
|---|---|
| 1 cup margarine | ½ teaspoon salt |
| 1 cup white sugar | 1 cup Rice Krispies |
| 1 cup dark brown sugar | 1 cup regular rolled oats |
| 2 eggs | 1 teaspoon vanilla |
| 2 cups sifted flour | 1 (6 ounce) package chocolate |
| 1 teaspoon soda | chips |
| ½ teaspoon baking powder | ½ cup chopped pecans |

Blend shortening and sugars in large mixing bowl. Add eggs and beat until fluffy. Sift together flour, soda, salt and baking powder. Add to other ingredients and blend. The mixture will be stiff to mix. By hand, stir in Rice Krispies, rolled oats, vanilla, chocolate chips and pecans. Drop by spoon on cookie sheet. Bake at 375 degrees for 12 to 15 minutes until lightly brown. Remove from cookie sheet immediately before cookie becomes crisp. Raisins may be substituted for chocolate chips.

*Mrs. Bud Erickson*

## DIMPLE COOKIE

*Great for a party*

| | |
|---|---|
| ¾ pound butter | 4 cups sifted flour |
| 1 cup sugar | 1 teaspoon vanilla |
| 2 egg yolks | Red currant jelly |
| Pinch salt | |

Cream butter and sugar; add egg yolks and salt. Beat till fluffy, then add sifted flour and vanilla. Shape in tiny balls. Place on cookie sheet and put a dimple in each ball by pressing a floured thimble in center of ball. Fill each with currant jelly. Bake at 300 degrees until brown.

*Mrs. William A. Nix, III (Grace Tate)*

## FRUITCAKE MINIATURES

| | |
|---|---|
| 1 cup coconut | 4 eggs |
| 1 pound chopped candied cherries | 3 cups plain flour |
| 1 pound chopped candied pineapple | 1 tablespoon cinnamon |
| 1 pound chopped candied dates | 1 tablespoon nutmeg |
| ½ pound chopped white raisins | 4-5 ounces orange juice |
| 6 cups chopped pecans | 3 teaspoons soda |
| 1 stick margarine | 3 teaspoons milk |
| 1 cup brown sugar | |

Chop fruit and nuts and mix with 1 cup of flour. Cream margarine and sugar. Add beaten egg yolks. Sift 2 cups of flour with the spices. Combine milk, soda and orange juice in a large cup as it will foam. Add alternately flour mixture and juice mixture to creamed butter and sugar. Add fruit and nuts. Fold in beaten egg whites. Bake in very small cupcake papers. Bake 300 degrees for 20 minutes. Garnish with ½ candied cherry.

Additional information: Up to 1 pound more fruit may be added; cookies may be made by dropping by spoon onto greased cookie sheet; sprinkle with bourbon and seal the mini-cakes tightly for several weeks before serving.

*Mrs. Richard Perry (Lucy)*

## GINGER COOKIES

*A grandmother's favorite*
*All little boys (especially husbands) really like these*

| | |
|---|---|
| 1  cup brown sugar | 5½ cups sifted flour |
| 1  cup granulated sugar | 2  teaspoons ginger |
| 1  cup butter or margarine | 1  teaspoon soda |
| 2  eggs | ½ teaspoon salt |
| ½ cup molasses | |

Cream sugars and butter. Add eggs and molasses, beat. Sift and add flour, ginger, soda, and salt. Chill. Roll into marble size pieces and bake 350 degrees for 12 minutes. Makes 5 dozen.

Dough also may be used for gingerbread boys. Makes 30.

*Mrs. T. G. Debreceni (Lois)*

## GINGERBREAD BOYS

| | |
|---|---|
| 1  cup butter | 3¼ cups flour |
| 1½ cups sugar | 2  teaspoons soda |
| 1  egg | 2  teaspoons cinnamon |
| 2  tablespoons dark corn syrup | 1  teaspoon ginger |
| 1  tablespoon water | |

Cream butter and sugar. Add egg and beat until fluffy. Add corn syrup and water, mix well. Sift dry ingredients and stir into creamed mixture and chill. On floured surface, roll out dough 1/8 inch thick and cut with cookie cutter. Place on ungreased cookie sheet and bake at 375 degrees for 8 to 10 minutes.

*Mrs. William N. Mitchell (Margaret)*

## LACE COOKIES

| | |
|---|---|
| 1 stick butter | 2 tablespoons flour |
| 1 cup brown sugar | 1 teaspoon vanilla |
| 1 cup oatmeal | Pinch of salt |

Mix all ingredients and chill. Roll into little balls about the size of a marble. Place on cookie sheet very far apart as they melt down as they cook. Bake at 375 degrees for about 7 minutes. Makes about 4 dozen.

*Mrs. Charles Bartenfeld (Deedy)*

## LEMON SQUARES

*Absolutely luscious*

| | |
|---|---|
| 1 cup all purpose flour | ½ teaspoon baking powder |
| ½ cup butter or margarine | ½ teaspoon salt |
| ¼ cup confectioners sugar | 2 or 3 tablespoons lemon juice |
| 2 eggs | Confectioners sugar |
| 1 cup granulated sugar | |

Heat oven to 350 degrees. Mix thoroughly, flour, butter and confectioners sugar. Press into square pan 8x8x2 building up ½ inch edge. Bake 20 minutes.

Beat remaining ingredients until light and fluffy. Pour over hot crust. Bake about 25 minutes longer or just until no imprint remains when lightly touched in center. Cool, sprinkle with confectioners sugar, cut into squares, Makes 2 dozen.

Note: For dessert, try cutting squares longer and put a scoop of lemon custard ice cream on top.

*Mrs. Edward R. Moore (Helen)*
*Mrs. C. J. Brown (Marian)*
*Mrs. E. Sam Jones, Jr. (Durand)*
*Mrs. Walter Butler (Mary Helen)*

## LEMON CRUMB SQUARES

| | |
|---|---|
| 1 (15 ounce) can condensed milk | ½ teaspoon salt |
| ½ cup lemon juice | 2/3 cup butter |
| 1 teaspoon grated lemon rind | 1 cup dark brown sugar |
| 1½ cups sifted flour | 1 cup uncooked oatmeal |
| 1 teaspoon baking powder | |

Blend milk, juice and lemon rind. Set aside. Sift flour, baking powder and salt together. Cream shortening, blend in sugar. Add oatmeal, flour mixture and mix until crumbly. Spread half of this mixture in 8x12x2 greased baking pan. Pat mixture down, then add condensed milk mixture on top and cover with remaining crumb mix. Bake 350 degrees about 25 minutes or until brown. Cool in pan 15 minutes before cutting into squares. Leave in pan until cool.

*Mrs. William Luesing (Carolyn)*
*Mrs. Ed Forio, Jr. (Phoebe)*

## MELTAWAY COOKIES

Crust:

| | |
|---|---|
| ¼ pound butter | 1 egg, beaten |
| 1 ounce unsweetened chocolate | 1 cup coconut |
| ¼ cup sugar | ½ cup chopped nuts |
| 1 teaspoon vanilla | 2 cups graham cracker crumbs |

Melt butter and chocolate. Blend in sugar, vanilla, eggs, coconut, graham cracker crumbs and nuts. Press into 9x13 inch pan. Refrigerate.

Filling:

| | |
|---|---|
| 4 tablespoons butter | 1 teaspoon vanilla |
| 1 tablespoon milk | 4 ounces unsweetened chocolate |
| 2 cups xxxx sugar | |

Cream butter. Slowly add xxxx sugar, milk and vanilla. Spread over crumb mixture. Chill. Melt chocolate. Pour over top of cookies. Refrigerate. Cut into squares before top gets too hard.

*Mrs. Fred Hayes (Anne)*

## MINCEMEAT COOKIES

| | |
|---|---|
| 3¼ cups sifted flour | 1½ cups sugar |
| ½ teaspoon salt | 3 eggs, well beaten |
| 1 teaspoon soda | 1 (9 ounce) package mince- |
| 1 cup shortening | meat (condensed) |

Sift together flour, salt and soda. Cream sugar and shortening until fluffy. Add eggs and beat until smooth. Add mincemeat broken into small pieces. Add flour and mix well. Drop by teaspoon 2 inches apart on greased cookie sheet. Bake about 12 minutes at 400 degrees. Makes 48 (3 inch) cookies.

*Mrs. Allan Strand (Anne)*

## PARTY COOKIES
*Quick and easy*

1¼ sticks butter
1 cup sugar
1 cup chopped dates

½ cup chopped pecans
3 cups Rice Krispies
Powdered sugar

Melt butter in electric frying pan or heavy duty pan. Add sugar and dates. Cook over low heat until sticky. Add nuts and Rice Krispies, mixing well. Roll into small balls and dust with powdered sugar.

*Mrs. Herbert Sodel (Jody)*

## PEANUT BUTTER CHEWS

1 cup peanut butter
1 cup corn syrup
1¼ cups nonfat dry milk

1¼ cup confectioners sugar
Coconut to roll balls in

In separate bowl, mix together peanut butter and corn syrup until well blended. Mix together dry milk and confectioners sugar. Combine mixtures and knead until evenly mixed. Pinch off enough to make a 1 inch ball. Roll in coconut. Chill before serving. Makes approximately 4 dozen.

*Mrs. David Vaughan (Vi)*

## PECAN BALL COOKIES

1 stick butter
2 tablespoons sugar
1 cup sifted flour
1 teaspoon vanilla

Pinch of salt
Confectioners sugar
1 cup finely chopped pecans

Cream butter, sugar; then blend in flour, vanilla and salt. Add pecans and work mixture with hands until it holds together well. Roll into one inch balls. Bake 350 degrees on a cookie sheet for 20 minutes. Dust with confectioners sugar while warm. Makes 20 cookies.

*Mrs. Edward C. Loughlin, Jr. (Bet)*

## HAWAII'S PINEAPPLE BARS

1 cup sugar
1¼ cups melted butter
2 eggs
1 large can crushed pineapple, drained
¾ cup chopped nuts

¾ cup flour
¼ teaspoon salt
¼ teaspoon soda
Powdered sugar

Mix sugar and butter. Add eggs and mix. Add flour, salt, soda; blend well. Mix in pineapple and nuts. Pour into greased 9x9 pan. Bake 350 degrees, 35 to 45 minutes. Remove from pan and cool. Cut into bars and sprinkle with sifted powdered sugar. Makes 12 bars.

*Mrs. Philip B. Bird (Jane Murray)*

## RASPBERRY TORTE
*Unusual and delicious*

2½ cups flour
2 sticks butter
2 tablespoons sugar
2 tablespoons sour cream
3 eggs separated (save whites)

1 jar raspberry preserves
 (1½ cups)
1½ cups chopped pecans
1 cup sugar

Mix the first five ingredients thoroughly by hand into one large ball of pastry. Then hand press onto a 15½x10½ pan. Bring up all the sides a little. Spread raspberry preserves on top of flattened pastry. Then sprinkle pecans on top of preserves. Beat egg whites, adding sugar until thick and foamy. Spread over preserves and nuts. Bake 320 degrees on lowest rack for 25 to 30 minutes or until meringue is lightly browned. Remove from oven and cut into small squares while still warm.

*Mrs. Donald Brown (Joan)*

## SUGAR COOKIES
*Perfect dough for cutting and decorating*

1 cup sugar
1 stick butter
1 egg
1 teaspoon vanilla

2 cups flour
½ teaspoon salt
1 teaspoon baking powder

Cream sugar and butter, Add egg and vanilla. Sift flour, salt, baking powder, and add. Chill 1 hour. (Hint: Leave dough not being used in refrigerator. It is easier to cut when cold.) Bake on cookie sheet at 375 degrees for 8 minutes. Makes 2 dozen.

*Mrs. Richard A. Allison (Judy)*

175

## SWEETMEATS

Base:
| | |
|---|---|
| 1 cup butter | 2 cups dark brown sugar |
| 2 cups flour | |

Topping:
| | |
|---|---|
| 1 cup dark brown sugar | 1 cup grated coconut |
| 4 beaten eggs | 2 cups chopped pecans |
| 2 tablespoons flour | Granulated sugar |

Base: Cream butter, flour and sugar. Spread with fingers on 15x10 baking sheet. Bake 375 degrees for about 15 minutes. Be careful it does not burn.

Topping: Mix brown sugar, eggs, flour, coconut and pecans. Pour over the baked layer base and bake for 20 minutes more. Remove from oven and sprinkle immediately with sugar. Cut while still warm. Store in air tight tin. Serves 10-12.

*Patti Marett Nunnally*


## ENGLISH TOFFEE SQUARES

| | |
|---|---|
| 1½ cups vanilla wafer crumbs | 2 sticks butter |
| 1½ cups chopped nuts | 3 squares bitter chocolate |
| 6 eggs, separated | 1 teaspoon vanilla |
| 2 cups confectioners sugar | |

Mix vanilla wafer crumbs and chopped nuts. Put 2 cups of this mixture in a buttered 12x7 pan. Set aside. Beat egg whites and set aside. Cream butter, sugar, then add beaten egg yolks. Beat till fluffy, then add melted chocolate and vanilla. Fold in beaten egg whites. Pour over wafer mixture and sprinkle remaining crumb mixture on top. Put in refrigerator overnight. Serve with whipped cream or Cool Whip. Serves 12.

*Mrs. William Horton (Carol Ann)*


## LOVING TOUCHES . . .

To make cookie tree ornaments; before baking, make a hole near the edge and insert a dry bean. When cookies cool, remove bean carefully. String on bright ribbons.

# Cakes

## BROWNIE CAKE

2 cups sugar
2 sticks butter
4 eggs
1½ cups flour
2 tablespoons cocoa
1 cup chopped nuts
1 teaspoon vanilla
Dash of salt

Icing:
1 package miniature marshmallows
1 stick butter
1 (6 ounce) package semi-sweet
   chocolate bits
1 pound confectioners sugar
1 teaspoon vanilla
Milk

Cream sugar and butter. Add eggs one at a time and mix well. Mix flour and cocoa. Mix all together with other ingredients. Bake in a 9x13 pyrex dish at 325 degrees for 45 minutes. Remove from oven and cover with layer of marshmallows. Return to oven just to melt marshmallows. Melt butter and chocolate bits over low heat. Add confectioners sugar. Thin with vanilla and a little milk until you can spread it on top of cake in pan. Serves 24.

*Mrs. Robert Dunlap (Mary Jane)*

## BUCHE de NOEL
### Christmas Log
*Troublesome-but heavenly*

5 eggs yolks
5 egg whites
1½ teaspoons lemon juice
¾ cup sugar
¾ teaspoon vanilla
¾ cup cake flour, sifted

Pinch of salt
Confectioners sugar
Coffee butter cream
Chocolate butter cream
Pistachio nuts, chopped

Beat egg yolks ten minutes. Beat egg whites until frothy, add lemon juice and beat till they hold soft shape. Add sugar, one tablespoon at a time, vanilla, and beat until stiff peaks form. Fold in egg yolks lightly. Sift flour and salt over egg mixture and fold it in until smooth. Pour into oiled jelly roll pan (10x15, lined with oiled wax paper) and bake at 400 degrees for 15 minutes. Sift confectioners sugar sparingly over top of cake and turn out on a board covered with two long overlapping sheets of waxed paper. Remove paper in strips from bottom of cake. Roll up cake lengthwise in the sheets of paper and let it cool. When cool, unroll, spread evenly with coffee butter cream and roll up again cutting paper away. Slide onto serving board and cover thickly with chocolate butter cream. Cover ends with coffee butter cream and swirl melted chocolate on ends. Sprinkle edges with finely chopped pistachio nuts. Serves 16.

### Chocolate Butter Cream

9 tablespoons sugar
1/3 cup water
¼ teaspoon cream of tartar
5 eggs yolks, beaten

2 sticks butter, slightly softened
3 ounces dark, sweet chocolate, melted
Rum to taste

Combine sugar, water and cream of tartar. Boil until candy thermometer registers 238 degrees F. Remove from heat. Gradually beat in egg yolks and continue beating until thick and cool. Beating still, add butter and chocolate. Flavor with rum. (For Coffee Butter Cream, substitute very strong coffee for water, omit chocolate, and flavor with 1 tablespoon rum).

*Mrs. Hall Ware (Mary)*

### CARROT CAKE

*This cake is absolutely foolproof and delicious!*

1½ cups corn oil
2 cups sugar
3 eggs
2 cups flour
2 teaspoons cinnamon
2 teaspoons soda

2 teaspoons vanilla
1 teaspoon salt
2 cups shredded carrots
1 cup chopped nuts
½ cup crushed pineapple

Combine all ingredients in large bowl and mix until well blended. Pour batter into 9x13 pan. Bake at 350 degrees for 1 hour. Cool. Ice with cream cheese icing in the pan.

### Icing

3 ounces cream cheese
1¼ cups powdered sugar
1 stick butter

1/8 cup crushed pineapple
¼ cup chopped walnuts

Cream butter, cheese, and sugar until slightly fluffy. Mix in pineapple and nuts. Spread on cake.

*Julie Briggs*
*Leslie Morgan*

179

## CHOCOLATE CHIP CAKE

½ pint sour cream
½ cup Crisco oil
1 small package chocolate instant pudding

1 small package chocolate chips
1 yellow cake mix
4 eggs
1 cup chopped nuts

Mix all ingredients (except nuts and chocolate chips) on high speed of mixer for five minutes and low speed for five minutes. Pour half of batter into well greased pan, then sprinkle on half of chips and nuts. Repeat and bake at 325 degrees for 55 to 60 minutes.

*Mrs. David L. Thomas (Betty)*

## CHOCOLATE SHEET CAKE

2 cups flour (sift before measuring)
2 cups sugar
½ teaspoon salt
1 cup water
½ cup shortening
1 stick margarine
3 tablespoons cocoa
2 eggs
½ cup buttermilk

1 teaspoon soda
1 teaspoon vanilla
Icing:
1 stick margarine
2 tablespoons cocoa
1 box confectioners sugar
1 cup chopped pecans
6 tablespoons milk
1 teaspoon vanilla

Sift sugar, flour and salt into a bowl. Mix water, shortening, margarine and cocoa in a saucepan and bring to a boil. Pour over dry ingredients, stir well, and add the eggs, buttermilk, soda and vanilla. Pour onto a greased cookie sheet (11x16) and bake about twenty minutes at 350 degrees. Icing: Melt, but do not boil the margarine, cocoa, and milk. Add the confectioners sugar, pecans and vanilla. Spread onto cake when it has cooled. Good to take as is on cookie sheet to picnics. Serves 24.

*Mrs. Robert F. Dennis (Peggy)*
*Mrs. Earle Duffey (Jacqueline)*

## DEVILS FOOD CAKE

¼ cup butter
2½ squares chocolate
1 cup sugar
1 egg

1½ cups cake flour
1 teaspoon soda
1 cup sour milk
1 teaspoon vanilla

Melt together butter and chocolate. Add sugar and mix well. Add one egg and mix well. Sift together flour and soda. Add alternately with sour milk. Mix in vanilla. Pour into two 8½ inch round pans which have been greased and floured. Bake at 350 degrees.

### Chocolate Icing

| | |
|---|---|
| 2½ squares chocolate | Pinch cream of tartar |
| 1/3 cup cold water | ¼ stick butter |
| 2 cups sugar | 1 teaspoon vanilla |
| ½ cup rich milk | |

Cut up chocolate into heavy pan. Add water and cook over low heat until consistency of heavy cream, stirring constantly. Add sugar, milk, cream of tartar and stir well until almost dissolved. Cook over medium heat to firm softball stage. Remove from heat and add butter and vanilla. Allow to cool. Beat until creamy, adding a few drops of hot cream, if needed.

*Mrs. Allan Strand, Sr. (Catharine)*

## CHOCOLATE CAKE WITH FUDGE ICING

*A fantastic cake that the men love!*

| | |
|---|---|
| 2 cups flour | 1 teaspoon vanilla |
| 2 cups sugar | ½ cup buttermilk |
| 2 sticks margarine | 1 cup Coca-Cola (8 ounces) |
| 2 eggs | 2 tablespoons cocoa (heaping) |
| 1 teaspoon baking soda | 2 cups miniature marshmallows |

### Fudge Icing

| | |
|---|---|
| 2 tablespoons cocoa (heaping) | 1 box confectioners sugar |
| 1 stick margarine | 1 cup chopped pecans |
| 2 ounces Coca-Cola | 1 teaspoon vanilla |

Put all dry ingredients into mixing bowl*. In saucepan, put margarine, cocoa, and Coca-Cola, and bring to a boil (watch carefully so it doesn't boil over). Pour over dry ingredients and mix thoroughly. Add eggs, vanilla, milk, marshmallows and mix. Pour into greased rectangular cake pan and bake at 350 degrees for 40 to 45 minutes (test with toothpick). When cake is done, prepare the icing as follows and ice the cake while still hot. Work fast since it hardens quickly. Bring Coca-Cola, cocoa, and margarine to a boil. Remove from heat. Add vanilla, sugar, and mix well. Pour over cake. If it hardens too quickly to spread, add few more drops of Coca-Cola. Can be made in square pans - then eat one and freeze the other.
*Can be mixed by hand - saves cleaning the mixer!

*Mrs. Donald Brown (Joan)*

181

## DATE–CHOCOLATE CAKE

1½ cups sifted flour
¾ teaspoon soda
½ teaspoon salt
1 package (8 ounce) dates, cut up
¾ cup brown sugar, packed
½ cup margarine
½ cup water

1 (6 ounce) package semi-sweet
  chocolate morsels
2 eggs, slightly beaten
½ cup orange juice
½ cup milk
1 cup chopped walnuts or pecans
  (walnuts add better flavor)

Sift together soda, salt and flour. Combine in saucepan dates, brown sugar, margarine and water. Cook, stirring constantly until dates soften. Stir in chocolate morsels and eggs. Add orange juice and milk to dry ingredients. Then add the date-chocolate mixture. Blend thoroughly. Bake in (13x9) greased and floured pan at 350 degrees for 30 minutes or until done. This cake is good iced with a white cream icing, but is also good plain cut into squares like brownies.

*Mrs. Kenneth P. Lynch, Jr. (Peggy)*

## PINEAPPLE CAKE

1 (No. 303) can crushed pineapple
1 butter pecan cake mix

1 stick margarine or butter
Whipped cream or ice cream

Grease square pan (9x9x2) with butter. Place crushed pineapple, juice and all, in bottom of pan. Sprinkle the dry cake mix in a layer over the pineapple. Melt the butter and pour over the cake mixture. Bake 45-50 minutes at 350 degrees. Cut into squares and serve warm with either whipped cream or vanilla ice cream. Serves 8. This dessert keeps people guessing what ingredients are used!

*Mrs. Gerrit C. Hagman (Ann)*

## CHEESE CAKE

3 (8 ounce) packages cream cheese,
  softened
1 cup sugar
4 egg whites
Dash of salt
1 teaspoon vanilla

Topping:
1 cup sour cream
3 tablespoons sugar
½ teaspoon vanilla

Beat together until stiff the four egg whites. In a separate bowl, with same beaters, cream together cream cheese, sugar and vanilla. Fold in egg whites and pour into a large buttered spring form pan which has been sprinkled with graham cracker crumbs. Cook 25 minutes at 350 degrees. Remove from oven and pour on the topping mixture and cook five minutes at 400 degrees. Remove and let cool. Refrigerate. Serves 8 or 10.

*Mrs. Thomas Bowers (Margaret)*
*Mrs. Robert C. Wade (Sue)*

## NEW YORK STYLE CHEESECAKE

*Very impressive looking!*

| | |
|---|---|
| 2 (8 ounce) packages cream cheese, softened | 3 tablespoons flour |
| | 1½ tablespoons lemon juice |
| 1 pound creamed cottage cheese | 1 teaspoon vanilla |
| 1½ cups sugar | 1 teaspoon grated lemon rind |
| 4 eggs, slightly beaten | ½ cup butter, melted |
| 3 tablespoons cornstarch | 1 pint sour cream |

Preheat oven to 325 degrees. Grease a 9 inch spring form pan. With electric mixer, beat the cream cheese with cottage cheese at high speed until well combined. Gradually beat in sugar, then eggs. At low speed, beat in cornstarch, flour, lemon juice, rind, and vanilla. Add melted butter and sour cream. Beat just until smooth. Pour into the greased pan and bake one hour and 10 minutes, or until firm around the edges. Turn off oven and let the pan stand in the oven for two hours. Then remove and let it cool completely. This takes at least two hours. Refrigerate the cake for three hours or until well chilled. To remove from pan, first run a spatula around side and then release clasp. Leave bottom of pan in place and put on serving plate. Can garnish with any fruit pie filling, cherry, blueberry or strawberry. Freezes well.

*Mrs. Donald Brown (Joan)*

## EASY COCONUT CAKE

*Almost as good as Mother's*

16 ounces sour cream
2 cups sugar

2 packages frozen coconut
1 yellow cake mix

The day before you bake the cake, mix together frosting ingredients and let stand in refrigerator overnight.
Bake cake mix. Slice the two layers in half making four thin layers. Frost. Keep refrigerated.

*Mrs. Oliver P. Ackerman, Jr.*

## DANISH TORTE

1 stick butter
1 cup chopped pecans or walnuts
1 cup flour
8 ounces cream cheese
1 cup confectioners sugar

1 pint Cool Whip
2 packages instant pudding
(any flavor)
3 cups milk

First layer:
Cream together butter, flour and nuts, press into bottom of 9x9 pan, bake 15 minutes at 350 degrees. Cool.
Second layer:
Cream together and add half of Cool Whip, cream cheese, and confectioners sugar. Put on top of cool crust.
Third layer:
Mix pudding with milk and beat until thick and put on top of second layer. Then top with rest of Cool Whip. Sprinkle with chopped nuts, coconut, or grated chocolate.
Refrigerate until ready to serve. Keep covered. Will keep several days.

*Mrs. John C. Portman, Jr. (Jan)*

## DUMP CAKE

1 can crushed pineapple (large size)
1 can cherry pie filling
1 box yellow cake mix

1½ sticks butter
½ cup pecans

Grease 2 inch deep casserole. Place all ingredients in order given. Bake in oven for one hour at 350 degrees.

*Mrs. Fritz Milner (Missy)*

184

## CRUNCH CAKE

*A family favorite*

1 cup Crisco
2 cups sugar
2 cups cake flour
6 large eggs

½ teaspoon salt
1 tablespoon lemon juice
1 small bottle almond extract

Pre-heat oven to 325 degrees. Mix all ingredients together and beat at medium speed for 10 minutes. Pour into greased and floured tube pan (not teflon) and bake one hour. Cool in pan for 10 minutes. Run knife around sides and center stem, invert and finish cooling. Freezes well.

*Mrs. William Harp (Charlotte)*

## FRUIT CAKE

2 cups sugar
½ pound butter or margarine
5 egg yolks
2½ cups, twice-sifted, plain flour
¼ cup wine
2 tablespoons rum
Juice of 2 large oranges
1 teaspoon grated orange rind
1½ cups mixed, candied, cut-up fruit, or cut-up:

¼ cup citron
¼ cup orange peel
½ cup cherries
½ cup pineapple
3 cups chopped pecans
½ cup dates
1 cup raisins
Blanched almonds, fruits, or pecans

Pre-heat oven to 250 degrees. Cream sugar and butter. Add egg yolks one at a time. Gradually add 1½ cups flour. Add other ingredients except fruit and nuts. Coat them with 1 cup flour and reserve for top. Pour batter into greased and floured 8½x3 inch aluminum loaf pan. Place cake on middle rack of oven and cover with brown paper. Put pan(s) of water above and below cake. Bake 3½ hours. Decorate with floured fruit and nuts while warm.

*Dr. David Stacy*

LOVING TOUCHES . . .

To make a large serving platter for cut-up cakes, cover heavy cardboard with aluminum wrap or brightly colored wrapping paper. Use saran wrap to hold the paper in place.

185

## ICE BOX CAKE

| | |
|---|---|
| 2 dozen unfilled lady fingers | 1½ cups sugar |
| 1 envelope Knox gelatin | 5 tablespoons lemon juice |
| ½ cup cold water | 1½ teaspoons grated lemon peel |
| 6 eggs | ¼ to ½ pint whipping cream |

Line the bottom and sides of a spring form pan with lady fingers. Cut off end of lady fingers (lining the sides) and use to wedge the bottom. Soak gelatin in cold water until soft. Beat 6 egg yolks, ¾ cup sugar, lemon juice, and lemon peel, and cook 15 minutes in double boiler, stirring occasionally. Remove from heat and stir in gelatin. Beat 6 egg whites, ¾ cup sugar until stiff. Fold in egg yolk and gelatin mixture. Pour into spring form pan and refrigerate for 6 hours. Whip cream and spread on top before serving. Remove sides of pan and serve, cutting between lady fingers on the side.

*Mrs. Thomas M. Barnett*

## BROWN SUGAR POUND CAKE

*Worth extra time and trouble!*

| | |
|---|---|
| 1 cup shortening | 3 cups cake flour |
| 1 stick margarine | 1 teaspoon baking powder |
| 1 pound soft light brown sugar | 1 teaspoon maple flavoring |
| 1 cup white sugar | 1 cup milk |
| 5 eggs | |

Cream shortening, margarine and sugars. Add eggs one at a time and beat well. Combine flour and baking powder and milk and flavoring. Add alternately to batter, beating very thoroughly. Bake at 325 degrees for 1½ hours in a large tube pan. (Bundt pan is not large enough.)

*Mrs. Robert Dunlap (Mary Jane)*

## CHOCOLATE POUND CAKE

| | |
|---|---|
| 1 cup butter | ½ cup cocoa |
| ½ cup margarine | ½ teaspoon baking powder |
| 3 cups sugar | ¼ teaspoon salt |
| 6 eggs | 1¼ cups milk |
| 3 cups cake flour | 2 teaspoons vanilla |

186

Cream butter and margarine; add sugar and cream well. Blend in eggs, one at a time. Sift flour, cocoa, salt and baking powder together. Alternate dry ingredients with milk to creamed mixture. Blend thoroughly. Add vanilla. Pour into tube or bundt pan and bake at 325 degrees for 1 hour and 20 minutes. Do not touch for one hour. Use your favorite chocolate frosting or sprinkle with confectioners sugar. It tastes great without any frosting. Serves 16-20. Freezes very well.

*Mrs. Bud Gould (Nancy)*

## CHOCOLATE POUND CAKE

½ pound butter  
2 cups sugar  
4 eggs  
1 (16 ounce) can Hershey's chocolate syrup  
2½ cups cake flour  

¼ teaspoon salt  
1 teaspoon vanilla  
1 cup buttermilk  
½ teaspoon soda  
1 (8 ounce) Hershey chocolate bar  

Cream butter and sugar. Add eggs one at a time. Add can of chocolate syrup. Add flour and buttermilk (soda added to buttermilk) alternately. Last add melted Hershey bar (melted with a little milk). Bake in preheated 325 degree oven for one hour, 30 minutes in tube pan.

*Mrs. Robert Richardson (Mary Anne)*
*Anne Wattles Constantine*

## COCONUT POUND CAKE

1½ cups Crisco  
2½ cups sugar  
5 eggs  
1 cup milk  
3 cups plain flour  
1 tablespoon baking powder  
¾ teaspoon salt  

1 box Angelflake coconut  
2 tablespoons coconut flavoring  
Sauce:  
1 cup sugar  
½ cup water  
2 tablespoons Karo syrup  
1 teaspoon coconut flavoring  

Cream shortening and sugar 10 minutes on high speed. Add eggs one at a time. Sift flour, salt, and baking powder. Add milk alternately with flour. Fold in coconut. Lemon and vanilla flavoring may be added. Bake at 325 degrees about one hour and 15 to 20 minutes in tube pan.

*Mrs. W. Joseph Biggers (Eathil)*

## WHIPPING CREAM POUND CAKE

½ pound butter
3 cups sugar
6 eggs
3 cups flour (sifted 3 times)
½ pint whipping cream

2 teaspoons vanilla (or 1 teaspoon vanilla and 1 teaspoon lemon, or 1 teaspoon butter flavoring)

Cream butter and sugar. Add eggs one at a time and beat. Add flour alternately with cream, not whipped. Blend until very smooth and add vanilla. Pour in greased and floured bundt pan. Place in cold oven. Bake at 325 degrees for one hour, 30 minutes. Serves 20 to 25. Freezes well.

*Mrs. Oliver P. Ackerman, Jr.*
*Mrs. John T. Glover (Sandra)*
*Mrs. Wood W. Lavell (Carolyn)*

## APRICOT POUND CAKE

*Brings raves from everyone!*

1 package lemon cake mix
¾ cup apricot nectar
¾ cup vegetable shortening
4 eggs

Sauce:
Juice from 2 or 3 lemons combined with 1 cup confectioners sugar

Mix all ingredients together. Then mix four minutes at medium speed with electric mixer. Bake at 350 degrees in greased tube pan for one hour. While cake is still hot (just out of oven, pour half of sauce on the top and let it soak in. Turn the cake upside down on a plate and pour the remaining sauce on the bottom half of cake. After it has soaked in, flip the cake right side up on another plate.

*Mrs. Gene Presley (Dianne)*

## SOUR CREAM POUND CAKE

1 cup butter
3 cups sugar
1 teaspoon vanilla
½ teaspoon salt

6 eggs, separated
¼ teaspoon baking soda
3 cups flour
½ pint sour cream

Cream butter and sugar thoroughly. Add vanilla and salt. Blend in egg yolks, one at a time beating well after each addition. Add sifted dry ingredients alternately with sour cream. Fold in beaten egg whites. Bake at 350 degrees for 1¼ hours in 10 inch greased tube pan. Cool in pan for 30 minutes before taking out of pan. (Do not invert pan.) Can be frosted.

*Mrs. Benjamin T. Selman, Jr. (Mary Jean)*

## SWEET POTATO CAKE

1½ cups cooking oil
2 cups sugar
3 eggs
3 cups self-rising flour
1 teaspoon cinnamon (scant)
1 teaspoon nutmeg (scant)

1 cup chopped nuts
1 small can crushed pineapple
  and juice
3 teaspoons vanilla
2 cups raw sweet potatoes,
  finely grated

### Icing

2½ sticks butter
8 egg yolks
2½ cups evaporated milk

2½ cups sugar
2 teaspoons vanilla
2½ cups coconut

Mix oil and sugar, add eggs and mix well. Add flour, cinnamon, nutmeg, nuts, pineapple, vanilla, and grated sweet potatoes. Mix well. Bake in six 9 inch pans for about 30 minutes at 350 degrees.

For icing: Place egg yolks, milk, butter, and sugar in double boiler and cook until thick (about 15 minutes). Then add vanilla and coconut. Ice cake when cool.

*Mrs. Richard Dukes*

## LOVING TOUCHES . . .

To cut: Insert the point of a serrated or a long thin knife into the cake, keeping the point down and handle up. Pull the knife toward you. If the frosting sticks, dip the knife into hot water or wipe with a damp paper towel after cutting each piece.
An 8 inch layer cake yields 10 to 14 servings.
A 9 inch layer cake yields 12 to 16 servings.
A 13x9 inch cake yields 15 to 18 servings.

## POPPY SEED CAKE

1 yellow butter cake mix
4 eggs
½ cup salad oil
1 cup water

1 large package instant
  vanilla pudding
¼ cup poppy seed
Confectioners sugar

Pre-heat oven to 375 degrees. Beat all ingredients together for ten minutes in electric mixer. Pour batter into generously greased and floured 10 inch tube pan. Bake for fifty-five minutes at 375 degrees. Cake will rise very high but will settle when cool. Sprinkle with confectioners sugar when cool.

*Mrs. M. R. Benson (Mildred)*

## PISTACHIO BUNDT CAKE

1 package yellow or white cake mix
4 eggs
1 cup orange juice

½ cup cooking oil
1 box instant pistachio pudding
¾ cup chocolate syrup

Place ingredients, except chocolate syrup, in a bowl and mix at low speed for one minute, and at a higher speed for about three minutes, or until well blended. Pour two-thirds of the batter into a well-greased and floured bundt pan. Add chocolate syrup to remaining batter. When well mixed, pour over the batter in the pan and run knife through batter to marble it. Bake one hour at 350 degrees. Allow to cool in pan fifteen minutes before turning out. Cool. Can freeze, but keeps nicely in tight container.

*Ruth Wright*

## STRAWBERRY ICE BOX CAKE

1 Sara Lee pound cake
2 cartons strawberries, sliced
  and sugared
3 egg yolks

1 cup confectioners sugar
Dash of vanilla
½ pint cream, whipped

Line an 8 inch square pyrex dish with slices of pound cake. Cover with layer of strawberries. Repeat. Then cover with the following custard: Beat egg yolks. Beat in confectioners sugar and dash of vanilla. Fold in whipped cream. Spread over cake and berries. Place in ice box several hours before serving. Serves 6-8.

*Mrs. John S. Stephens (Jane)*

## PRUNE CAKE

1 cup Wesson oil
1½ cups sugar
3 eggs
2 cups flour
1 teaspoon soda
1 teaspoon ground cloves

1 teaspoon vanilla
1 teaspoon salt
1 teaspoon cinnamon
1 cup prunes, cooked, drained
   and chopped
1 cup nut meats

### Sauce

1 1/3 cups sugar
2 tablespoons Karo syrup
1 teaspoon vanilla
1/3 cup butter
½ teaspoon soda

½ cup buttermilk (may make
   buttermilk by adding few
   drops cider vinegar into
   sweet milk and letting stand
   few minutes)

Mix oil, sugar, eggs. Add flour, salt, soda, cloves, cinnamon to mixture. Add prunes, vanilla, nuts. Bake in greased and floured tube pan at 350 degrees for 50-60 minutes. Make sauce by boiling ingredients two minutes. Pour over piping hot cake and let cool completely in pan. Only when cool, invert and place on plate. To prepare prunes use pitted prunes in water with fresh lemon slices. Simmer until tender and chop after draining. This cake freezes beautifully and makes a wonderful Christmas gift.

*Mrs. William A. McClain, III (Rose)*


## PLUM NUTTY CAKE

2 cups self-rising flour
2 cups sugar
3 eggs
1 cup Wesson oil
½ teaspoon cinnamon

½ teaspoon cloves
½ teaspoon nutmeg
2 jars junior baby food plums
½ cup chopped pecans or
   raisins

### Glaze

2 tablespoons lemon juice with confectioners sugar added to spreading consistency

Mix all above ingredients well and pour into greased and floured tube pan. Bake 1 hour, 15 minutes at 300 degrees. Let cool 15 minutes. Remove from pan. Top with glaze.

*Mrs. Clayton D. McLendon (Inez)*
*Mrs. William Whitaker (Susan)*

191

## SHERRY CAKE

*Popular, quick and easy*

| | |
|---|---|
| 1 package yellow cake mix | 4 eggs, unbeaten |
| ¾ cup sherry | 1 teaspoon nutmeg |
| ¾ cup Wesson oil (or Mazola) | 1 package vanilla instant pudding |

Beat together five to ten minutes. Pour into a greased and floured tube or bundt pan. Bake 45 minutes at 350 degrees. Cool and sift confectioners sugar over cake. Freezes well. Flavor improves with standing. Wrap in saran and heavy foil, and "age" for two days.

*Mrs. Richard C. Estes (Becky)*
*Mrs. Coley L. Evans, Jr. (Mary)*

## VIENNESE TORTE

| | |
|---|---|
| 6 ounces semi-sweet chocolate pieces | 4 egg yolks, slightly beaten |
| ½ cup margarine | 2 tablespoons confectioners sugar |
| ¼ cup water | 1 teaspoon vanilla |
| | 1 frozen loaf pound cake |

Heat together chocolate, butter and water over medium heat. Stir until blended. Cool slightly. Add yolks, sugar and vanilla; stir until smooth. Chill until mixture is of spreading consistency. (About 45 minutes in refrigerator). Slice cake horizontally into 6 layers. Spread about 2 large tablespoons chocolate between each layer; then frost top and sides. Chill at least 45 minutes or make it the day before serving. Serve thin slices, topped with Kahlua and-or whipping cream. (It's wonderful alone, too!)

*Mrs. Charles Bouis (Lois)*

## LOVING TOUCHES . . .

A teaspoon of coconut flavoring added to a pound cake recipe creates a special taste.

Make candle holders for cakes by using candy circle mints, candied cherries or other fruits, marshmallows or large, brightly colored gumdrops. Make a criss-cross cut in gumdrops in order to insert the candle easily.

# Pies

DAVID SAPP

## DEEP DISH APPLE PIE

| | |
|---|---|
| 1 stick butter | ¾ cup sugar |
| 1 can sliced apples | ½ cup milk |
| ¾ cup flour | ½ teaspoon baking powder |

Cut butter into pieces and put in bottom of 1½ quart casserole dish. Add can of apples. Mix remaining ingredients and pour over apples. Bake at 450 degrees for one hour. Serves 8.

*Mrs. William Voegeli (Dorothy Ann)*


## BANANA BAVARIAN PIE

| | |
|---|---|
| 4 cups miniature marshmallows | 1 cup heavy cream, whipped |
| 1 (1 ounce) square unsweetened chocolate | 2 bananas, sliced diagonally |
| | Lemon juice |
| ¼ cup milk | ¼ cup chopped pecans |
| 2 eggs, beaten | 1 (9 inch) pie crust |

Melt marshmallows with chocolate and milk in saucepan over low heat, stirring frequently. Stir small amount of hot mixture into eggs: return to hot mixture. Cook 2 minutes over low heat, stirring constantly. Chill until slightly thickened. Fold in whipped cream. Line bottom and sides of 9 inch pie plate with banana slices dipped in lemon juice. Pour filling into banana shell. Top with nuts. Freeze until firm. Place pie in refrigerator one hour before serving. Serves 8.

*Mrs. John W. Wright (Joanne)*


## BUTTERSCOTCH PIE

| | |
|---|---|
| 1 graham cracker pie crust | 4 teaspoons sugar |
| 2 eggs, separated | 1 cup dark brown sugar |
| ½ teaspoon salt | 1 teaspoon vanilla |
| 1½ cups milk | Meringue: |
| 4 tablespoons butter | Whites of 2 eggs |
| 4 tablespoons flour | ½ cup sugar |

Combine egg yolks, salt, milk, and butter in a saucepan. Add flour, white sugar and brown sugar. Stir constantly over low heat until thickened, about 15 minutes. When cold, add vanilla and pour into pie shell. Make meringue by beating egg whites and ½ cup sugar together until stiff. Spread over pie. Cook at 350 degrees for 15-20 minutes. Serves 8.

*Mrs. Bryan Marshall*

## CHERRY PIE

| | |
|---|---|
| 1 cup sugar | ¼ teaspoon almond extract |
| 3 tablespoons cornstarch | ½ teaspoon red food coloring |
| ¼ teaspoon salt | 2 tablespoons butter |
| ¾ cup cherry juice | 3 cups red tart cherries, drained |
| 1½ teaspoons fresh lemon juice | Top and bottom 9 inch pie crusts |

Mix in a saucepan ¼ cup sugar, cornstarch and salt. Add cherry juice and cook until thick. Add remaining sugar and cook until glossy. Remove from heat and stir in lemon juice, almond extract, food coloring and butter. Gently mix in cherries. Place in pie shell, top with crust. Bake at 450 degrees for 10-15 minutes. Lower heat to 350 degrees and bake for 30 minutes. Serves 8.

*Mrs. Jane Blume*

## BLACK FOREST CHERRY PIE

*Elegant four-layer pie. Easy to make.*

| | |
|---|---|
| 2/3 cup sugar | 1/3 cup Nestle's chocolate chips |
| 3 tablespoons cornstarch | 1 (8 inch) baked pastry shell |
| ¼ teaspoon salt | 1 (16 ounce) can pitted dark, sweet cherries, drained and halved |
| 2 cups milk | |
| 2 eggs, beaten slightly | |
| 2 tablespoons butter | |
| 1 teaspoon vanilla | ½ cup whipping cream |

Combine sugar, cornstarch and ¼ teaspoon salt. Gradually stir in milk. Cook and stir until bubbly; cook 2 minutes more. Stir small amount of hot mixture into eggs. Return to hot mixture and cook 2 minutes more. Remove from heat. Add butter and vanilla. Stir ½ cup egg mixture into melted chocolate. Spread into pastry shell. Cover vanilla mixture with waxed paper. Cool 30 minutes. Arrange cherries, cut side down, on chocolate, reserving 8 halves. Spread vanilla mixture over this. Chill. Whip cream. Spoon around edges. Add cherry halves to top of custard. Serves 6-8.

*Mrs. Russell Grove, Jr. (Charlotte)*

## FRENCH CHERRY PIE

*This is delicious and not too heavy - great in summer.*

1 (3 ounce) package cream cheese
¾ cup sugar
½ pint whipping cream

1 tablespoon sherry
1 can cherry pie filling
1 baked pie crust

Cream sugar with cream cheese. Add sherry and mix well. In another bowl whip cream until peaks form. Fold cream into sugar mixture and pour into pie crust. Spread cherries over top. Refrigerate. Serves 6.

*Mrs. John B. Mobley (Mary)*


## CHESS PIE

3 eggs
1½ cups sugar
½ cup butter

1 teaspoon vanilla
1½ teaspoons vinegar
1 unbaked pie shell

Melt butter on low heat. Add sugar. Add unbeaten eggs one at a time and cook until blended and creamy. Remove from heat and add vinegar and vanilla. Pour into pie shell. Bake at 325 degrees for 45 minutes. Serves 6.

*Mrs. William A. Nix, III (Grace Tate)*


## INDIVIDUAL CHESS PIES

12 Pet-Ritz frozen, uncooked
    tart shells
4 eggs, beaten lightly
2 cups sugar

¼ pound butter
¼ cup whipping cream, unbeaten
Pinch salt
Scant teaspoon vanilla

Mix pie ingredients. Pour into uncooked shells. Bake at 350 degrees for 30 minutes, then let stand another 30 minutes with oven off and oven door closed. Be sure filling is firm. Serves 12.

*Mrs. James H. Wildman (Pat)*


## LEMON CHESS PIE

4 eggs
1½ cups sugar
1 tablespoon flour
1 tablespoon cornmeal

¼ cup melted butter
¼ cup milk
¼ cup fresh lemon juice
1 (9 inch) pie shell, unbaked

Mix eggs and add sugar, flour and cornmeal. Add butter, milk and lemon juice. Pour into pie shell and bake at 325 degrees for 30 to 35 minutes. Note: To insure a firm middle, add a collar of foil around pastry edge and bake at 325 degrees for 45 to 50 minutes. Remove foil last 10 minutes.

*Mrs. Tom C. Campbell (Dot)*

## CHOCOLATE ANGEL PIE

Crust:

| | |
|---|---|
| 2 egg whites | 1/8 teaspoon cream of tartar |
| ½ cup chopped pecans | 1/8 teaspoon salt |
| ½ cup sugar | ½ teaspoon vanilla |

Filling:

| | |
|---|---|
| 1 ounce German chocolate | 1 teaspoon vanilla |
| 3 tablespoons hot water | ½ pint whipping cream |

Beat egg whites, adding cream of tartar and salt, until stiff. Add sugar gradually beating until very stiff. Fold in nuts and vanilla. Shape into greased 9 inch pie plate and bake at 275 degrees for 45 minutes. Turn off oven and leave crust inside for 15 minutes. Cool thoroughly. Whip cream until peaks form. Melt chocolate in double boiler. Add hot water and blend well. Cool. Add vanilla. Fold in whipped cream. Pour into cooled pie crust. Refrigerate. Serves 8. Make the day before serving.

*Mrs. John B. Mobley (Mary)*

## EASY CHOCOLATE NUT PIE

*Ellen, age 10, can make this pie*

| | |
|---|---|
| 2 eggs, slightly beaten | 1 cup chocolate chips |
| 1 cup sugar | 1 tablespoon vanilla |
| 1 stick melted butter | ½ cup flour |
| 1 cup chopped pecans | 1 unbaked pie shell |

Combine eggs, sugar, butter, vanilla, nuts and chocolate chips. Mix, add flour, and mix again. Bake in pie shell 30 minutes at 350 degrees. Serves 6-8.

*Mrs. William O'Neill (Nancy)*

197

## COCONUT PIE

*This recipe makes two pies and forms its own crust*

4 eggs
½ stick margarine
2 cups milk
½ cup self-rising flour

1¾ cups sugar
1 teaspoon vanilla
7 ounces coconut

Cream together sugar and margarine. Add flour. Mix well-beaten eggs with milk and vanilla. Combine two mixtures and add coconut. Pour into 2 well-greased 8 inch pie plates and bake at 350 degrees for 30 minutes. Serves 12.

*Mrs. Speer Mabry (Judy)*

## COFFEE SUNDAE PIE

*Children of all ages love this!*

18 Oreo cookies or chocolate
   refrigerator cookies
½ cup butter, melted
2 squares unsweetened chocolate
½ cup sugar

1 tablespoon butter
2/3 cup Pet milk
1 quart coffee ice cream
1 cup whipping cream, whipped
Crushed walnuts

Crush cookies, add ½ cup melted butter. Put in 9 inch pie pan and chill. Melt chocolate over warm water, add ½ cup sugar and 1 tablespoon butter. Slowly add Pet milk. Stir until thick. Cool. Spread coffee ice cream into crust and freeze. Pour cooled chocolate mixture over ice cream and freeze. Top with whipped cream and crushed walnuts and return to freezer until ready to serve.

*Mrs. Albert Redd (Sue)*

## RITZ CRACKER PIE

3 egg whites
1 cup nuts
1 cup sugar

1 cup crushed Ritz crackers
1 teaspoon vanilla
1 teaspoon baking powder

Beat 3 egg whites stiff and mix all together. Pour into greased pie plate. Bake 25 minutes at 325 degrees. Chill and add whipping cream to top. Serves 6-8.

*Mrs. Robert Evans (Shirley)*

## FROZEN CREME de MENTHE PIE (GRASSHOPPER PIE)

24 Oreo cookies, finely crushed
¼ cup butter, melted
¼ cup creme de menthe

1 (7 ounce) jar marshmallow creme
2 cups whipping cream

In medium bowl toss cookie crumbs with butter. Reserve ½ cup for top of pie. Press remaining in bottom of 9 inch spring form pan. Gradually add creme de menthe to marshmallow creme, mixing well until blended. Whip cream until it holds its shape. Fold into marshmallow mixture. Pour into crumb-lined pan. Sprinkle reserved crumbs over top of pie. Freeze until firm. Serves 6.

*Mrs. Bert Oastler (Belitje)*

## DATE NUT PIE

½ cup margarine or butter
1½ cups granulated sugar
3 eggs, separated
1¼ cups milk

1 cup chopped dates
1 cup chopped nuts
  (English walnuts or pecans)
2 (9 inch) pie crusts

Cream together butter and sugar. Add well-beaten egg yolks. Add milk, dates and nuts, and mix well. Add well-beaten egg whites and pour into the two pie crusts. Place pies on cookie sheet and bake at 375 degrees for 30 - 45 minutes, until centers are set.

*Mrs. Virgil Wolff (K. Eileen)*

## LOVING TOUCHES ...

Easy Ice Cream Pie: Fill a chocolate cookie crust with softened ice cream (any flavor). Freeze. Slice and serve with Johnson's Hot Fudge Sauce (sold in packages - ready to heat and serve).

## FRENCH SILK PIE

*Delicious and very rich*

½ cup butter
¾ cup sugar
1 square unsweetened chocolate

1 teaspoon vanilla
2 eggs
1 baked pie shell

Cream together butter and sugar. Add vanilla. Add melted, cooled chocolate. Add 1 egg and beat 10 to 15 minutes. Add other egg and beat 10 to 15 minutes. Pour into pie shell and chill. May be served with whipped cream topping and shaved chocolate as garnish.

*Mrs. J. Randall Akin (Vicki)*
*Mrs. Coy Lander (Pat)*
*Mrs. Timothy Trivers (Helen)*

## FRESH FRUIT PIE

4 egg whites
1 cup sugar
¼ teaspoon salt
½ teaspoon vanilla

½ teaspoon cream of tartar
1 pint fresh fruit
1 pint whipping cream
1 frozen pie crust, baked

Beat egg whites that have reached room temperature. When they are almost stiff, add sugar, salt and vanilla. Pour mixture into baked pie crust. Shape meringue up the sides of the crust to form a cavity in center. Bake at 275 degrees for 1 hour. Cool meringue. Fill cavity with fresh fruit, either peaches, strawberries or blueberries. Top with whipped cream. Refrigerate for 12 hours before serving.

*Mrs. John Dearing (Gail)*

## HEAVENLY PIE

1 pint whipping cream, whipped
1½ cups sugar
¼ teaspoon cream of tartar
4 eggs, separated

3 tablespoons lemon juice
1 tablespoon lemon rind
1 pie shell, unbaked

Sift together 1 cup sugar and cream of tartar. Beat egg whites, and add sifted ingredients to beaten egg whites. Shape mixture into pie shell. Bake at 275 degrees for 1 hour. Beat egg yolks slightly. Stir in ½ cup sugar, lemon juice and rind. Simmer until thick. Fold in ½ of the whipped cream. Fill shell, top with remaining whipped cream. Refrigerate 24 hours.

*Mrs. George Hopkins (Betty)*

## EASY LEMON CHIFFON PIE

1 (6 ounce) can lemonade (or limeade)  1  can Eagle Brand milk
1 (9 ounce) carton Cool Whip   1  graham cracker crust

Mix together ingredients and pour into shell. Refrigerate 10-15 minutes.
May also be served frozen. Serves 8.

*Mrs. William Voegeli (Dorothy Ann)*
*Mrs. John O. Mitchell (Beverly)*


## KEY LIME PIE

1  can condensed milk     4  egg whites, beaten
½ cup lime juice (small yellow   6  tablespoons sugar
   Key limes, if possible)    ½ teaspoon cream of tartar
4  egg yolks, beaten     1  (9 inch) pie shell, baked

Mix together first three ingredients. Beat one egg white until stiff. Fold
into lime mixture. To make meringue, beat remaining 3 egg whites and
gradually add sugar and cream of tartar. Pour lime mixture into pie shell
and top with meringue. Bake at 350 degrees for 8 to 10 minutes.

*Mrs. David Stacy (Beverly)*


## LIME PIE

2  small cans Pet milk     Juice of 1 lemon
¾ cup boiling water     1  box vanilla wafers
1  small package lime gelatin    ½ pint whipping cream
1  cup sugar

Refrigerate 2 cans Pet milk overnight. Dissolve lime gelatin in boiling
water. Add 1 cup sugar and lemon juice; cool. Whip milk, then combine
with above mixture. Line pie plate with vanilla wafers. Pour in lime
mixture. Whip the cream for topping. Refrigerate for several hours.

*Mrs. John Glover (Sandra)*


## LOVING TOUCHES . . .

Little feather brushes from gourmet cooking shops are great to brush
jelly on the bottom crust before filling, or mustard for a quiche or meat
and vegetable pie. (This holds filling away from crust and prevents
sogginess.)

## MYSTERY PIE

1 can Eagle Brand condensed milk
1 large can crushed pineapple, drained
1 large can bing cherries, drained
½ cup chopped pecans
1 tablespoon lemon juice
1 large container Cool Whip
2 graham cracker pie crusts

Mix first 6 ingredients together. Divide mixture and pour into the two pie crusts. Either freeze or refrigerate overnight. Serves 12.

*Mrs. Charles Beard (Mary)*

## PARADISE PIE

2 cups confectioners sugar
1 stick margarine, softened
1 large egg
¼ teaspoon salt
¼ teaspoon vanilla
1 cup whipping cream
1 cup crushed pineapple, drained
½ cup chopped nuts
2 (9 inch) pie crusts, baked

Cream together sugar and margarine. Add egg, salt and vanilla. Beat until fluffy. Spoon evenly into pie crusts; chill. Whip cream until stiff. Blend in pineapple and nuts. Spoon on top of filling. Chill thoroughly. Makes two pies.

*Mrs. Erik Collett (Pat)*

## COOKIE PEACH PIE

*So good, and easy too*

1 can sliced peaches
¾ cup sugar
1½ tablespoons flour
Dash salt
1/3 stick butter
1 package refrigerator sugar cookies (or butterscotch nut cookies)

Fill 9 inch shallow pan with peaches. Mix sugar, flour and salt. Sprinkle over peaches. Dot with butter. Top with refrigerator cookies, sliced ¼ inch thick. Bake at 350 degrees for 45 minutes. Top with whipped cream or ice cream. Serves 6-8.

*Mrs. Bengt Stromquist (Alison)*

## PEANUT BUTTER PIE

1 (3 ounce) package cream cheese
1 cup confectioners sugar
1/3 cup milk
1/3 cup peanut butter

1 teaspoon vanilla
1 (9 ounce) container Cool Whip
1 (9 inch) graham cracker crust

Cream together first 4 ingredients. Add vanilla and fold in Cool Whip. Pour into crust and freeze. Serves 6-8.

*Mrs. Richard Lea (Robin)*

## PECAN PIE

*Old South recipe*

1 cup white Karo syrup
½ cup sugar (white)
4 tablespoons melted butter
1 teaspoon vanilla

3 eggs
1 cup pecans
1 (9 inch) pie crust, unbaked

Combine syrup, sugar, butter and vanilla. Add eggs, one at a time, beating each with a fork when added. Sprinkle nuts over pie crust. Add egg mixture. Bake at 275 degrees for 1¼ to 1½ hours on low shelf. Serves 6-8.

*Mrs. James Magbee (Tia)*
*Mrs. William Drumheller (Carol)*

## STRAWBERRY PIE

1 pound frozen strawberries, thawed
½ pound marshmallows

¼ cup of juice from strawberries
½ pint whipping cream
1 baked and cooled pie crust

Drain berries and reserve juice. Combine ¼ cup juice and marshmallows in double boiler, and heat until marshmallows are melted. Cool and add berries. Whip cream and fold into mixture. Pour over baked pie crust and refrigerate to set. Serves 6-8.

*Mrs. Solon Patterson (Marianna)*

LOVING TOUCHES...

Freezing a pie crust before adding fillings ensures crispness every time. (especially for quiche)

## STRAWBERRY PIE

1 quart strawberries
1 cup sugar
3 tablespoons cornstarch
1 (3 ounce) package cream cheese

Milk or cream
1 pint whipping cream (optional)
1 baked and cooled pie crust

Clean berries; set aside half. Cook the other half in saucepan over low heat. Stir in sugar combined with cornstarch. Cook until mixture is thick and clear. Cool. Soften cream cheese with a little milk or cream, and spread on bottom of pie crust. Arrange reserved berries on cheese, and pour cooked berries over them. Cool. Serve with or without whipped cream. Serves 6-8.

*Mrs. Richard McCamey (Betsy)*

## LOVING TOUCHES . . .

Cut out shapes of apples, leaves, etc. from pastry dough, bake and add to finished pie for a special touch.

For browning top crust, brush with egg white, evaporated milk, butter, salad oil or cream. For a sparkling, sugary top, sprinkle with granulated sugar.

# Desserts

DAVID SAPP

## ANGEL PUDDING

4 eggs, separated
½ cup sherry
1 cup sugar

1 envelope Knox gelatin
1 small angel food cake
½ pint whipping cream

Beat egg yolks, add ½ cup sugar and ½ cup of sherry. Cook in double-boiler until thick. Soak gelatin in 1 tablespoon of cold water. Dissolve over hot water. Beat egg whites and add ½ cup of sugar. Whip ½ pint cream and add to whites. Add dissolved gelatin to the cooked egg yolk mixture. Break cake in small pieces and add to whipped cream, egg white mixture and egg yolk mixture. Put in any size bowl and chill. Serve with a little whipped cream on top. Serves 8.

*Mrs. Edward E. Jackson (Dot)*

## APRICOT SOUFFLE

2 (30 ounce) can peeled apricots
2 envelopes unflavored gelatin
½ cup cold water
6 eggs
1½ tablespoons lemon juice
¾ cup apricot syrup

¾ teaspoon salt
¾ teaspoon almond extract
¾ cup sugar
1½ cups whipping cream
1 small can mandarin orange
  sections

Before mixing ingredients add a 3-4 inch collar around inside top of a 2 quart souffle dish using wax paper or foil and scotch tape. Put tape on outside of dish. Remove collar before serving. Sprinkle gelatin over cold water to soften. Separate eggs. Mix yolks, lemon juice, apricot syrup and salt in top of double boiler. Cook over boiling water, stirring constantly, until mixture is thick and custard-like. Remove from heat. Stir in gelatin and almond extract. Chill in refrigerator but do not let mixture get firm. Blend apricots in blender and stir into gelatin mixture. In a large bowl beat egg whites to a soft shape. Gradually add sugar and continue beating until mixture looks shiny and holds precise points. Beat cream, then pile on top of egg whites. Fold apricot mixture into cream and egg whites. Pour into souffle dish and chill at least 4 hours before serving. Garnish top with mandarin orange sections. Serves 12.

*Mrs. Hix Green , Jr. (Beverly)*

## LOVING TOUCHES. . .

Serve fresh blueberries on lemon sherbet.

206

## BANANA WHIP

*Quick, easy, good*

4 bananas
1 cup whipping cream

¼ cup sugar
1 teaspoon lemon juice

Cut up bananas and blend until smooth. Whip cream until stiff, adding sugar and lemon juice. Fold into bananas. Pour into sherbert dishes and refrigerate for two hours. Garnish with mint leaves or lemon peel. Serves 6.

*Mrs. Coy Lander (Pat)*

## BRANDY ICE

*Simple yet elegant*

1 quart vanilla bean ice cream          ½ cup brandy

Place ice cream in blender. Add brandy. Blend until smooth. Pour into stemmed crystal glasses. Serves 6.

*Mr. Robert F. Dennis*

## BROWNIES ALASKA

*Fun dessert to serve*

1 small package Duncan Hines
   brownie mix
½ cup of pecans

4 egg whites
½ cup sugar
1 quart coffee ice cream

Bake brownies as directed (adding pecans) in a well-greased 10 inch round pan. Let cool 20 minutes and turn out on foil-covered cookie sheet. Pile on ice cream and freeze. Beat egg whites, gradually adding sugar, until they form peaks. Cover ice cream with meringue and bake in hot oven 500 degrees five minutes. Serves 8. Refreeze, wrapped in foil.

*Mrs. R. Joseph Dietrich (Joanne)*

## LOVING TOUCHES . . .

Serve orange sherbet with:
   Black walnuts - Pass a pitcher of bourbon.
   Undiluted frozen lemonade and pineapple preserves

## CHOCOLATE TOFFEE DESSERT

20 vanilla wafers
2/3 cup soft butter
1 1/3 cups confectioners
  sugar
2 egg yolks

2 (4 ounce) bars of German
  chocolate
2/3 cup pecans
1 teaspoon vanilla
2 egg whites

Roll wafers until very fine. Cream together butter and sugar. Stir in egg yolks, melted chocolate, nuts and vanilla. Beat egg whites until stiff, and fold in. Sprinkle half of crumbs on bottom of 9 inch square pan. Spread chocolate mixture over crumbs. Sprinkle remaining crumbs on top. Chill. Cut and serve in a small square with a dab of whipped cream on top. Serves 9-12.

*Mrs. William Teem, III (Betty)*

## COEUR A'LA CREME

*The very best*

6 (3 ounce) packages cream
  cheese
1 pint whipping cream
1 envelope plain gelatin

½ cup cold water
1¼ cups sugar
½ cup sweet sherry
1 cup coffee cream

Soften cream cheese. Blend with whipping cream. Add sugar and sherry. Dissolve gelatin in water. Heat coffee cream. Add dissolved gelatin to coffee cream. Let cool and add to cheese mixture. Pour into oiled mold. Chill at least 3 hours. Serve with strawberries or any fruit. Serves 12.

*Mrs. William Farr, III (Linda)*

## COMPANY'S A'COMIN'

3 egg whites
½ teaspoon cream of tartar
1 cup sugar
18 saltine crackers
1 cup chopped pecans

1 teaspoon vanilla
1 large container Cool Whip
½ pint pineapple preserves
1 package frozen coconut

Beat egg whites until frothy. Add cream of tartar and sugar and beat until stiff. Crumble saltines and add pecans and vanilla to egg whites. Place in buttered 14x8 pan and cook 35 minutes at 350 degrees. Allow to cool. Mix pineapple preserves and Cool Whip. Spread over meringue and sprinkle package of coconut over top. This dessert is better if it is made a day before serving. Keep refrigerated. Serves 20.

*Mrs. Walter G. Canipe (Virginia)*

## FIGS SUPREME

12 black figs, fresh        ¾ cup roasted almonds
½ cup cointreau        1 quart vanilla ice cream

Soak figs in cointreau after peeling and quartering. Just before serving, mix figs and almond mixture with softened ice cream. Turn into silver bowl. Sprinkle with remaining almonds and return to freezer for 5 to 10 minutes. Serves 6.

*Mrs. Jay Gilbreath (Skee)*

## FLOATING ISLAND CUSTARD

*Delicious*

4 eggs        3 teaspoons sugar
½ cup sugar        ½ teaspoon vanilla
1 quart milk

Beat egg yolks and ½ cup sugar. Scald milk in top of double boiler. Add egg mixture to the milk. Cook and stir until it begins to thicken. (Mixture will not get very thick.) Whip egg whites until stiff. Add sugar and vanilla. Spoon egg whites into a bowl. Pour mixture over. Serves 6.

*Mrs. Hill Robertson, Jr. (Betty)*

## CHOCOLATE FONDUE

*Great for bridge club*

6 ounces semi-sweet chocolate chips    ½ cup smooth or crunchy
½ cup sugar                     peanut butter
½ cup milk

Melt chocolate, sugar and milk in sauce pan. Add peanut butter. Put ingredients in fondue dish and keep on low heat while serving. Serves 6. Condiments: Bananas, strawberries, marshmallows, pound cake cubes.

*Mrs. John Williams (Donna)*

## FUDGE

*Fantastic*

1 (6 ounce) package chocolate chips
1 cup chopped nuts
1 stick butter
2 cups sugar

10 large marshmallows
1 tablespoon water
2/3 cup canned evaporated milk

Mix chocolate chips, nuts and butter in bowl. Cook marshmallows and water in double boiler until fluffy. Add to chocolate mixture and blend together. Cook milk and sugar on low heat and bring to boil for 7 minutes. Add to chocolate mixture. Pour into greased 9x13 casserole and refrigerate when cooled. Makes 24 pieces.

*Linda Murphy Finsthwait*
*Mrs. William Bradshaw (Carolyn)*
*Mrs. Clayton McLendon (Inez)*

## HOT FUDGE SAUCE

5 squares unsweetened chocolate
½ cup butter
1¼ teaspoons vanilla

3 cups confectioners sugar
1 can evaporated milk

Melt chocolate and butter; remove from heat. Mix in sugar and milk alternately. Bring to boil over medium heat stirring constantly. Cook and stir 8 minutes or until thick. Remove from heat and stir in vanilla. Serve warm. Yields 3 cups. Can be stored in refrigerator and reheated.

*Mrs. Dale Harmon (Kathy)*
*Mrs. W. H. Bennett (Louise)*

## LEMON SPONGE PUDDING

1 cup sugar
1 tablespoon butter
2 tablespoons flour
2 egg whites, stiffly beaten

1 lemon, juice and rind
1 cup milk
2 egg yolks

Cream butter, sugar and flour. Add lemon, milk and egg yolks. Fold in egg whites. Pour into buttered dish and place in a pan of boiling water. Bake at 375 degrees for approximately 40 minutes. Serve warm with whipped cream. Serves 4-6.

*Mr. T. Gordon Little*

## MARSHMALLOW DESSERT

½ pound miniature marshmallows
¼ pound raisins
½ pint whipping cream

½ cup pecans, chopped
Sherry

Soak overnight marshmallows, raisins and pecans in a tumbler of sherry. Whip cream and fold into sherry mixture. Let stand in refrigerator 2 to 4 hours before serving. Serves 10.

*Mrs. John R. Strother, Jr. (Elsie)*

## LEMON MOUSSE
*Quick and easy*

1 can evaporated milk
1 cup sugar

½ cup lemon juice
1 graham cracker crust

Prepare crust in a 10 or 12 inch tart pan. Chill. Empty evaporated milk into a small, deep bowl. Place in freezer (uncovered) until crystals form. Remove from freezer. Beat on high speed with electric mixer, gradually adding sugar and lemon juice. Beat until fluffy. Pour over crust, spread flat. Sprinkle lemon rind or graham cracker crumbs on top to decorate. Place in freezer until firm. (3-4 hours). Serves 8-10.

*Pam Poole Payne*

## QUICK CHOCOLATE MOUSSE

4 large eggs, separated
6 ounces semi-sweet chips
2 tablespoons sugar

½ cup whipping cream
1 teaspoon vanilla or brandy

Beat egg yolks slightly with fork. Melt chocolate chips over hot water. Add egg yolks to chocolate chips. Beat egg whites until foamy. Add sugar and beat whites until stiff. Carefully fold egg whites into chocolate mixture. Add vanilla or brandy. Spoon into 1 large bowl or six small compotes. Chill several hours. Top with whipped cream, crushed almonds or grated chocolate. Serves 6.

*Mrs. Dave Davis (Joan)*

## LOVING TOUCHES . . .

In a hurry? Serve a tray of "store-bought" chocolates (wrappers removed) on a pretty tray. Everyone loves candy!

## MOCHA MOUSSE

*Rich and good!*

½ pint whipping cream
1½ teaspoons instant coffee

1 teaspoon cocoa
½ cup confectioners sugar

Whip ingredients together until thick. Serve in pot de cremes or demi-tassee cups. Serves 6-8.

*Mrs. James Cushman (Elkin)*

## EASY POT de CREME

¾ cup milk
6 ounces semi-sweet
  chocolate bits

1 egg
2 tablespoons sugar
Pinch salt

Heat milk to boiling. Put all ingredients, including milk, in blender. Blend until smooth. Pour into pot de creme pots. Let stand in refrigerator for several hours before serving. Serves 4.

*Mrs. H. Eugene Williams*

## BRANDY POT de CREME

1 cup semi-sweet chocolate
  chips
1¼ cups light cream

2 egg yolks
3 tablespoons brandy
  (brandy extract is fine)

Put chocolate chips, egg yolks, and brandy in blender. Scald cream in double-boiler. Add to blender. Turn blender on high and blend till smooth. Pour into 6 small cups. Chill. Serve with a dab of whipped cream on top.

*Mrs. Thomas Johnson (Benita)*
*Mrs. Thomas Bowers (Margaret)*

## DR. LOGUE'S POT de CREMES

*Easy and great*

1½ cups half and half
¾ cup sugar
Dash of salt

4 egg yolks
4 tablespoons creme de cocoa
Sprinkle of nutmeg

Scald half and half with sugar. Add slowly to beaten egg yolks, stirring constantly. Add creme de cocoa. Bake in custard cups in pan of water at 350 degrees for 30 minutes. Chill. Can make ahead of time. Serves 6.

*Mrs. William Luesing (Carolyn)*

## SYRUP PUDDING

*Family recipe that has been around for 5 generations*

¾ cup sorghum syrup
1 cup sugar
1 teaspoon soda
1 cup hot water
½ cup melted shortening

1 egg
1½ cups flour
¾ teaspoon allspice
¾ teaspoon ginger

Dissolve soda in hot water. Mix with all other ingredients. Grease and flour an 8x12 pyrex dish. Cook at 350 degrees for 30 minutes. Tastes like a moist gingerbread. Serves 12.

*Mrs. I. C. Rolader (Mif)*

## TOMBSTONE PUDDING

1 small box instant vanilla pudding
1 teaspoon almond extract
1 package lady fingers

1 tablespoon sherry
½ pint whipping cream
1 jar maraschino cherries

Make pudding as directed on box. Add almond extract to pudding. Whip cream. Line a round bowl with lady fingers. Sprinkle sherry over lady fingers. Spoon pudding over lady fingers and then cover pudding with whipped cream. Decorate with cherries. Refrigerate. Slice into wedges to serve. Serves 8.

*Mrs. Neal Williams (Virginia)*

## SHERBET SUPREME

*Elegant and easy*

½ gallon mint sherbet
2 boxes Birdseye frozen mixed fruit

¾ cup sweet red sherry

Six hours prior to serving, thaw fruit and mix with sherry. Let stand at room temperature, about 4 hours. Refrigerate approximately 1½ hours prior to serving. Spoon fruit mixture over individual servings of mint sherbet. Serves 10.

*Mrs. John S. Dodd, Jr. (Marie)*

## STRAWBERRIES ROMANOFF

1 quart strawberries        1 cup whipping cream
¼ cup sugar        1 pint vanilla ice cream
¼ cup liqueur (triple sec, grand manier, or cointreau)

Wash and hull berries. Drain. Sprinkle with sugar and chill for 3-4 hours. When ready to serve, remove ice cream from freezer and allow to soften. Meanwhile, whip cream until stiff. Fold ice cream into whipped cream. Gently mix in liqueur and strawberries. Serve immediately in crystal, long-stemmed compotes or wine glasses. Serves 6-8.

*Mr. Robert F. Dennis*

## FRAISES PORTO

*Strawberries in wine*

1 quart small, sweet strawberries        1 cup good port wine

Clean and chill the berries. Pour the port over the berries directly before serving. This dessert may be served alone or with: Profiteroles au Chocolat (small cream puff shells stuffed with vanilla ice cream, topped with a thick, home-made chocolate sauce).

*Mrs. Joseph Conant (Olympia)*

## LOVING TOUCHES . . .

Combinations that are smooth and refreshing after a rich entree:
Oranges and grand marnier or curacao
Blueberries and gin        Strawberries and chartreuse
Pineapple and pernod        Sliced grapes and brandy
Pineapple and anisette        Peaches and champagne
Serve vanilla ice cream with:
Raisins marinated in rum
Crushed Heath Bar and rum

A small amount of cornstarch added to whipping cream makes it just right every time.

# Potpourri

## SCALLOPED APPLES

4 cups diced apples
¾ cup sugar
3 cups bread crumbs or cubed bread

Cinnamon, nutmeg or any
desired spice
½ cup melted butter

Combine apples, sugar and spice. Mix butter and bread. Place alternate layers in baking dish beginning with apples and ending with crumbs on top. Cover and bake at 350 degrees for 30 minutes. Remove cover and brown about 5 minutes. Serves 6.

*Mrs. Lamar Roberts (Shirley)*

## APRICOT CASSEROLE

2 large cans apricots
Juice of 1 can
1 stick of butter

1 small box Ritz crackers
½ box brown sugar

Mash apricots, add melted butter, sugar and crumbled crackers, saving some crackers for bottom and top of casserole. Add juice. Pour into buttered casserole. Bake 325 degrees for 30 to 40 minutes. Serves 8.

*Mrs. James Magbee (Tia)*
*Mrs. Frank Owens, Jr. (Marguerite)*

## BANANAS IN A BLANKET

*Delicious*

Bananas
Pineapple, sliced

Bacon

Pre-heat broiler. Cut banana into lengthwise halves. Place canned sliced pineapple between the banana halves. Wrap with bacon and broil until bacon is crisp.

*Mrs. Stuart Wilson (Mimi)*

## CURRIED FRUIT

*Looks great in a chafing dish; good with chicken, lamb or ham*

1 large can pear halves
1 large can pineapple chunks

1 large can apricots
1 small jar cherries

216

Sauce

½ cup butter                          ¾ cup brown sugar
1 teaspoon curry (or a little more if desired)

Cut pears into quarters. Drain fruit well, arrange in baking dish and pour melted butter on top. Mix sugar and curry and sprinkle over fruit. Bake at 350 degrees for 1 hour. Serves 10.

*Mrs. Earle Duffey (Jacqueline)*
*Mrs. William Voegeli (Dorothy Ann)*

## GRANOLA

*Health food*

3 cups grated coconut              1½ cups water
5 cups wheat germ (1 large jar)    1½ cups oil
2 cups chopped nuts (mixed)        1½ tablespoons salt
3 pounds oatmeal (regular)         3 teaspoons vanilla
1½ cups brown sugar

Mix dry ingredients in large baking pan. Melt syrup ingredients over medium heat in saucepan to dissolve the sugar. Pour over dry ingredients mixing well and bake in oven 275-325 degrees for 45 minutes turning every 10 minutes. Additions: Sunflower seeds, sesame seeds, raisins.

*Mrs. Wade Mitchell (Mary Lu)*
*Mr. Stan Gumble*
*Mrs. Harry Lange (Dottie)*

## BAKED PINEAPPLE

1 (No.2) can crushed pineapple     3 tablespoons flour
  (do not drain)                   5 slices of bread, cubed
3 eggs                             1 stick margarine, melted
½ cup sugar

Blend together eggs, flour and sugar. Mix with pineapple. Pour into well-buttered casserole. Top with bread cubes. Melt butter and drizzle on top of bread. Bake at 350 degrees for 40 minutes covered and 20 minutes uncovered. Serves 8.

*Mrs. James Dunlap (K-Jo)*

## PEACH BRANDY PUNCH
*Makes 18 thirsty ladies very happy*

1 cup peach brandy
4 fresh peaches
2/3 cup sugar
1 cup lemon juice

1 cup orange juice
1 bottle sauterne
1 bottle rose wine
2 quarts ginger ale

Puree in blender the first four ingredients. Strain if desired. Chill several hours. Add remaining ingredients and serve over block of ice in punch bowl. Serves 18.

*Mrs. T. G. Debreceni (Lois)*

## WASSAIL PUNCH
*Perks itself*

1 cup grapefruit juice
2½ cups orange juice
2 cups apple cider
¼ cup water

¼ cup sugar
6 whole cloves
1 cinnamon stick

Combine fruit juices, cider and water in bottom of clean 12 cup coffee-maker. Place sugar and spices in coffeemaker basket. Perk until signal light indicates punch is ready. Remove spices and serve hot from coffee-maker. Serves 12.

*Mrs. Oliver P. Ackerman, Jr.*

## FRIENDSHIP TEA

1 small jar Tang
¼ cup instant tea
1¼ cups sugar

1 package Wyler's lemonade mix
1 teaspoon cinnamon
½ teaspoon ground cloves

Mix together all ingredients. Store in tightly closed jar. Use 3-4 teaspoons to one cup of boiling water. Great alternate to coffee.

*Linda Miner Carswell*

## MINT TEA

3 tablespoons tea
6 sprigs of mint

2 lemons, juice only
1 cup sugar

Pour 2 cups boiling water over mint and tea. Pour 2 cups boiling water over lemon juice and sugar. Let each stand for 15 minutes. Strain and mix. Add 1 quart water. Great for keeping in the refrigerator in summer. Makes 2 quarts.

*Mrs. David Adams (Elizabeth)*

## ORANGE CHAMPAGNE COOLER

Orange juice                    Champagne

Mix orange juice and champagne in equal amounts. Serve in tall glasses over ice.

*Mrs. William A. McClain, III (Rose)*


## HOT CHOCOLATE MIXTURE

1  (8 quart) box powdered milk      1  (6 ounce) jar Coffee-Mate
1  (16 ounce) box of Nestle's Quick    1½ cup confectioners sugar

Mix above ingredients together in an air tight container. Use 2 heaping tablespoons in cup of boiling water for a delicious drink.

*Mrs. James Magbee (Tia)*
*Mrs. John K. Snellings (Beverly)*


## ORANGE–GLAZED PECANS

1½ cups granulated sugar       2  tablespoons orange juice
½ cup water                    1  pound whole pecans
Rind of 2 oranges, grated      Pinch of salt

Put sugar and water in pot. Heat until it forms a soft ball in water. Add rind and juice, salt and nuts. Stir until well coated. When cloudy, spread on wax paper and separate. Serve, or store in tin, when glaze is hard.

*Mrs. Bruce Dick (Sylvia)*


## EGG NOG

*Thick and rich*

12 large eggs, separated         ¾ cup bourbon
1  pint whipping cream, whipped    1¾ cups sugar

Whip cream and set aside. Wash beaters. Beat egg whites till stiff but not dry, adding sugar gradually. In large bowl beat egg yolks until light colored, adding whiskey gradually. Fold cream into yolk mixture using a spatula, then fold in whites. Serves 8.

*Mrs. David Stacy (Beverly)*

219

## HERB BUTTER

¼ pound butter
1 tablespoon lemon juice
2 teaspoons finely chopped parsley
1 small clove garlic, pressed

2 teaspoons finely chopped chives
2 teaspoons finely chopped tarragon

Add herbs and juice to softened butter and cream all together. Cover and store in refrigerator for seasoning to blend. Delicious with wheat thins or spread on sliced French bread and lightly brown under broiler.

*Mrs. Bud Gould (Nancy)*


## CHEESE FONDUE

1 bottle German white wine
2 heaping teaspoons cornstarch
3 ounces kirsch
1 pound gruyere cheese, grated

Dash of salt
Ground nutmeg
1 pound Swiss cheese, grated
Garlic clove

Mix first two ingredients and let sit. Rub pot with garlic. Heat wine, but do not boil. Add 2 dashes of nutmeg. Add cheeses, dash of salt. Stir in one direction with wooden spoon till thick - approximately 5 minutes. Add starch and kirsch mixture. Serve with cubes of French bread and a green salad.

*Mrs. Frank Millians (Helen)*


## CHEESE GRITS

*A brunch favorite*

1 cup uncooked grits
1 stick butter
½ pound grated sharp ceddar cheese

¼ cup milk
2 eggs, well beaten

Cook grits as directed. Melt butter and cheese. Combine beaten eggs and milk. Add all ingredients to grits. Pour into buttered 1½ quart casserole. Bake at 425 degrees for 45 minutes. Serves 6-8.
Variations:  Add garlic salt.
Substitute 1 roll Kraft garlic cheese for cheddar cheese.

*Mrs. Robert Dunlap (Mary Jane)*
*Mrs. William Niall Mitchell (Margaret)*
*Mrs. William A. McClain, III (Rose)*

## SURPRISE GRITS

| | |
|---|---|
| 1 quart milk | 1 cup grated gruyere cheese |
| ½ cup butter | 1 cup grated parmesan |
| 1/3 cup butter (for top) | 1 teaspoon salt |
| 1 cup grits (regular) | 1/8 teaspoon pepper |

Bring milk to boil. Add ½ cup butter; gradually stir in grits. Cook and stir till thick. Remove from heat and add salt and pepper. Beat with mixer at high speed till creamy. Pour into ungreased casserole, 13x9x2, and allow to set in refrigerator overnight. When ready to bake, cut into squares and place like fallen dominoes in greased casserole. Pour 1/3 cup melted butter over squares and sprinkle with the grated cheeses. Bake at 400 degrees for 35 minutes. Serves 6.

*Mrs. Ross Shaw (Mimi)*
*Mrs. John W. Wilcox, Jr. (Susan)*

## CHEESE SOUFFLE

*No - fall*

| | |
|---|---|
| 3 tablespoons butter | Dash of pepper |
| 5 tablespoons flour | ½ pound grated sharp cheese |
| 1 1/3 cups hot milk | 4 eggs, separated |
| 1 teaspoon salt | ¼ teaspoon baking powder |

Make a cream sauce of first five ingredients in saucepan over medium heat. When it starts to thicken, add cheese and stir until cheese melts. Cool the mixture. Then add well-beaten egg yolks. Fold in stiffly-beaten egg whites, to which baking powder has been added. Pour into greased 1½ quart baking dish. Place in pan of hot water and bake at 350 degrees for 1 hour. Serves 4 generously.

To make cream sauce: use wire whisk, melt butter, stir in flour and slowly pour in hot milk while stirring.

*Mrs. Thomas Johnson (Benita)*

## LOVING TOUCHES ...

Using a small glass, cut a round from a piece of stale bread. Fry bread and round in butter, drop in an egg and fry slowly. Don't turn until almost done.

221

## CHEESE SOUFFLE CASSEROLE

8 slices white bread, remove crusts     Salt to taste
½ pound sharp cheddar cheese     3 eggs
¼ cup melted butter     2 cups milk
½ teaspoon dry mustard

Quarter the bread. Layer the ingredients in a high-sided souffle dish. Pour butter over. Beat eggs and milk. Pour over ingredients. Let stand overnight. Cover and bake at 350 degrees 1 hour. Serves 6.

*Mrs. Robert F. Dennis (Peggy)*
*Mrs. Frank Owens, Jr. (Marguerite)*
*Mrs. James R. Harland (Teenie)*

## HEAT – AND – HOLD SCRAMBLED EGGS
*Buffet delight*

¼ cup butter     1 tablespoon each, chopped
12 eggs     parsley, pimientos, chives
1 1/3 cups milk     1 teaspoon salt
2 tablespoons flour     1/8 teaspoon pepper

Melt butter in large skillet over low heat. Combine remaining ingredients in large bowl. Beat with rotary beater until smooth and well-blended. Pour into skillet and stir from outside edge to center, allowing uncooked egg in center to flow to outer edge of skillet. Continue stirring until all the mixture has been cooked and has creamy appearance. Will hold up to 2 hours in covered chafing dish or electric skillet set at 200 degrees or in 200 degrees oven. Serves 6-8.

*Mrs. Dennis Mollenkamp (Jane)*

## APPLIANCE OMELET
*A flat omelet to serve to many*

4 eggs     Salt

Preheat electric griddle to 300 degrees. Make a plug of aluminum foil for the drainhole. Put eggs in iced tea glass; beat well with a fork. Pour on the griddle and let it run out to the corners and make a rectangle. Sprinkle with salt and quickly roll up while still wet. Slice and serve.

*John Wall*

## BREAKFAST QUICHE

2 (9 inch) pie shells
8 ounces shredded mozzarella cheese
12 ounces bulk sausage, browned
8 eggs, beaten

1½ cups of milk
1 teaspoon salt
½ teaspoon pepper

Line shells with sausage, then cheese. Combine eggs, milk, salt and pepper, divide and pour over sausage. Bake at 375 degrees for 25-30 minutes. Serves 8 well.

*Mrs. Fred Hayes (Anne)*

## COTTAGE CHEESE PANCAKES

*Children love them*

1 egg
Salt and pepper to taste

2 heaping tablespoons flour
1 pint cottage cheese

Beat egg. Add salt and pepper and flour. Stir in cottage cheese. Cover and let stand 20 minutes. Drop mixture by tablespoon into pan of hot grease. Fry until brown. Serves 2.

*Mrs. Myles J. Gould (Lynn)*

## SOUR DOUGH PANCAKES OR WAFFLES

*Students make these at school when studying food chemistry*

1 cup starter*
1 egg
1 tablespoon oil
½ teaspoon salt

1 tablespoon sugar
½-1 teaspoon baking soda
1½ cups flour
1 cup warm water

To one cup starter beat in egg, oil, salt, sugar. Fold in ½-1 teaspoon baking soda (amount depends on the "age" of your starter). Cook on hot oiled griddle or waffle iron. Serves 4.

*To get your starter - ask a friend to share some or make your own. The night before you use it, add flour and water to remaining starter and beat until smooth. Store in warm place.

**Starter:**

3½ cups flour
1 tablespoon sugar

1 package yeast
2 cups warm water

Beat well. Cover with loose lid in an earthenware, glass or plastic container. (Not metal). Let ferment for two days in a warm place.

*Mrs. Robert A. Hatcher (Carolyn)*

223

## PEPPER JELLY

6 large hot peppers, or ½ cup ground    1½ cups vinegar
6 large bell peppers, or ¾ cup ground    1 bottle Certo or Sure-Jel
6½ cups sugar

Blend in blender two hot peppers, two bell peppers, no seeds, with ½ cup vinegar for one minute. Repeat with remaining peppers as above. Add Sure-Jel or Certo and bring to rolling boil. Add sugar and boil one minute till jelled. You may add green food coloring, stir and skim or leave it amber colored with bits of red and green showing. Pour into 8-10 sterilized jelly glasses and seal with paraffin. (Rubber gloves should be worn when working with pepper.) Delicious with cream cheese and crackers or as an accompaniment with meat and vegetables.

*Mrs. Robert Dunlap (Mary Jane)*
*Mrs. William A. McClain, III (Rose)*

## PICKLED OKRA

*Crisp and yummy*

3 pounds young, fresh okra    ½ cup salt (not iodized)
6 cloves garlic    1 cup sugar
6 teaspoons celery seed    1 quart white vinegar
6 pods hot pepper    1 quart water
6 teaspoons dill seed

Pack washed okra into pint jars. Divide garlic, celery seed, hot pepper and dill seed among the six jars. Combine salt, sugar, water and vinegar in large saucepan. Bring to boiling, then pour into jars within ½ inch of top. Seal jars and place in hot water bath (water to cover jars) and cook 7 minutes. Remove to wire racks to cool. Yield: 6 pints.

*Mrs. Richard Estes (Becky)*

## PICKLED ONIONS

4 quarts small white onions    1 quart white vinegar
3 pints boiling water    ¼ cup sugar
1 cup salt    3 tablespoons whole allspice
3 pints cold water    3 tablespoons mustard seed
3 tablespoons peppercorns

Cover onions with the boiling water. Let stand five minutes; drain and cover with cold water and peel. Dissolve salt in cold water; add onions and let stand 12-24 hours. Drain; cover with cold water and drain. Mix together vinegar, sugar, allspice, mustard seed, peppercorns and boil one minute. Remove spices; add onions; heat to boiling. Pack onions in sterilized jars. Fill to overflowing with hot vinegar, then seal. (Spicier if left sealed for about 10 days). Makes 6 to 7 pints.

*Mrs. John E. Anderson (Mary Gray)*

## SQUASH PICKLES

*Fantastic*

8 cups thinly sliced squash (small ones)
2 cups sliced onions
4 bell peppers, sliced
2 cups vinegar
3 cups sugar
2 teaspoons celery seed
2 teaspoons mustard seed
1 jar pimientos

Combine squash and onions in large container or sink. Cover squash with ice and salt. Set aside for 1 hour. Put bell peppers on top of ice for 5 minutes; then drain and rinse squash, onions and peppers well. Combine sugar, vinegar and spices and bring to a boil. Add squash, onions and peppers and bring to full boil. Sterilize jars. Pour into jars while hot and seal.

*Mrs. John Sineath (Nancy)*

## SWEDISH NUTS

1 pound pecans, or a mixture of pecans, English walnuts and almonds
1 cup sugar
Dash salt
2 egg whites, stiffly beaten
½ cup butter

Toast nuts in 325 degree oven until light brown. Fold sugar and salt into egg whites and beat until stiff peaks form. Fold nuts into meringue. Melt butter in a 15x10x1 jelly-roll pan. Spread nut mixture over butter. Bake at 325 degrees for about 30 minutes. Stir every 10 minutes, or until nuts are coated with a brown covering and no butter remains in the pan. Cool. Makes 4 cups.

*Mrs. Jane Blume*

## CHOCOLATE MINT PATTY PUNCH

¼ cup white creme de menthe          1 quart chocolate ice cream
¼ cup creme de cacao

Put liquers in blender. Add ice cream a spoonful at a time, blending smoothly after each addition. Pour into stemmed glasses and serve immediately. Garnish with mint sprigs, chocolate curls and/or crushed peppermint candy. Serves 6.

*Mrs. George F. Longino, III (June)*

## SIMPLE COFFEE PUNCH

1 gallon strong chilled coffee          1 quart whipping cream
2 quarts coffee or chocolate ice cream   ¼ cup sugar
4 teaspoons vanilla

Put chilled coffee in punch bowl and stir in melting ice cream and vanilla. Whip cream, add sugar, and fold into punch just before serving. Serves 30-35.

*Mrs. Charles E. Brown (Lorenna)*

## LOVING TOUCHES . . .

Raw turnips cut into strips make a good snack or hors d'oeuvre.

Marinate fresh broccoli and cauliflower floweretts in Wishbone Italian Dressing.

Hot dog relish spread over a block of cream cheese is delicious served with Waverly crackers.

Top a large block of cream cheese with black or red caviar.

One of the most elegant "befores" of all: lightly salted, lightly buttered and lightly toasted pecans.

226

**LOVING TOUCHES. . .**

## FREEZER CHART

1. Fruits and fruit juice concentrates - 1 year

2. Vegetables - 8 to 10 months

3. Breads, cakes, doughnuts - 2 to 3 months

4. Pies (fruit filled) - 8 months

5. Meats:
   Beef:   Hamburger or chopped thin steaks - 3 months
   Roast and steaks - 1 year
   Lamb: Patties - 4 months
           Roast - 1 year
   Pork:   Cured - 2 months
           Roast - 8 months
           Sausage - 2 months
   Veal:   Cutlets, chops - 6 months
           Roast - 8 months
           Cooked meat - 3 months
   Poultry:  Cut up chicken or turkey - 6 months
           Whole chicken - 1 year
           Whole turkey - 6 months
           Cooked chicken or turkey pies - 1 year
           Cooked chicken or turkey dinner - 6 months
           Fried chicken - 3 months
   Fish:   2 to 4 months

6. Ice cream and sherbet - 1 month

*Mrs. E. T. Griffith*

## JUG WINE LIST

Some excellent, yet inexpensive "jug" wines:

RED
> Sebastiani Mountain Cabernet Sauvignon
> Inglenook Zinfandel
> Gallo Hearty Burgundy
> Gallo Barbera

WHITE
> Inglenook Chablis
> Almaden French Colombard
> Sebastiani Pinot Chardonnay
> Gallo Chenin Blanc
> Gallo Sauvignon Blanc

MISC.
> Italian Swiss Colony - Pink Chablis
> Folonari Sauve
> Folonari Valpolicella

## DRY POTPOURRI

Dry rose and colorful flower petals and leaves on a large screen. To 1 quart dried petals, add the following mixture:

> 1 ounce ground cinnamon
> 1 ounce ground nutmeg
> 1 ounce ground cloves

Add:
> 1 ounce sliced gingerroot
> ½ ounce anise seed
> 2 ounces powdered arrowroot

Mix with dried petals and keep in covered jar. If kept out, occasionally add a few whole cloves and crushed whole cinnamon sticks to mixture to restore fragrance.

# Students'
## Recipes

## BANANA PROTEIN SHAKE

1 ripe banana  
½ teaspoon vanilla  
1 cup milk  
¼ cup nonfat dry milk  
1 tablespoon honey  
Ice (6-8 cubes)

In a blender, blend whole milk, honey, vanilla, and dry milk. Turn blender on high and add ice cubes until crushed and blended. Add banana and mix one minute. Powdered milk will make shake thicken without the fat and sugar of ice cream.

*Kimberly Arp - Kindergarten*

## BUTTER "SHAKE"

1 empty baby food jar  
Whipping cream

Take 1 baby food jar. Fill ½ full with whipping cream. Add a bunch of kids dancing and shaking with jars in hand and Bingo! Butter! Add a little salt and spread on sandwich bread. It's delicious! (1 teaspoon sour cream per ½ pint of whipping cream can be added).

*Mrs. Vaught's Pre-kindergarten class*

## BUTTERFLY SANDWICHES

*Sandwiches for kids*

1 small can of tuna  
Mayonnaise  
Onion flakes (optional)  
1 tablespoon pickles  
Salt  
Pepper  
1 tablespoon lemon juice

Put drained tuna in a bowl. With a fork, mix mayonnaise, onion, salt, pepper and lemon juice with tuna. Use as sandwich filling. Cut bread crosswise. Turn the corner sides in and place the pickle in between. Decorate with olives, carrots, etc. Makes 3 or 4 sandwiches.

*Elizabeth Aquino - Form I*

## BREAD

1 yeast package  
7 cups flour  
½ cup sugar  
3 tablespoons butter  
1 tablespoon salt  
2 cups warm water  
1 egg, beaten

Mix yeast, 3½ cups flour, sugar, salt, water, and egg. Add remaining 3½ cups flour with 3 tablespoons butter. Knead and let dough rise until it doubles in size. Knead again and make into 2 loaves. Let rise again. Bake 400 degrees for 10 minutes, then 350 degrees for 40 minutes.

*Emilie Morgan - Form I*

## RAGGEDY ANN SALAD

| | |
|---|---|
| 1 fresh or canned peach half | Tiny piece red cherry |
| 4 small celery sticks | Grated yellow cheese |
| 8 raisins | Ruffled leaf lettuce |
| Half a hard-cooked egg (cut lengthwise) | |

Make a Raggedy Ann using above ingredients in the following way: body - peach half; arms and legs - small celery sticks; head - egg half; eyes, nose, shoes, buttons (on the peach half) - raisins; mouth - cherry; hair - grated cheese; skirt - ruffled lettuce leaves.

*Marianne Dennis - Grade 3*

## WOODSMAN STEW

| | |
|---|---|
| 2 pounds ground chuck | 1 can water |
| 1 large onion, chopped | ¼ cup margarine |
| 2 cans vegetable soup | |

Place margarine in large vessel over campfire. Brown onion in margarine with ground chuck. Add vegetable soup and water. Heat thoroughly. Serve generously to 6 hungry scouts or 6 fishermen who lost their catch. Serves 6.

*John Mill Walker - Form II*

## CHOCOLATE CHIP PANCAKES

| | |
|---|---|
| ½ cup milk | 2 teaspoons baking powder |
| 2 tablespoons melted butter | 2 tablespoons sugar |
| 1 egg | ½ teaspoon salt |
| 1 cup all-purpose flour | ½ cup semi-sweet chocolate morsels |

Place milk, butter, and egg in mixing bowl. Beat lightly. Sift flour, baking powder, sugar and salt. Add to milk mixture all at once. Stir enough to dampen flour. Add enough milk to make batter as thick as heavy cream. Pour batter on moderately hot griddle and arrange several chocolate morsels on top of pancake. Cook until bubbles form and undersurface is nicely browned. Brown on other side. Serve immediately. Serves 2 to 3.

*Rob Dennis - Grade 5*

## QUICKIE DONUTS

1 (8 ounce) can refrigerated
buttermilk biscuits
Fat for frying

1 cup confectioners sugar
2 tablespoons water
½ teaspoon vanilla extract

Cut a small hole in center of each biscuit. Fry in hot fat (360 degrees) until golden brown on both sides, turning once. Drain on paper towel. Combine sugar, water and vanilla and heat till dissolved. Dip hot donuts in mixture to glaze. Makes 10 donuts.

*Tom McClain - Grade 2*

## PORTUGUESE FRENCH TOAST

2 eggs
4 pieces of bread
1 teaspoon ground cinnamon

1 tablespoon sugar
2 tablespoons butter

Beat eggs and salt together. Soak bread in mixture. Fry bread at medium high heat in a large buttered frying pan. Sprinkle cinnamon and sugar over bread while frying. Brown on both sides. Serves 4.

*Bill McClain - Grade 6*

## JAY'S CHOCOLATE CHEWIES

2/3 cup margarine
1 box brown sugar
3 eggs
2¾ cups flour

1½ teaspoons vanilla
½ teaspoon salt
2½ teaspoons baking powder
1 (12 ounce) package chocolate chips

Melt butter, add sugar, stir and cool. Add eggs, one at a time and beat well. Add remaining ingredients and mix well. Pour into well greased and floured pan (12x8). Bake at 350 degrees for 30 minutes. Cool. Cut into squares. Makes 5 dozen.

*Jay Forio - Form VI*

## CHOCOLATE COVERED "WORMS"

1 package (6 ounce) semi-sweet
chocolate chips
1 package (6 ounce) butterscotch
chips (or omit butterscotch and
use 2 packages of chocolate chips)

1 can (3 ounce) Chinese
noodles
¼ cup chopped nuts

Melt chips in a saucepan over low heat. Remove from heat. Add noodles and nuts. Stir carefully, and cover noodles completely. Drop by teaspoonfuls onto waxed paper. Let cool. Makes about 36 pieces.

*Twyla Finch - Grade 4*

## M & M COOKIES
*Our favorites*

| | |
|---|---|
| 1 cup butter, softened | 2¼ cups sifted all-purpose flour |
| 1 cup firmly packed brown sugar | 1 teaspoon baking soda |
| ½ cup granulated sugar | 1 teaspoon salt |
| 2 teaspoons vanilla | 1½ cups (¾ pound) M&M plain |
| 2 eggs | chocolate candies |

Mix butter, brown sugar and granulated sugar. Beat in vanilla and eggs. In another bowl, sift flour, baking soda, and salt together. Add dry ingredients to sugar-egg mixture. Blend well. Stir in ¾ cup M&M's. Drop rounded teaspoons of dough 2 inches apart on ungreased cookie sheet. Decorate tops with M&M's. Bake at 375 degrees for 10 minutes. Cool on wire rack.

*Saunders Glenn - Grade 1*
*Amanda Glenn - Kindergarten*

## COCO–NOT COOKIES

| | |
|---|---|
| 1 stick butter or margarine | 1 package Spudflakes (instant |
| 1 cup sugar | mashed potatoes) |
| 1 teaspoon coconut extract | 1 small egg |
| 1 package Bixmix | |

Cream together butter, sugar and coconut extract. Add egg and beat. Stir in Bixmix and Spudflakes. Cover bowl and chill for about 1 hour. (To save time, melt butter in frying pan and add all other ingredients. It should become stiff enough to shape into marblesized balls.) Place cookies 2 inches apart on ungreased cookie sheet and bake at 375 degrees 12 to 14 minutes. Makes 4 dozen cookies.

*Twyla Finch - Grade 4*

## PEANUT BUTTER COOKIES

| | |
|---|---|
| 1 cup shortening (Crisco) | 1 cup sugar |
| ½ teaspoon salt | 1 cup brown sugar |
| 1 teaspoon baking soda | 2 eggs |
| 1 (8 ounce) jar of crunchy | 2 cups flour |
|   peanut butter | 2 tablespoons water |

Mix together Crisco, salt, soda, and peanut butter. Then add sugar, brown sugar, eggs, flour, and water. Mix together thoroughly. Drop from a teaspoon onto a cookie sheet and flatten with fork. Bake at 325 degrees for 15 minutes. Makes 5 dozen. Freezes well.

*Amy Brown - Form IV*

## AUNT DOT'S ROCK COOKIES

| | |
|---|---|
| 2 cups dark brown sugar | 1 teaspoon baking powder |
| ½ pound melted butter | ½ teaspoon nutmeg |
| 2 eggs | 3 cups all-purpose flour |
| 1 teaspoon soda | 2 cups raisins |
| 1 teaspoon cinnamon | 1 cup chopped pecans |

Cream butter and sugar. Add eggs one at a time. Combine cinnamon, baking powder, and nutmeg with sifted flour. Add all ingredients together with soda (that's been dissolved in a little water), raisins, and nuts. Mix well and drop by teaspoon onto greased cookie sheet. Bake at 350 degrees for about 15 minutes. Makes 5 dozen.

*Phoebe Forio - Form IV*

## APRIL FOOLS ICE CREAM CONES
### or
## FLOWER POT CAKES

| | |
|---|---|
| 1 package cake mix, any flavor | 1 can prepared frosting |
| 10 flat bottom ice cream cones | |

Mix your favorite cake mix by package directions. Fill cones ½ full. Bake on cookie sheet at 350 degrees for 25 minutes. Frost with any flavor frosting. To make "Flower Pots", stick in a lollipop and use green gumdrops for leaves.

*Mrs. Caswell's Kindergarten class*

## NUTTY GINGERBREAD

¾ cup brown sugar
¾ cup melted shortening
¾ cup molasses
2 eggs
2¼ cups flour
2½ teaspoons baking powder
2 teaspoons ginger

1½ teaspoons cinnamon
¾ teaspoon baking soda
½ teaspoon nutmeg
½ teaspoon ground clove
¾ cup chopped pecans
1 cup boiling water
Whipped topping, optional

In large mixing bowl, combine sugar, shortening and molasses. Add eggs and beat well. Stir dry ingredients and nuts together. Add to sugar mixture and mix well. Stir in water and pour into greased 13x9x2 pan. Bake in preheated 350 degree oven for 40 minutes. Serve with whipped topping.

*Anne Fitten Glenn - Grade 6*

## BUNNY CAKE

1 box cake mix
Coconut
1 can prepared or homemade vanilla icing

Jelly beans
Licorice strips

Bake two 9 inch cake layers. Use one layer for body and cut ears from other layer. Use middle part of layer for bowtie. Frost with white icing, sprinkle with coconut. Jelly beans for eyes and nose. Licorice strips for whiskers.

*Georgia Ware - Grade 4*
*Molly Ware - Grade 1*
*Ginny Ware - Pre-kindergarten*

## HALLOWEEN CAKE

*A ghostly dessert*

1 box yellow cake mix
1 can vanilla frosting
Licorice jelly beans

Orange food coloring
Orange sprinkle stuff

Concoct the cake and bake in two 8 inch round pans. Just before spreading frosting on the cake, add food coloring. Then, ice the cake and decorate with jelly beans and sprinkles. Kids will love this.

*Mrs. Matthew's Kindergarten class*

## GRANDPARENTS' DAY POUND CAKE

*A special treat for pre-school grandparents*

1  box powdered sugar                6  eggs
3  sticks butter or margarine        1  teaspoon vanilla
Cake flour (enough to fill empty powdered sugar box)

Preheat oven to 325 degrees. Grease and flour pan. Mix and mash powdered sugar with butter. Add eggs, flour and vanilla and blend well with mixer. Bake about 1 hour.

*Mrs. Calhoun's Kindergarten class*

## GREAT GRANNY'S POUND CAKE

1  cup lightly salted butter         2  cups flour (sifted 4 times)
1½ cups sugar (sifted 4 times)       5  eggs

Cream butter and sugar. Beat and add one egg at a time. Add flour slowly. Beat 5 minutes. Pour into a greased and lightly floured cake pan. Bake 1 to 1½ hours in a pre-heated 350 degrees oven. The true butter flavor is so delicious that no flavoring or icing is needed.

*Debbie Stacy - Grade 2*
*Elizabeth Stacy - Kindergarten*

## FUDGE PIE

*Freezes beautifully*

½ cup butter                         1  cup sugar
2  squares unsweetened chocolate     ¼ cup all-purpose flour
2  eggs                              Pinch of salt

Melt butter and chocolate together over warm water. Beat eggs in a bowl; gradually add sugar. Add flour and salt, then combine with chocolate mixture. Pour into ungreased 8 inch pie plate and bake at 350 degrees for 20 to 25 minutes. Cool. Serve with ice cream.

*Sarah Redd - Grade 4*
*Miles Redd - Grade 1*

## LOLLIPOPS

1  cup sugar                         Flavoring extract
½ cup light corn syrup               Food coloring

Combine sugar, corn syrup and ½ cup of water in a saucepan. Cook without stirring until candy thermometer reads 300 degrees. Add flavoring and coloring-stir just to mix. Arrange wooden sticks on a buttered pan. Pour candy over top of each stick. When cold, wrap lollipop in waxed paper. Faces on lollipops can be made with raisins, cinnamon drops, etc.

*Jeffrey Shaw - Kindergarten*

## PINK CLOUD BISQUE

*This is a dessert my grandmother,*
*Mrs. George Little, taught me to make.*

1 package fruit gelatin
  (cherry or strawberry)
1½ cups boiling water
½ cup sugar
Graham cracker pie crust

Juice and rind of one lemon
Tall can of chilled
  evaporated milk
Pinch of salt

Put fruit gelatin, sugar, and salt in a bowl and pour 1½ cups boiling water over mixture until dissolved. Cool. Squeeze juice and grate rind of one lemon. Add to first mixture. Whip 1 tall can of evaporated milk. Fold into mixture until custard forms. Pour over graham cracker crust in an 8x8 pan. Chill in refrigerator. Surprise Dad!

*Cathryn L. Walker - Grade 6*

## PUDDING POPSICLES

*A delicious and creamy treat*

1 box instant chocolate pudding mix    Milk

Take one package of instant chocolate pudding and mix according to directions on box. Pour into popsicle molds or ice tray and freeze.

*Susanne Estes - Grade 1*

## HOMEMADE SNOW AND HONEY

2 tablespoons honey, warmed    1 tray ice cubes

If you have an ice crusher, crush the ice cubes to a powdery snow. By hand: put the ice in 2 or 3 plastic bags and cover with a double fold of foil. Hammer until the ice is a powdery snow. Pour the warm honey over the snow and eat.

*Anne Crowder - Grade 5*

237

## STRAWBERRIES IN THE SNOW

½ can Eagle Brand condensed milk    1 package (2 cups) grated
1 (3 ounce) package strawberry gelatin    coconut

Mix ingredients. Shape into strawberries and roll in another dry package of strawberry gelatin. Garnish with mint leaves or cut green cherries. Chill. Line a basket with a doily and serve.

*Elizabeth Strand - Kindergarten*

## GINGER ALE AND ICE CREAM

1 glass ginger ale            1 teaspoon honey
1 large scoop ice cream    1 ice-teaspoon

Put the scoop of ice cream in a tall glass. Spoon the honey over it. You may stir ice cream and honey together or leave as is. Add ginger ale. Drink and eat.

*Anne Crowder - Grade 5*

## CHOCOLATE SAUCE

*Serve this delicious sauce immediately over pound cake,
ice cream or anything.*

¼ cup sugar                  2 tablespoons butter
2 tablespoons water         1 teaspoon vanilla
1 tablespoon unsweetened cocoa

Put the sugar, water and cocoa in a small pan. Bring these ingredients to a rapid boil. On low heat, stir in butter and vanilla. Serves 5-6.

*Elizabeth Aquino - Form I*

## HOMEMADE PLAY DOUGH

*DO NOT EAT!*

½ cup salt                   1 cup water
1 cup flour                 1 tablespoon oil
2 tablespoons cream of tartar    Food coloring

Combine salt, flour, cream of tartar. Add water and oil. Add food coloring of your choice. Cook over medium heat for 5 minutes - until consistency of cream puff pastry. Store in plastic bag. (Use as you would use commercial play dough.)

*Kathy Van Natter Young*

# Manners

From: *Rhymes For Good Times And Some Other Verses*
By Kate F. Edwards

### Going to the Dinner Table

"I'll wash my hands and comb my hair —
I'll make myself quite nice and neat —
And then I'll stand behind my chair
Till every grown-up has a seat."

### At Table

"Although the dinner looks so fine —
Potatoes cooked with roasted pork —
Until the others all are served
I will not even touch my fork."

### At Table Again

"We'll use our forks — and not our spoons —
To eat our peas — or pie —
We'll sip soup from the sides of spoons —
There're several reasons why.

In drinking liquids — eating food —
We'll be the silent kind —
We'll try to keep our elbows in —
A thing to bear in mind.

Some children use their thumbs to help
Their forks pick up their food —
We'll keep our thumbs away from this —
A plan that's very good."

### In Eating My Food

"In eating my food
I must shut my lips tight —
An open-mouthed eater
Is no pleasant sight."

239

# Grade School Parties

"... For in the dew of little things the heart finds its morning ..."
*The Prophet* Kahlil Gibran

A loving touch and a sense of children will make a party a happy memory. Children of all ages love the special touches and know the difference between "making do" and "doing your best".

These party guidelines and suggestions, hopefully, will aid mothers who often are responsible for planning and executing classroom parties for their young children. With the exception of the "End-of-the-Year Parties", the other party ideas are for an indoor situation and should be planned for a time period of about one hour.

Many of the games can be varied to suit almost any holiday theme and some of them can be adapted to almost any grade level. Even though offered as "classroom party" suggestions, these ideas may well be used for children's parties everywhere — in various situations and for many occasions.

Please refer to the bibliography at the end of the chapter for further help and more detailed game instructions if needed.

## Guidelines For Classroom Parties:

1. Remember that parties, in addition to being fun, can be invaluable learning situations.
2. Keep the party simple and on the proper age level for the class for which you are planning.
3. Plan a party that is swiftly paced and as diversified as possible. Consult with the teacher in advance.
4. Let your child help as much as possible in the advance planning at home. Getting ready is so much fun.
5. Plan too many rather than too few activities. Be organized and follow through on each game, explaining it clearly.
6. Active games can be alternated with quiet ones, but one should keep in mind that outdoor games cannot be successful in an indoor classroom situation.
7. Supervise the party yourself rather than expecting the teacher to do it.
8. Have enough mothers present to insure a smoothly functioning party and invite different mothers from time to time.
9. Take all the necessary materials and equipment needed. (A stop watch may be useful and a large bag for trash is a must.)
10. Keep the refreshments as simple and as nutritious as possible. Serve them last.
11. Always use plates, napkins, cups, candy, etc. that coordinate in color and theme with the holiday for which you are planning.

12. When possible, ask the children themselves for ideas regarding their parties. At the beginning of the year, you might provide them with a brief questionnaire to complete regarding their preferences.
13. Prizes are a traditional part of parties and, with a little effort on your part, they can become secondary in importance if the actual playing of the game is emphasized instead. Search for prizes and favors that are inexpensive but meaningful. An alternative to giving individual prizes at a school party is to award a class prize that can be left in the classroom and used and enjoyed by the entire class. (This is a particularly good idea when planning games that involve teams.)
14. If balloons are given to small children, blow them up. Small children can choke on deflated ones.
15. Don't use time at school parties to discuss your child with the teacher!
16. Don't use this time as an opportunity for mothers to visit among themselves.
17. Allow for some clean-up time at the end of the party.
18. It is thoughtful if the children write the mothers responsible for the party a note of thanks.

The following refreshments, games, prizes, and favors are offered as suggestions. Choose from among them, according to the age level of the party being planned.

## HALLOWEEN PARTIES

*Refreshments:*

Oranges with a straw to suck the juice
Black and orange jelly beans wrapped in saran and tied with orange ribbons
"Pumpkin cookies": sugar cookies, orange icing, raisin eyes, nose and mouth
"Mysterious Hollows": doughnuts with orange icing
Apples cored and filled with peanut butter
"Witches Brew": chilled cider
"Ghostly Popcorn": parmesan cheese — sprinkled popcorn in brown paper bags decorated with Halloween stickers and black ribbon

*Games:*

Bean Bag Toss: pumpkin-shaped bean bags and large cardboard Jack O'Lantern with triangle nose

Dot-to-Dot-Alphabet: connected letters reveal witch, pumpkin, etc.

Jack-O-Lantern: Decorate cut-out paper pumpkins (or small real ones)

Gone Fishing: Teams "fish" for black and orange construction paper fish (magnetized with paper clip)

(continued)

Pin The Nose On The Pumpkin

Make your own mask: paper bag animal masks from necessary items tucked inside

Identifying Months: from mounted magazine pictures placed at random around room

Feel it: guessing the contents of numbered, fabric-wrapped items

Fortunes

*Prizes:*

Horn, noisemaker, mask, Glow-in-the Dark Pick-up Sticks, Halloween lollipop, tube of "Scar Stuff", Halloween stickers, tube of vampire "blood", magic trick cards

*Favors:*

Trick or Treat Bags, paraffin teeth or lips; 3 Fortune cookies (wrapped in orange tissue, tied with black ribbon), Crackerjacks

# CHRISTMAS PARTIES

*Refreshments:*

Reindeer or Snowman Cake
Red Holly Brownies
Christmas Cookies
Pink Milk
Lime Sherbet Punch
Hot Chocolate — marshmallow with red or green cherry trim

*Games:*

Picture Lotto: Like a picture bingo — using inexpensive, identical picture books to make the cards and pieces

Simple Simon

Dot-to-Dot Numbers: Connect numbers to reveal Christmas objects.

Hot, Warm, Cold: Finding hidden objects around room

Concentration Box (Memory Teaser): From a quick peek, remembering the most tiny Christmas items glued inside a shoe box

Portable Tick-Tack-Toe: Made from kitchen matchboxes, decorated in Christmas colors (put X's and circles in box drawer)

Make a boxwood Christmas tree (to take home).

Make a pomander ball.

*Prizes:*

Kaleidoscope, spinning top, Christmas record, inexpensive copy of *The Night Before Christmas,* tiny glass reindeer, angel or Santa, Christmas puzzle, "Crazy Straw", Word Search booklet, box of Christmas cards or stationery

*Favors:*

Tiny Christmas tree ornament, Christmas cookie ornament, small Santa mug filled with candy, candy cane ball point pen, a jingle bell

## VALENTINE PARTIES

*Refreshments:*

Large heart-shaped sugar cookies "glued" with icing to paper doilies
Cranberry-lemon-lime punch
Gingerbread squares decorated with red hots
Pink lemonade
Cupcakes with child's initial in "red hots" on white icing

*Games:*

Passing Comic Heart: Like "Hot Potato"
Valentine Puzzles: Team competition to complete cut-up puzzles
Make Valentine Bean Bags: With heart-shaped felt pieces, glue, and beans
Valentine Crossword Puzzles

Hearts-a-Plenty: Guessing the number of conversation hearts in a heart-and-ribbon-decorated apothecary jar (winner keeps it)

(continued)

243

Bingo: Use cinnamon or conversation hearts for markers

Trace the Hearts: From a given cut-out, to trace the most complete hearts on a sheet of paper

Valentine Word Jumble

*Prizes:*

Finger puppets, tiny valentine stickers, valentine puzzles, red felt-tip pens, small set of magic markers, package of red pencils, small green plant tied in red ribbons

*Favors:*

Red and white checked gingham "tooth fairy" pillows, valentine lollipops, tiny straw baskets tied in red ribbon and filled with conversation hearts

## END-OF-THE-YEAR PARTIES

*Suggested places to go:* Zoo, Park, Pool

*Refreshments:*

Sack lunches from home

Giraffe cake

Hawaiian lemonade: lemonade, apricot nectar, pineapple juice and ginger ale

Class Name Cake: Each child's name written in a square on the cake

Flower Pot Cakes (see index)

*Games:*

Animal Hunt: Finding hidden paper animals

Feeding the Elephant: Tossing peanuts into elephant's trunk (a roll of pink and grey construction paper)

Ribbon Hunt: Hunting for ribbons of varying lengths (The longest collection wins.)

Stringing Straws: Using string, pieces of straws and squares of paper

Relays: Running; Run, Jump, Hop; Dress-up Relay

Soft Ball Toss

Shoe Scramble

Drop the Penny: Squarely on a half-dollar in pail of water

*Prizes:*

Animal puzzle, helium balloons, animal-shaped basket, coloring book of animals, play dough, "Crazy Straw", sugarless gum, small packages of peanuts or pumpkin seeds, small sand pail, boat, or balsa airplane, small travel games, yo-yo, tiny sachets, ball and jacks, nerf ball, foam rubber frisbee

*Favors:*

Bottles of "bubbles", boxes of animal crackers, a class picture (from an earlier school function, if possible)

# GRADE SCHOOL PARTIES
## Other Ideas

*Favors or Prizes:*

Inexpensive school supplies: Metric ruler, tiny pencil sharpener, unusual erasers, scissors, assignment pads, etc.

Calendar

Autograph of a famous person who is popular with the children

Unusual snack foods from a health food store

*Class Prizes:*

(Always check with the teacher on these!)

A plant

Educational Puzzle

*Guiness Book of World Records*

Frisbee

Balls

A pet gerbil, hamster, mice, etc.

(continued)

*Favors or Prizes:*

Fill a basket with colorful foil-wrapped English walnut shells which have been filled with tiny toys, candy, new dime or penny, short "fortune", etc. (shells are glued back together). Each child chooses one to take home.

*Class Prizes:*

Terrarium

Ant Farm

Educational games (Scrabble, Chess, Spill and Spell)

Puppets

Long Jump Rope

A kite

*Activities:*

Plan a Christmas party with an international theme in keeping with Lovett's annual Christmas trees of the world display. Ex: Mexico: Pinata, Mexican cookies, cocktail size tacos. Research some Mexican games and their special Christmas traditions.

## BIBLIOGRAPHY OF BOOKS WHICH MAY BE HELPFUL

Betty Chancellor, *A Child's Christmas Cookbook* (Nevada City, California, Berliner and McGinnis, 1964).

Betty Crocker's *Cakes Kids Love* (New York, Golden Press, Western Publishing Company, Inc., 1969).

Virginia H. Ellison, *The Pooh Party Book* (New York, E. P. Dutton and Co., Inc., 1971).

Lois M. Freeman, *Betty Crocker's Parties For Children* (New York, Golden Press; Racine, Wisconsin, Western Publishing Company, Inc., 1974).

Florence Hamsher, *Party Cues For Teens* (Garden City, New York, Garden City Books, 1957).

Eva Moore, *The Cookie Book* (New York, The Seabury Press, 1973).

Margaret E. Mulac, *Games and Stunts for Schools, Camps and Playgrounds* (New York, Harper and Row, 1964).

Virginia W. Musselman, *Making Children's Parties Click* (Harrisburg, Pennsylvania, Stackpole Books, 1967).

Alvin Schwartz, *The Rainy Day Book* (New York, Trident Press, 1968).

Ursula Sedgwick, *My Learn To Cook Book* (New York, Golden Press; Racine, Wisconsin, Western Publishing Company, 1967).

# Regional Foods

These "regional menus," representing the major regions of our country, are introduced by two typical English dinners from two of Lovett's English exchange students.

Assuming you may have some of the recipes in these menus, we have included only the ones hard to find or the ones straight from the kitchens of the particular region.

## TYPICAL ENGLISH DINNER

Roast beef

Roast potatoes

Green peas

*Apple slices with custard sauce

Louise Axton, our exchange student from just south of London (Oxton, Surrey) says that this is her favorite dinner.

## WARM APPLE SLICES WITH CUSTARD SAUCE

*Sauce:*
1 cup milk
2 egg yolks
3 tablespoons granulated sugar
Dash salt
½ teaspoon vanilla extract

*Apple Slices:*
1 can (1 pound, 4 ounces)
  apple slices
½ cup granulated sugar
2 tablespoons lemon juice
WHIPPED TOPPING
½ cup heavy cream
2 tablespoons confectioners sugar

Make custard sauce by heating milk in top of double boiler, until bubbles form around the edge of the pan. Stirring constantly, add slightly beaten egg yolks with granulated sugar and salt. Cook and stir constantly, over simmering water until mixture coats a metal spoon. Add vanilla. Pour in small bowl, cover and refrigerate until chilled. Place drained apple slices in medium saucepan. Stir in sugar and lemon juice. Heat to boiling, reduce heat and cook, uncovered for 20 minutes, or until apples are glazed and liquid has evaporated. Keep warm. Serves 4.

# TYPICAL ENGLISH DINNER

*Steak and kidney pie

Mashed potatoes

Cabbage

*Shortbread

Richard Shearman, an exchange student from England, finds this his favorite dinner. Richard is from the northeastern part of England.

## STEAK AND KIDNEY PIE

2½ packages pie crust mix
2 pounds chuck, cut into 2x1 inch strips
¼ cup unsifted all purpose flour
6 tablespoons butter or margarine
2 veal kidneys, thinly sliced
1 can (7 ounce) frozen oysters, thawed and drained
2 cans (10¾ ounce) beef gravy
¼ pound fresh mushrooms, washed and halved
1 cup chopped onion
2 tablespoons chopped parsley
½ bay leaf
1 teaspoon dried thyme leaves
1 tablespoon salt
¼ teaspoon pepper

Prepare pie crust as directed, refrigerate. Roll chuck in flour to coat, brown well on all sides in butter. Place around sides of large baking dish. In a large bowl combine remaining ingredients, pour over steak in dish. Roll dough ¼ inch thick and cut into 1 inch wide strips. Place strips around inside top edge of baking dish. Dampen edges slightly with water. Roll remaining pastry to a 14 by 10 inch rectangle. Place over pastry strips sealing edge: press edges firmly with tines of fork. In center of pie cut out small hole to form an air vent. Bake 1¾ to 2 hours at 350 degrees or until beef is tender. Serves 8.

## SHORTBREAD

1 cup butter or margarine, softened
½ cup sugar
2 tablespoons almond paste
2¼ cups sifted all purpose flour
1 teaspoon vanilla extract
¼ teaspoon almond extract

It is not necessary to use vanilla or almond extract

Cream butter, sugar and almond paste, (also extracts if used). Stir in flour until smooth and well blended. Dough will be stiff. Refrigerate for 1 hour or so. Preheat oven to 300 degrees. Press dough very thin into an ungreased, flat pan. Bake for 25 minutes or until light golden. Cut into strips about 1x4 inches, remove to rack and cool. Makes about 4 dozen.

## PENNSYLVANIA DUTCH MENU

*Corn chowder

Chicken pot pie

Red cabbage

Scalloped potatoes

Traditional condiments

| Seven sours | Seven sweets |
|---|---|
| Bean salad | Stewed tomatoes |
| Chow chow | Grape conserve |
| Corn relish | Rhubarb jam |
| Pepper relish | Quince jelly |
| Pickled beets | Apple butter |
| Mustard pickles | Bread and butter pickles |
| Watermelon rind pickles | Spiced peaches |

Bread

Dessert

Shoofly pie    Apple cake

Coffee

## CORN CHOWDER

| | |
|---|---|
| 4 tablespoons butter | 1 cup finely cut carrots |
| 2 tablespoons minced onion | 2 cups creamed style corn |
| 1 cup boiling water | 2 cups milk |
| 2 cups finely diced potatoes | 1 teaspoon salt |
| 1 cup finely cut celery | ⅛ teaspoon pepper |

(continued)

Melt butter and saute onions until yellow. Add water, potatoes, celery and carrots. Heat until slow boil. Just before serving add corn, milk, salt and pepper. Bring to boil, stirring occasionally. Serve immediately. Serves 6.

## TYPICAL NEW ORLEANS DINNER

Appetizer

*Oysters bienville

Entree

*Stuffed flounder

Fresh asparagus

Mixed green salad

Dessert

Bananas foster

Cafe au lait

*Ann Brandau*

## OYSTERS BIENVILLE

¼ cup butter
3 tablespoons flour
1 clove garlic, minced
1 tablespoon onion juice
1 tablespoon worcestershire sauce
1 teaspoon celery seed
1 (2 ounce) can mushrooms
  (stems and pieces)

¾ cup liquid (juice from
  mushrooms and shrimp
1 dozen shrimp, cooked and
  chopped
1 tablespoon sherry
1½ pints oysters
Parmesan cheese
Paprika
Salt to taste

Make sauce of butter, flour, garlic, onion juice, worcestershire sauce, celery seed, and liquid. Add mushrooms, shrimp and sherry. Slide oysters under broiler until edges just curl. Pour off liquid. Sprinkle liberally with parmesan cheese; then cover with sauce. Sprinkle with paprika. Slide back under broiler for 5 to 8 minutes, until bubbly. (This sauce may also be used for Trout Marguery.) Serves 4 to 6.

# BAKED FLOUNDER WITH CRAB STUFFING

3 or 4 large flounders      Salt to taste
(¾ to 1 pound)      1 stick butter

## Stuffing

1 cup crab meat      1 teaspoon salt
2 tablespoons bacon drippings      ½ teaspoon pepper
1 medium onion, chopped fine      ⅛ teaspoon thyme
1 shallot, chopped      1 tablespoon parsley, chopped
2 cloves garlic, minced      1 egg
2 tablespoons celery, chopped      ¾ cup bread crumbs
2 tablespoons bell pepper, chopped

Have butcher slit a big pocket in each fish. Place generous amount of stuffing (made by sauteing vegetables in drippings, then mixing with remaining ingredients) into each slit. Melt butter in pan or pans to lay fish, not overlapping. Place fish dark side down: then flip. This butters stuffed side, too. Bake at 375 degrees or 400 degrees, covered for 30 minutes. Uncover last 5 or 10 minutes.

## NORTHWESTERN MENU

Fried chicken - gravy

Creamed new potatoes and green peas

Green beans

Pickled beets

Hot baking powder biscuits

Apple pie ala mode

Coffee

This menu came from Mrs. Willis Stirk's Cookbook, containing recipes which are more than 75 years old.

# MIDWESTERN MENU

*Meat pastry

Slaw with boiled dressing

Sliced tomatoes

Pickles

*Eskimo pie

These recipes came from the upper peninsular of Michigan and the cookbooks of Mrs. Jerre Enberg.

## MEAT PASTRY

| | |
|---|---|
| Prepared pie crust | 2 medium onions, chopped |
| ¾ pound lean beef | 4 medium potatoes, diced |
| ¾ pound lean pork | 3 carrots, shredded |

Cut meat into small pieces. Mix potatoes, onions, carrots, salt and pepper. Roll out crust, place mixture on half of it, adding a slice of butter, "a shake of water," (dripped from finger tips). Fold crust over making an oval, pinching.the sides together. Bake at 350 degrees for 1½ hours, but check in 1¼ hours. Do not overcook. Serves 6.

## ESKIMO PIE

| | |
|---|---|
| 16 large marshmallows | ½ cup fruit (strawberries, |
| ½ cup milk | raspberries or cherries) |
| ½ pint whipped cream | |

Melt marshmallows and milk together. Cool. Add whipped cream and fruit.

Crush 12 plain chocolate cookies, mix with 4 tablespoons butter. Press into pie tin, saving some for the top of the pie. Pour top mixture into pie shell. Sprinkle crumbs on top and chill. Toasted nuts (almonds or pecans) make it especially delicious. Serves 6 to 8.

# SOUTHWESTERN MENU
## (Texas)

### APPETIZER

Nachos

*Barbecued cabrito
(Young goat)

### SALAD

*Tomato slices topped with guacamole

Chile beans

*Catherine Dennis*

## BARBECUED CABRITO
### (Young goat)

1 cabrito 7-8 pounds, cut into sections

Sauce:

| | |
|---|---|
| 1 cup Wesson oil | 6 tablespoons worcestershire |
| 1½ cups chopped onion | 4 tablespoons prepared mustard |
| 1½ cups water | 4 teaspoons salt |
| ⅔ cup lemon juice | 1 small (2 ounce) box of black |
| 6 tablespoons sugar | pepper. (Important) |

Saute onion in hot oil. Add remaining ingredients. Simmer 15 to 20 minutes.

Place cabrito on grill about 12 inches above charcoal, oak, or hickory coals (medium heat). Baste and turn frequently. A small dish mop is ideal for basting. Cook for 1½ to 2 hours until meat is done and nicely browned.

## TOMATO SLICES WITH GUACAMOLE

| | |
|---|---|
| 2 very ripe avocados | Salsa jalapeno or green chiles |
| 2 medium tomatoes | (peppers, chopped) |
| 1 medium onion or use green | Wine vinegar or lemon juice |
| onions, chopped | Salt to taste (generous) |

Mash avocados with a fork. Add other ingredients, except tomatoes. Top each tomato slice with the guacamole and serve on a bed of lettuce. Makes 3 cups.

# *Menus*

## SPECIAL OCCASIONS

The special occasions in our lives should be special for the "cook", too and they are if the menus are planned with advance preparation in mind. The following menus have been very successful for special times and almost everything may be pre-cooked one or two days ahead. (Starred * items may be found in the index.)

### CHRISTMAS DINNER

Le Duc and orange juice

or

Le Duc or Asti Spumante

Salted nuts

*Shrimp parfaits

Roast beef au jus    *Gallo Barbera*

Roasted onions

*Yorkshire pudding

*Spinach mimosa

*Buche de noel    *Le Duc or Asti Spumante*
(French Yule Log)

With such a colorful and festive meal, keep table decorations simple: Candles, holly and bright red napkins.

254

# CHRISTMAS OPEN HOUSE

A Sunday morning family party — a week or so before Christmas

Wassail

Camembert or brie with sweet crackers
Cream haverti and port salut with crackers
Pears, apples, pineapple — cubed and sliced

Salted nuts

Baked ham with rye bread
Mayonnaise — horseradish sauce

Christmas cookies and red punch
(for the children)

With your house already decorated for Christmas, this is an easy and enjoyable party for entire families.(Children are so happy to be included in a holiday party to which their parents seem always to be going.)

# CHRISTENING PARTY

Served as a buffet luncheon after the church ceremony

Le Duc or Asti Spumante

Cheese straws

*Curried shrimp and condiments     *Gallo Chenin Blanc*

Rice

Spinach and avocado salad

*Coeur a la creme with melba sauce

Table decorations: Baby's breath and sweetheart roses in a glass bowl; organdy napkins and delicate china

# EASTER BRUNCH MENU

*Cold cucumber and watercress soup

*Ham braised in madeira sauce      *Gallo Sauvignon Blanc*

*Cheese-grits souffle

Baked spinach ring molds

Curried fruits

Hot biscuits

*Bunny cake
(Children make this)

Table decorations: Pastel linen mats and napkins with delicate china and crystal

Centerpiece: Children's dyed eggs and spring tulips in a straw Easter basket


# SURPRISE BIRTHDAY DINNER

Seated Buffet

*Pate and toast rounds      *Le Duc or Asti Spumante*

*Roast fillet of beef and *bordelaise sauce      *Gallo Barbera*

*Crab and avocado salad

Wild rice

Tomatoes stuffed with creamed spinach

*Danish torte      *Le Duc or Asti Spumante*

NOTE: Cook the fillet of beef in the afternoon and serve with the hot bordelaise sauce.

Seating tip: Two card tables placed together creates an "extra" dining table. Place cards, with gentlemen guests' names at both tables, allows for changing partners for dessert.

256

# BUFFET MENUS

These menus have been successful "after" party menus — after an evening event such as the theatre, a concert, an art exhibit or any special entertainment.

Almost everything can be prepared well in advance and easily served buffet style after arriving home. The foods are so decorative, little embellishment is needed. (Starred * items appear in the index.)

## COLD BUFFET SUPPER

After a Spring or Summer opening night, such as Opera

*Vichyssoise
(passed in mugs or cups on a tray)

*Lobster salad in lobster shell

Sliced Virginia ham (very thin)

Croissants
(split, buttered and toasted)

Fresh fruits with kirsch
(served from large brandy snifter)

White wine

## INFORMAL BUFFET SUPPER

Served from kitchen after a movie or play

*Curried tomato soup
(served from a tray of cups or mugs on counter)

*Chicken crepes
(Hostess fills crepes as each guest is ready.)

Green salad tossed with raw broccoli flowers and asparagus tips
(served from salad bowl on counter)

*Mocha mousse

White wine

257

# BUFFET DINNER

After an early event such as the Antique Show Opening

Bouillon with lemon slice

*Fillet of beef or *Beef wellington

and                    and

*Tomato garnish  *Vegetable garnish

Watercress salad

Homemade rolls

Fresh strawberries in champagne        -


# BUFFET COCKTAIL SUPPER

Bowl of fresh shrimp

Snow crab claws

Cocktail sauce

Virginia ham (chipped)

*Angel biscuits

Cheese platter with fruit

Water biscuits

*Steak tartare mold
(watercress and cherry tomatoes garnish)

Wheat crackers

Cold artichokes with hollandaise sauce

or

Curry mayonnaise

Bite size chicken pieces in cream, wine, tarragon

Small chocolate eclairs

Demi-tasse

# PICNIC MENUS

## TAILGATE PICNIC

Elegant for Steeplechase, Hunter-Jumper Classic or Pops in the Park

*Carrot soup

*Cornish hens stuffed with fruit

*Le seur pea salad

Cherry tomatoes, celery sticks

*Marinated black olives

*Vegetable sandwiches

*Beer muffins and whipped butter

*Lemon squares

Whole strawberries with powered sugar

Decorations: Orange linen tablecloth and napkins, vase of daffodils, orange, yellow, green pottery plates and mugs


## CHANGE OF PACE PICNIC

*Cream cheese soup

Sliced cold leg of lamb

Preserved fig wrapped in prosciutto

*Vegetable salad

Sliced rye and pumpernickel bread

Fresh fruit (apples, pears and grapes)

*Viennese torte

Decorations: Brown and green earthenware plates and mugs, ecru linen cloth, Chablis wine glasses, green plant set in wicker basket

259

# PATRIOTIC PICNIC

*Gazpacho

Fried chicken

Old fashioned cole slaw

*Potato salad

Deviled eggs

Pimiento cheese sandwiches

Cucumber sandwiches

*Apple pie


Decorations: Blue and white large-checked gingham cloth, red and white small-checked gingham napkins, red lacquered paper plates, cups with stars and stripes, white vase filled with red poppies and blue bachelor's buttons


# "LET'S GO FLY A KITE" PICNIC

*Hot tomato soup

Sliced turkey sandwiches

Potato chips

Carrot and celery sticks

*Sugar cookies

Boxes of raisins

Individual cartons of milk


Decorations: Individual paper bags with names drawn with colorful magic markers or crayons. Tuck in bright bandana — print paper napkins and matching hot cups to sip soup.

Take along: Large beach towels for seating

## LOVING TOUCHES...

Unusual invitations to a "picnic party": Written on a small brown paper bag, folded in thirds and sealed with an attractive sticker

"CANNED PICNICS": Assembled as instant picnic fare from the nearest grocery store or the "emergency shelf" in your pantry

"HEALTH FOOD PICNICS": Assembled from the delicious variety of foods in Health Food Stores

A decorative touch for these "instant picnics": A bouquet of fresh flowers from a street vendor along the way

"AROUND-THE-WORLD PICNICS":
Select a particular country, plan the food accordingly and seek out an appropriate location. By all means, take the children along. Check out library books, get travel posters and brochures, etc. Use this as a pleasant opportunity to learn and to teach your children about another culture of the world.

# Picnic Spots of Interest In and Around Atlanta*

## DOWNTOWN:

### GEORGIA PLAZA PARK

*Nearby points of interest:*

Capitol Building: Gilded with Georgia-mined gold

City Hall: Site of General Sherman's headquarters in 1864

State Government Buildings

Central Presbyterian Church and Immaculate Conception Shrine: Both were spared by Sherman.

(continued)

---

*Similar points of interest in any city would be suitable for the picnic menus and ideas suggested in this book.*

# CENTRAL CITY PARK

*Nearby points of interest:*

Urban walls project: Colorful paintings on walls of buildings

Five Points: In a drugstore here in 1886, Coca-Cola was first served

Candler Building: Atlanta's first skyscraper, 17 stories high

Margaret Mitchell Square

Lowe's Grand Theatre: Famous for world premiere of "Gone With The Wind"

Andrew Carnegie Library: Display of memorabilia of Margaret Mitchell and "Gone With The Wind"

Commerce Building: Chamber of Commerce films of Atlanta

Atlanta Stadium: Home of the Braves and Falcons

## HURT PARK

*Nearby points of interest:*

Hurt Building and Flatiron Building — Two of Atlanta's oldest structures

Rich's — Atlanta's most famous "institution"

Omni International: Six theatres, ice skating, shops, fantasy world of Sid and Marty Kroft, world's longest escalator, basketball, hockey and soccer

## CABLE CAR IN UNDERGROUND ATLANTA (reserve)

*Nearby points of interest:*

Underground Atlanta: "City beneath the City"

Zero Mile Post: Where Atlanta began

## PEACHTREE CENTER

*Nearby points of interest:*

Hyatt-Regency: Atlanta's most famous hotel

Davison's: One of Atlanta's oldest and finest department stores

Peachtree Plaza Hotel: The world's tallest hotel

262

## PLAZA LEVEL-COLONY SQUARE
### or
## WINN PARK IN ANSLEY PARK

*Nearby points of interest:*

Colony Square: "Atlanta's city within a city"; shops, ice skating

Fairmont Hotel

Atlanta Memorial Arts Center — Art museum, symphony hall, theatre, ballet

Rhodes Mansion: Peachtree branch of the Georgia Department of Archives

## AROUND TOWN
## PIEDMONT PARK

*Nearby points of interest:*

Playscapes: "Art in the Park" — sculptural play environment (near 12th street entrance)

Spring Arts Festival in the park

Civic Center

## PEACHTREE BATTLE CREEK PARK

*Nearby points of interest:*

Governor's Mansion

Swan House and Tullie Smith House

Atlanta Historical Society

## OTHER PLACES TO PICNIC:

Stone Mountain Park

Grant Park: Zoo, Cyclorama

Inman Park

Chastain Park

Historic Roswell

Chattahoochee River: Rafting; Nearby Sunday Polo matches

Vinings: "Turn of the century" village; antique shops

Wren's Nest: Home of Joel Chandler Harris of "Uncle Remus" fame

Kingdoms 3 — Formerly Lion Country Safari

Kennesaw Mountain Battlefield Park

Six Flags Over Georgia

Monastery at Conyers, Georgia

Callaway Gardens

Fernbank Science Center

# Cooking for a Crowd

Use this table as a guide when planning and shopping for food for a large group. The size of one serving has been listed for each item. For hearty eaters, plan approximately 1½ servings per person. Add accordingly for second helpings.

| FOOD | SERVINGS | UNIT | AMOUNT |
|---|---|---|---|
| Beverages | | | |
| Coffee | 25 | 1 cup | ½-¾ lb. |
| Tea-Hot | 25 | 1 cup | 1 oz. |
| Tea-Iced | 25 | 1 glass | 3 oz. |
| Coffee Cream | 25 | 1 Tbsp. | 1 pt. |
| Milk | 24 | 1 8-oz. glass | 1½ gals. |
| Breads | | | |
| Bread | 25 | 1 oz. slice | 1¼ lbs. |
| Casseroles | 25 | 1 cup | 6¼ quarts |
| Cake | 24 | 1/12 cake | 2 (9-inch) layers |
| | 24 | 2½ in. square | 1 (15½x10½x1) sheet |
| Pie | 24 | ⅛ pie | 3 (9-inch) pies |
| Canned Fruit | 24 | ½ cup | 1 (6½ to 7¼ lb.) can |
| Relishes | | | |
| Carrot Strips | 25 | 2 to 3 strips | 1 to 1¼ lbs. |
| Cauliflowerets | 25 | 2 oz. sliced, raw | 7 lbs. |
| Celery | 25 | 1 (2 to 3) in. piece | 1 stalk |
| Olives | 25 | 3 to 4 | 1 quart |
| Pickles | 25 | 1 oz. | 1 quart |
| Radishes | 25 | 2 | 5 bunches |
| Tomatoes | 25 | 3 oz. sliced | 5 to 6¼ lbs. |
| Salads | | | |
| Cottage Cheese | 25 | ⅓ cup | 5 lbs. |
| Fruit | 24 | ⅓ cup | 2 qts. |
| Gelatin | 25 | ½ cup liquid | 3 qts. |
| Potato | 24 | ½ cup | 3 qts. |
| Tossed | | | |
| Vegetable | 25 | ¾ cup | 1¼ gals. |
| Vegetables | | | |
| Canned | 25 | ½ cup | 1 (6½ to 7¼ lb.) can |
| Potatoes | 25 | ½ cup mashed | 6¾ lbs. |
| | 25 | 1 med. baked | 8½ lbs. |
| Frozen | | | |
| Beans | 25 | ⅓ cup | 5¼ lbs. |
| Carrots | | | |
| or | | | |
| Peas | 25 | ⅓ cup | 5 lbs. |
| Potatoes | | | |
| French fried | 25 | 10 pieces | 3¼ lbs. |

264

# Metric Conversion

## ENGLISH TO METRIC CONVERSION TABLE
### (Units to Volume)

| English Unit | Approx. Metric Conversion (based on metric cup) | Exact Metric Conversion |
|---|---|---|
| 1 tsp. | 5 milliliters (ml) | 4.9 ml |
| 1 tbsp. | 15 ml | 15 ml |
| 1 fluid oz. | 30 ml | 30 ml |
| ¼ cup | 60 ml | 59 ml |
| ½ cup | 125 ml | 118 ml |
| 1 cup | 250 ml | 237 ml |
| 1 quart | 950 ml | 946 ml |
| 1 gallon (= 4 qts.) | 3.8 liters | |

REMEMBER: A liter is just a little bigger than a quart (1.06 quarts per liter) 1000 milliliters = 1 liter.

### (Units of Weight)

| | | |
|---|---|---|
| 1 ounce | 28 grams | 28.35 grams |
| 1 pound (= 16 oz.) | 454 grams | 453.59 grams |

REMEMBER: A gram is an extremely light weight. 1000 grams = 1 kilogram (kg). The kilogram is the most commonly used metric unit of weight. One kilogram weighs a little more than 2 pounds (1 kg = 2.2 pounds).

### (Conversion of Temperature)

| Conventional Fahrenheit Temp. | Metric (Celsius or Centigrade) Temp. |
|---|---|
| 200 F. | 100 C. |
| 250 F. (very low) | 130 C. |
| 300 F. (low) | 150 C. |
| 350 F. (moderate) | 180 C. |
| 400 F. (hot) | 200 C. |
| 450 F. (very hot) | 230 C. |
| 500 F. (extremely hot) | 250 C. |

REMEMBER: The metric temperature is approximately ½ the Fahrenheit equivalent.

# Low Cholesterol Guide

Arteriosclerosis is one of the most serious health problems in our contemporary society. It is a fact that the average American diet, high in cholesterol and other saturated fats, is a contributing factor. Therefore, it is in the interest of many to modify their diet and restrict those foods that may be harmful. Let's begin by defining terms frequently used.

*Polyunsaturated fat:* Usually a fat of plant origin. Most liquid vegetable fats are unsaturated. However, ounce for ounce, they contain the same number of calories as saturated fats.

*Saturated fat:* Usually a fat of animal origin. A solid vegetable shortening (hydrogenated) may be highly saturated.

*Cholesterol:* A fatty substance manufactured by the human liver. It is present in foods of animal origin.

The average American diet contains more than 600 mg. of cholesterol per day. A desirable objective is to restrict the daily cholesterol intake to less than 300 mg. This means the elimination of those foods containing "high saturation" fat such as cream, whole milk, butter, chocolate, egg yolk, pork, luncheon meats, and shellfish. Below is a list of common foods and their cholesterol content.

| Food | Amount | Cholesterol Content in MG. |
|---|---|---|
| Whole milk | 1 glass | 22 |
| Skim milk | 1 glass | 6 |
| Whole milk cheese | 100 gm. | 100 |
| Cottage cheese | 100 gm. | 15 |
| Butter | 1 tablespoon | 38 |
| Eggs | 1 yolk | 300 |
| Eggs | 1 white | 0 |
| Shellfish | 100 gm. | 100-200 |
| Organ meat | 100 gm. | 150-350 |
| Lean meat | 100 gm. | 75 |
| Poultry, fish | 100 gm. | 75 |

What is arteriosclerosis? It is a process in which cholesterol deposits become enmeshed in the lining of the artery wall. These deposits accumulate over many years and result in narrowing and roughening of the channel through which the blood flows. Eventually an artery may be closed off completely. When this occurs in a major artery serving the heart muscle (coronary artery), the result is a "heart attack". Remember that this process of arteriosclerosis begins early in life; therefore, good dietary habits are as important for children as for adults.

Below is a summary of foods that should be included and excluded (or eaten in moderation) in a low cholesterol diet.

| *INCLUDED* | | *EXCLUDED* (Avoid or use sparingly) |
|---|---|---|
| Beverages: | Coffee, tea, carbonated drinks, fruit juice | |
| Breads: | Whole wheat, rye or white bread, saltines, graham crackers | Pancakes, French toast, potato chips, cornbread |
| Cereals: | All commercial cereals, rice, spaghetti, macaroni, noodles | |
| Dairy Products: | Skim milk, nonfat buttermilk, dry cottage cheese | Whole milk, cream, condensed milk, "hard" cheese |
| Desserts: | Angel food cake, jello, cakes and pies made with skim milk and egg white | All commercial cakes, pies, cookies, ice cream |
| Fats: | Safflower oil, corn oil, "soft" margarine, mayonnaise | Butter, lard, "hydrogenated" margarine, coconut oil |

(continued)

| *INCLUDED* | | *EXCLUDED* (Avoid or use sparingly) |
|---|---|---|
| Fruit: | All fruits, avocado in small amounts | |
| Meats: | Fish, poultry, lean beef, veal, lamb | "Cold cuts", hot dogs, sausage, bacon, shellfish |
| Misc: | Olives, pickles, salt, mustard, catsup | Chocolate, coconut, cashew and macadamia nuts |
| Vegetables: | Any fresh, frozen or canned | Creamed or fried |

## TIPS FOR THE "LOW CHOLESTEROL" SHOPPER

*Meats:* Select the lean cuts of beef, i.e., rump, round, and tenderloin. Trim away all extra fat before the meat is served. Hamburger should be ground to order from lean round. Avoid pork and luncheon meats. Avoid "marbled" cuts of meat.

*Fish and Fowl:* These are very low in saturated fats (except shellfish). The light meat of chicken and turkey is especially "cholesterol free".

*Dairy products:* Almost all dairy products are high in saturated fats and cholesterol. Exceptions include skim milk and low-fat cottage cheese. Egg substitutes are available at most supermarkets. Cheeses made with skim milk and unsaturated fats are also available.

*Fruits and Vegetables:* Almost all foods in this group are essentially "fat free".

*Desserts:* Gelatin desserts, cornstarch pudding, angel food cake, sherbet, and fruit are examples of "low fat" desserts.

*Margarine:* "Soft" margarine, high in unsaturated fat, should be used.

For a complete selection of low cholesterol recipes, consult: *The American Heart Association Cookbook* (David McKay Company, Inc., New York, 1973)

# Herbs for Gourmet and Gardener

"And on his left he held a basketful
Of all sweet herbs that searching eye could cull;
Wild thyme, and valley-lillies whiter still
Than Leda's love, and cresses from the rill."

John Keats

Grocery store shelves burst with a diversity of bottled or packaged herbs, but many gourmets prefer to grow fresh herbs because of their subtlety and delicacy in seasoning. Herbs are naturals for even "brown thumb" gardeners because they require minimal care and culture. Countless books are available describing the many uses of herbs, how to grow them, how to preserve them. Please note a small bibliography at the end of this chapter that might spark a beginning to what could be a fascinating, lifetime study.

## Herb Culture: Outdoors

Herbs prefer a well-drained area, so that water does not stand around the roots. A neutral to slightly alkaline or "sweet" soil is best for most herbs. If your azaleas and rhododendron thrive, chances are your soil is acid, so you will need to add limestone, bonemeal or woodashes each spring to the soil. (Allow 100 lbs. of lime for a garden 12 by 18.) Compost is the best fertilizer for herbs, but commercial manure can be used. Herbs profit from having eight hours of sun. If you have moderate shade, most herbs will grow well, but will be taller and less flavorful than those grown in the sun.

Hardy perennial herbs are generally bought as plants. Biennials and annuals are usually grown from seed sown in the garden plot. However, if you want to have plants early, start them in February or March in the sunniest and coolest window you have or under fluorescent lights. Seed catalogues have impressive lists of available herb seeds, both culinary and medicinal. In the Atlanta area, our greenhouses during April and May are now good sources for healthy, perennial, biennial, and annual plants of popular herbs.

The herb garden plan may be a formal patterned one ("knot", "butter-fly", or "stain-glass form", etc.) or a simple doorway garden of culinary

(continued)

269

favorites. A wheel pattern, either with or without the actual wooden wheel, is an easy form to design and execute. Terra cotta tubs, wooden barrels, planter boxes, or strawberry jars are but a few containers that can be adapted for devising a small "herb garden". Certainly, careful note of the scale of plants at maturity is critical when planning an herb garden of any size.

A few herbs lend themselves to hanging baskets: trailing thymes and a special cascading variety of rosemary. Planting thyme between railroad-tie steps or stepping stones is a delightful way to enjoy a "perfumed" morning walk. Several varieties of thyme spilling over a rock wall or santolina covering a sunny hill are other possibilities for an informal use of herbs. Underplanting with parsley a patio tomato plant makes an interesting and useful addition to the deck or terrace.

## Herb Culture: Indoors

Chives, dill, lemon balm, lemon verbena, mint, parsley, rosemary, sage, sweet marjoram, thyme, winter savory seem to adapt particularly well indoors. Select a well-lighted place with at least five hours of direct sun. Provide fresh air every day, not by a direct draft, but through a partly opened window or door in an adjoining room. Adequate humidity (about 30 to 50 percent) and a fairly cool atmosphere (never above 75) are important. Herbs need a pot of adequate size and one prepared for drainage. They thrive in a mixture of equal parts of garden loam, sand, peat moss, well-rotted pulverized manure. Keep the soil evenly moist, never soggy and never bone dry. Feel soil before watering. Fertilize with a soluble houseplant food about once a month. Place pots on pebbles.

Delightful combinations for indoor planting include: a planter box of citrus scents . . . lemon balm, lemon verbena, lemon geraniums, and lemon thyme; a pot of rosemary shaped to topiary form; thyme trained over a wire to form a handle for an oval planter. The possibilities are unlimited . . . and the pleasure given to the nose, palate, and eye throughout the winter makes the effort well worth it.

## Popular Culinary Herbs to Grow

Basil (Ocimum basilicum), Burnet (Sanguisorba minor), Dill (Anethum Grabeolens), Chervil (Anthriscus cereforium), Chives (Allium Schoenoprasum), Sweet Marjoram (Majorana Hortensis), Mint (Spearmint: Mentha spicata; orange: Mentha Citrana; peppermint: Mentha pereita; curly: Mentha crispa; Pennyroyal: Mentha pulequim; apple: Mentha rotundifolia); Lemon Balm (Melissa officinalis), Lemon verbena (Lippia citriodora), Oregano (Origanum vulgare), Parsley (Petroselinum crispum), Common Sage (Salvia offincinalis), Summer Savory (Satureja hortensis), Tarragon (Artemnesia Dracunculus), Thyme (Lemon: Thymus serpyllum; Common: Thymus Vulgaris; Golden Thyme: Thymus serpyllum aureus).

## HERB GARDENS IN THE ATLANTA AREA:

Conyers Monastery, Conyers, Georgia

Tullie Smith House Gardens

Sources for purchasing herb plants:

    Hastings

    Sears

    Green Brothers

    Cloudts

## BIBLIOGRAPHY

Clarkston, Rosetta E. *Herbs: Their Culture and Uses* (The MacMillan Company, New York, 1944).

Foster, Gertrude B. *Herbs For Every Garden* (E. P. Dutton and Company, New York, 1944).

Fox, Helen Morganthau. *Gardening With Herbs For Flavor and Fragrance* (Dover Publications, New York, 1970).

Hogner, Dorothy Childs. *Herbs From The Garden To The Table* (Oxford University Press, New York, 1953).

Simmons, Adelma Grenier. *Herb Gardening In Five Seasons* (D. Van Nostrand Company, Inc., Princeton, N. J., 1964).

Sunset Books. *How To Grow Herbs* (Lane Books, Menlo Park, California).

Periodical: *The Herb Gardener* (Falls Village, Connecticut, 06031).

## LOVING TOUCHES . . .

*Lemon Sugar:*

Layer lemon geranium leaves with sugar in tightly covered container. Use in tea, in cookie recipes, sprinkle on top of cookies, breads, etc.

271

# Gifts From the Kitchen

"Blessed are those who can give without remembering and take without forgetting"
Elizabeth Bibesco

Gifts from your kitchen are truly gifts from and to the heart and are cherished gifts for any person or for any occasion. The gift suggestions in this section offer some creative ways to say:

"Happy Birthday — Anniversary"

"Merry Christmas — or Merry whatever holiday"

"I'm sorry you're sick."

"I'm thinking of you at a time of stress."

"Welcome to the street, church, club, etc."

"Thank you for that favor you did for me."

"Here's my dish for the bridge supper — or for our cooperative dinner."

or      "I just learned to make something so fabulous I have to share it with you." (and even "half a loaf is treasured, too")

1. A big, beautiful shell (maybe one you found at the beach last summer) filled with a gorgeous seafood salad

2. A pretty basket filled with tiny jars of assorted homemade pickles, chutneys, relishes (Use baby food containers with "pinked" circles of calico fabric applied to the tops.)

3. A homemade cheese mixture in a small porcelain or lacquered bowl for a favorite male on your list (He can later use the container for paper clips on his desk.)

4. A special congealed salad molded in individual colorful paper cupcake liners set in a new muffin tin

5. A delicious pound cake made beautiful by filling the center hole with a tiny bouquet of fresh flowers, backed with a lace doily

6. A favorite recipe tucked inside the appropriate pan or mold in which to make it (bundt, spring form, quiche, sauce, iron skillet, cookie jar, fish mold, etc.). Tie it with a gingham fabric ribbon. (To go the extra mile — tuck in a pot holder or a tea towel.)

7. A golden baked turkey dressed up in leg frills made by fringing two pieces of white tissue paper or foil

8. Small cookies, candies or nuts in berry baskets (saved from the summer) woven with ribbons (Children love to help here.)

9. Fancy candies and small decorated cookies displayed individually in egg cartons (Cut away tops, line with paper or fabric and garnish with clear cellophane and a perky bow.)

10. Jars (attractive peanut butter size) of special salad dressings or sauces

11. A lucite photo cube filled with nuts for perhaps another special man (Food gifts for men are also fun tucked into a chef's hat or in a male apron pocket.)

12. Refrigerator boxes, especially three stacked on top of each other (with striped cord holding them together) make most welcomed gifts — whether food filled or not.

13. A miniature loaf of bread, simply wrapped, with an attached tiny Beatrix Potter-type print card (not in an envelope)

14. A tall bottle of special barbecue sauce wrapped in solid glossy paper tied with one of the grand looking extra large "to-from" tags — with a bow to complement it.

15. Small, glossy shopping bags filled with cookies (Add a cookie cutter and a bow to the side handles.)

16. A bag of dried herbs added to the bow around an Italian dish (Write the card in Italian.)

17. Fill a basket with a crepe pan, a crepe recipe, a wire whisk and perhaps a salad dressing for a salad to complement the crepes.

18. A dozen perfect artichokes or eggplants nestling in a beautiful basket — maybe with a favorite recipe

19. A dozen meringues to be served with fresh berries and ice cream (Put them in a clear glass container, maybe with a cork top.)

20. All the ingredients for a specific, special drink — *everything* necessary for the making of it with perhaps a beautiful glass

21. A basket filled with all kinds of salamis, sausages and cheeses

(continued)

22. A trio of special liqueurs — bundled in a shallow basket with fresh apricots or other fruit tucked in the basket around the bottles

23. Great sauce for pasta — with the pasta necessary for completing the dish

24. Lots of unusual breads — in perhaps a beautiful basket

25. Really terrific paper napkins — or cloth ones

26. Fresh herbs — a big bag of basil — perhaps tiny pots of fresh basil · and rosemary plunked in a small basket

27. A series of teas — in painted wooden boxes

28. A burlap-lined basket filled with whole coffee beans

29. Four large wine glasses filled with candied ginger, pistachio nuts, nougats, chocolate mints, etc (Tie a bright ribbon around each one.)

30. A beautiful enameled colander filled with packages of various shaped pasta or other food you know the receiver will love

31. Homemade tarragon vinegar or other herb vinegars put up in empty wine bottles with hand-drawn labels

32. *All* the ingredients for a homemade apple pie in a fluted French baking tin

33. A natural wood cutting board with a wedge of Bel Paese, Stilton, Roquefort, or other favorites with several pieces of a special fruit that's in season

34. A really fine pate made in a bright enameled loaf pan

35. Make a huge pot of basic brown sauce or other. Freeze it in eight-ounce jars and give to friends who love sauces but don't have time to prepare them.

36. Make sherried walnuts and pile them in a charlotte mold. Add a tiny wooden serving scoop.

37. Stuff a big salad bowl with your own bouquet garni — little cheese-cloth squares filled with a small bay leaf, pinch thyme, 1 tsp. dried parsley and tied with a white string.

38. Stack a series of salad oils — walnut, grape seed, peanut, French olive — in a handwoven basket.

39. A set of different kinds of mustard

40. Tie a small can of black truffles around the neck of a bottle of Madeira or Marsala.

41. Stuff marshmallows with apricot halves and stack them in a beautiful handwoven basket.

42. A copy of *Cook and Love It* plus a dish you prepared from it (Footnote the recipe on your tag.)

## GIFTS FOR CHILDREN

Don't forget gifts for children (and especially your own). When you want a child to know you love him, bake him something special or fix an exciting basket to open. Here are a few suggestions:

1. A basket filled with a box of gingerbread mix, a rolling pin, the cookie cutter, plus the condiments for the features

2. A party hat filled with a bag of corn to be popped and a recipe for popcorn balls

3. A gold fish bowl filled with Christmas (or any holiday) cookies

4. A house-bound child would enjoy receiving a hobo bag tied on a stick which has his special sandwich, cookies, juice and a comic book.

5. A simple bag of peanuts (in the shell) yarn, needle, and an easy recipe for peanut butter cookies (He can craft them, eat them or bake them.)

6. A child on a special diet would be charmed to receive a sandpail stuffed with apples and an apple cutter. (Including a package of construction paper and a magic marker will add hours of fun — making designs by tracing that cutter.)

7. Measuring spoons, ice cream scoops, timers, cake testers, pizza cutters are among kitchen gifts the younger set adores attached to packages of goodies from you.

. . . And by doing so, you may be planting the seeds for a future Cordon Bleu Chef who will treat you mightily with his gourmet wonders when you are elderly and on soup and custards.

# Index

*(Alphabetized both by main ingredient and general category)*

278

279

281

284

Be sure to check the LOVING TOUCHES (helpful suggestions) which run throughout the book. See: LOVING TOUCHES under "L" for page numbers.

# 1976 Cookbook Committee

Chairman . . . . . . . . . . . . . . . . . . . . . . . . . . . . . Mrs. Vincent L. Sgrosso
Recipe Collection and Organization . . . . . . . . . Mrs. Richard B. Jones
Art . . . . . . . . . . . . . . . . . . . . . . . . . . . . . . . . . . . . . . . . . . . . . . David Sapp
Publicity . . . . . . . . . . . . . . . . . . . . . . . . . . Mrs. John E. Anderson, Jr.
Circulation . . . . . . . . . . . . . . . . . . . . . . . . Mrs. Charles G. Bartenfeld
Mrs. John C. Portman, Jr.

## COMMITTEE MEMBERS

| | | |
|---|---|---|
| Mrs. J. Randall Akin | Mrs. Hix Green, Jr. | Mrs. Richard Mattison |
| Mrs. Sam Allen | Mrs. William Harp | Mrs. William Mellen |
| Mrs. Ed Andrews | Mrs. Hal Hatcher | Mrs. Frank Millians |
| Mrs. David F. Apple, Jr. | Mrs. J. S. Havermale | Mrs. Waldo Moore |
| Mrs. Hunter Bell | Mrs. Fred Hayes | Mrs. Frank Morris |
| Mrs. Jon Paul Bell | Mrs. John Hirsh | Mrs. Michael C. Murphy |
| Mrs. William Benton | Mrs. Lindsey Hopkins | Mrs. Paul Pater |
| Mrs. Charles Bouis | Mrs. Lynn Humphries | Mrs. Richard Perry |
| Mrs. Howard Busbey | Mrs. James Hunter | Mrs. William Pulliam |
| Mrs. Richard Childs | Mrs. John Jackson | Mrs. Hill Robertson, Jr. |
| Mrs. Thomas Clyatt, Jr. | Mr. Charles Jess | Mrs. I. C. Rolader |
| Mrs. Erik Collett | Mrs. George Johnson | Mrs. Vernon Sanders |
| Mrs. James Crist | Mrs. Fred Keith | Dr. Vernon Sanders |
| Dr. James Curtis | Mrs. Donald Keough | Mr. Clinton Schaum |
| Mrs. James Cushman | Mrs. Clifford M. Kirtland, Jr. | Mrs. Ross Shaw |
| Mrs. Robert F. Dennis | Mr. Clifford M. Kirtland, Jr. | Mrs. Frank Stevenson |
| Mr. Robert F. Dennis | Mrs. Graydon Leake | Mrs. J. W. Travis |
| Mrs. Thomas Eddins | Mrs. George Longino III | Mrs. L. Newton Turk |
| Mrs. Frank F. Ford | Mrs. Edward C. Loughlin, Jr. | Mrs. John N. Wall, Jr. |
| Mrs. Ed Forio, Jr. | Mrs. Richard McCamey | Mrs. H. Hall Ware III |
| Mrs. Dorothy George | Mrs. Bert Madden | Mrs. James Wilcox, Jr. |
| Mrs. John Gillespie | Mrs. James Magbee | Mrs. Ralph Williams |
| Mrs. Edward P. Gould | Mrs. Robert Malone | Mrs. Charles Wood |

A special "thank you" to Dr. Allan Strand, whose interest and support made possible the publication of this book.

*We sincerely appreciate every recipe of the hundreds submitted. Regretably, we were unable to incorporate all the wonderful recipes and ideas due to a lack of space.*

# COOK AND LOVE IT

4075 Paces Ferry Road, N.W.
Atlanta, Georgia 30327-3099

Please send me _____ copies of COOK AND LOVE IT

at $16.95 per copy, plus $3.25 per copy for handling. Enclosed is my check or

money order for $ _____ . Georgia residents add .96¢ sales tax.

Name _____

Street _____

City _____ State _____ Zip _____

*All proceeds from the sale of this cookbook are to benefit the Lovett School. Make check payable to Cookbook — Lovett School. Price is subject to change.*

---

# COOK AND LOVE IT

4075 Paces Ferry Road, N.W.
Atlanta, Georgia 30327-3099

Please send me _____ copies of COOK AND LOVE IT

at $16.95 per copy, plus $3.25 per copy for handling. Enclosed is my check or

money order for $ _____ . Georgia residents add .96¢ sales tax.

Name _____

Street _____

City _____ State _____ Zip _____

*All proceeds from the sale of this cookbook are to benefit the Lovett School. Make check payable to Cookbook — Lovett School. Price is subject to change.*

---

# COOK AND LOVE IT

4075 Paces Ferry Road, N.W.
Atlanta, Georgia 30327-3099

Please send me _____ copies of COOK AND LOVE IT

at $16.95 per copy, plus $3.25 per copy for handling. Enclosed is my check or

money order for $ _____ . Georgia residents add .96¢ sales tax.

Name _____

Street _____

City _____ State _____ Zip _____

*All proceeds from the sale of this cookbook are to benefit the Lovett School. Make check payable to Cookbook — Lovett School. Price is subject to change.*